Scrum

2nd Edition

by Mark C. Layton
MBA[2], CST, PMP, SAFe SPC
and

David Morrow
CSP, ICP-ACC

A Wiley Brand

Scrum For Dummies®, 2nd Edition

Published by: **John Wiley & Sons, Inc.**, 111 River Street, Hoboken, NJ 07030-5774, www.wiley.com

Copyright © 2018 by John Wiley & Sons, Inc., Hoboken, New Jersey

Published simultaneously in Canada

For general information on our other products and services, please contact our Customer Care Department within the U.S. at 877-762-2974, outside the U.S. at 317-572-3993, or fax 317-572-4002. For technical support, please visit https://hub.wiley.com/community/support/dummies.

Wiley publishes in a variety of print and electronic formats and by print-on-demand. Some material included with standard print versions of this book may not be included in e-books or in print-on-demand. If this book refers to media such as a CD or DVD that is not included in the version you purchased, you may download this material at http://booksupport.wiley.com. For more information about Wiley products, visit www.wiley.com.

Library of Congress Control Number: 2018938627

ISBN: 978-1-119-46764-9 (pbk); 978-1-119-46768-7 (ebk); 978-1-119-46769-4

Manufactured in the United States of America

10 9 8 7 6 5 4 3 2 1

Contents at a Glance

Table of Contents

Introduction

Welcome to *Scrum For Dummies.* Scrum is an agile project management framework with proven results in decreasing time to market by 30–40 percent, improving product quality, and heightening customer satisfaction — all while lowering costs 30–70 percent. Scrum accomplishes these results through integration of business and development talent, improved communication models, increased performance visibility, regular customer and stakeholder feedback, and an empirically based inspect-and-adapt mentality. You can manage even the most complex project more effectively by using scrum to increase your bottom line.

About This Book

The goal is to demonstrate explicitly how you can use scrum for any project, not just software development. This book is intended to be a field manual for the application of scrum in real-world situations. Although it covers scrum fundamentals in detail, this book also delves into how to get out and experience the amazing benefits of scrum.

Scrum is by design easy to explain, but application and mastery are often difficult. Old habits and organizational mindsets need to be shifted and new ways embraced. For this reason, we've included success stories so that you can see how scrum can fit into your situation.

The main thrust of understanding scrum lies in the three roles, three artifacts, and five events that form its foundation and that we cover thoroughly. We also include common practices that we use and that others in the field use so that you can choose what works best for your project.

Scrum isn't technical. In fact, its basic tenet is common sense. In many cases, we've wrapped this information within the world of technology and have used technical terms to help explain this. Where useful, we've defined these terms.

We also cover common practices from scrum experts throughout the world. You can learn so much from others who use this framework in a seemingly limitless spectrum of projects.

Scrum falls under an umbrella of project management called *agile project management*. Neither scrum nor agile practices is a proper noun. *Scrum* is a framework for organizing your work, whereas *agile* is an adjective used to describe a variety of practices that conform to the values of the Agile Manifesto and to the 12 Agile Principles. Scrum and agile are not identical or interchangeable, but you frequently see them written in many sources, especially online, interchangeably. In this book, you will see terminology from both descriptions, because scrum is a frequently used subset of agile practices.

Foolish Assumptions

Several books about scrum are available, but this one differs in its practicality. Each of the authors has more than a decade of experience with agile methods and scrum, and we bring this experience to you in a practical guide. We make no assumptions about what you already know: You don't need to be a rocket scientist or a whiz programmer; all you need are a project and passion to get it done in the best way possible. We give you examples from building jet fighters to a family organizing a vacation. We focus on the steps necessary to get scrum's magic working for you.

Our audience includes code programmers, sales professionals, product manufacturers, executives, and midtier managers, as well as educators who are looking for a way to engage their students.

If you're in a technology industry, you've probably heard the terms *agile* and/or *scrum.* Maybe you've even worked in a scrum environment but want to improve your skills and vocabulary in this area and to bring others in your firm along with you. If you're not in technology, you may have heard that scrum is a great way to run projects, which is true. Perhaps scrum is new to you, and you're searching for a way to make your project more accessible, or maybe you have a great idea burning inside and don't know how to bring it to fruition. Whoever you are, an easy way exists to run your project, and that way is called scrum. Within these pages, we show you how to use it.

Conventions Used in This Book

If you do an online search, you may see the words *agile* and *scrum*, roles, meetings, and documents and various agile methodologies and frameworks (including scrum) capitalized. We shied away from this practice for a couple of reasons.

To start, none of these items are really proper nouns. *Agile* is an adjective that describes a number of items in project management: agile projects, agile teams, agile processes, and so on. But it is not a proper noun, and except in chapter or section titles, you will not see us use it that way.

For readability, we did not capitalize agile-related roles, meetings, and documents. Such terms include agile project, product owner, scrum master, development team, user stories, product backlog, and more. You may, however, see these terms capitalized in places other than this book.

Some exceptions exist. The Agile Manifesto and the Agile Principles are copyrighted material. The Agile Alliance, Scrum Alliance, and Project Management Institute are professional organizations. A Certified ScrumMaster and a PMI-Agile Certified Practitioner are professional titles.

Icons Used in This Book

The following icons in the margins indicate highlighted material that we think will be of interest to you.

TIP

Tips are ideas that we'd like you to take note of. These ideas are usually practical advice that you can apply to the given topic.

WARNING

This icon is less common than the others in this book. The intent is to save you time by bringing to your attention some pitfalls that you're better off avoiding.

TECHNICAL STUFF

If you don't care much about the technical stuff, you can skip these paragraphs without missing much. If technical stuff is your thing, you may find these sections fascinating.

REMEMBER

This icon marks something we'd like you to take special note of, such as a concept, idea, or best practice that we think is noteworthy.

Beyond the Book

You can find an online Cheat Sheet for this book at www.dummies.com. The Cheat Sheet covers the Agile Manifesto; the principles behind scrum and the Agile Manifesto; the roadmap to value that we reference frequently throughout this book; a snapshot of various definitions for roles, artifacts, and activities related to scrum; and a summary of resources you can find in the scrum community. Go to www.dummies.com and type the title of the book into the search field to find the Cheat Sheet.

Where to Go from Here

To start getting scrum working for you, you can begin applying it on smaller projects to get the feel of it. Soon, you'll be handling your most important projects in the same way. This book applies to a diverse set of readers and is organized in a way that allows you to find specific areas of interest that are relevant to you. Each chapter can be a reference any time you have a technical question or want to see an example of scrum in real life.

If you're new to scrum, begin with Chapter 1 to understand introductory concepts and terminology; then work your way through Chapter 7 to find out about the entire framework. As you continue past Chapter 7, you see how to apply scrum in any situation.

If you're familiar with scrum and want to find out more about how it applies to many industries, check out Chapters 8 through 11, and read about scrum being practiced in a variety of industries.

If you're a product owner, scrum master, or business leader and want to know more about scrum on a larger scale, start by reading Chapter 13 and all of Part 6 for valuable resources.

If you're familiar with scrum and want to know how it can help you address daily life, read Chapters 17 and 18 to get inspiration and examples.

1
Getting Started with Scrum

Connect scrum with the principles of agile project management.

Use constant feedback through transparency and quantification to elevate success rates of projects.

Become tactically flexible to create strategic stability.

Chapter 1

The Basics of Scrum

Scrum is an empirical exposure model, which means that people who employ the scrum model have gained knowledge from real-life experience and make decisions based on that experience. It's a way of organizing your project — whether it be releasing a new smartphone or coordinating your daughter's fifth-grade birthday party — to expose whether your approach is generating intended results. If you need to get something done, scrum provides a structure for increased efficiency and faster results.

Within scrum, common sense reigns. You focus on what can be done today, with an eye toward breaking future work into manageable pieces. You can immediately see how well your development methodology is working, and when you find inefficiencies in your approach, scrum enables you to act on them by making adjustments with clarity and speed.

Although empirical exposure modeling goes back to the beginning of time in the arts — in sculpting, for example, you chisel away, check the results, make any adaptations necessary, and chisel away some more — its modern-day usage stems from computer modeling. The empirical exposure model means observing or experiencing actual results rather than simulating them based on research or a mathematical formula and then making decisions based on these experiences. In scrum, you break your project into actionable chunks and then observe your results every step of the way. This approach allows you to immediately make the changes necessary to keep your project on the best track possible.

The Bird's-Eye Basics

Scrum isn't a methodology; it's a new way of thinking. It isn't a paint-by-numbers approach in which you end up with a product; it's a simple framework for clearly defining roles and organizing your actionable work so that you're more effective in prioritizing work and more efficient in completing the work selected. Frameworks are less prescriptive than methodologies and provide appropriate amounts of flexibility for processes, structures, and tools that complement them. When this approach is used, you can clearly observe and adopt complementary methods and practices, and quickly determine whether you're making real, tangible progress. You create tested, usable results within weeks, days, or (in some cases) hours.

Like the process of building a house brick by brick, scrum is an iterative, incremental approach. It gives you early empirical evidence of performance and quality. Roles are distinct and self-ruling, with individuals and teams being given the freedom and tools required to get the job done. Lengthy progress reports, redundant meetings, and bloated management layers are nonexistent. If you just plain want to get the job done, scrum is the approach to use.

TECHNICAL
STUFF

Scrum is a term that comes from the rough-and-tumble game of rugby. Huddles, or scrums, are formed with the forwards from one side interlocking their arms, heads down, and pushing against the forwards from the opposing team who are also interlocking arms with their heads down. The ball is then thrown into the midst of this tightly condensed group of athletes. Although each team member plays a unique position, all team members play both attacking and defending roles, and work together to move the ball down the field of play. Like rugby, scrum relies on talented people with varying responsibilities and domains working closely together in teams toward a common goal.

We want to emphasize, and have written two thirds of this book on, an overlooked concept of scrum: its amazing versatility. People who know about scrum commonly think that it's customized for software, information technology (IT), or tech use, but that's just the tip of the scrumberg. Absolutely any project — large, small, tech, artistic, social, personal — can be productively placed within the scrum framework. In Chapters 8 through 18, we show you how. Be forewarned! Scrum is such an addictive framework that you'll be using it to coach your kid's soccer team, plan your Neighborhood Watch, and even ratchet up your exercise routine.

Roadmap to value

Throughout this book, we discuss techniques some expert scrum practitioners apply as common practice extensions to scrum. These techniques complement, not replace, the scrum framework. We point out the differences when they occur.

All the common practices that we include and recommend are tried and tested — always with the clear understanding that these practices are outside of the basic scrum framework and are suggested for your consideration in your own situation.

We call this aggregation of scrum and vetted common practices the *"roadmap to value."* This roadmap consists of seven stages that walk you through the vision stage of your project to the task level and back again in a continual process of inspection and adaptation. In other words, the stages help you see what you want to achieve and progressively break that vision into pieces through an efficient cycle that leads to real results every day, week, and month.

You know that billion-dollar idea that's been lurking in the back of your head for years? Follow the seven stages. They show you the feasibility and fallacy of your idea and where to make your improvements — step by step, piece by piece.

Figure 1-1 shows a holistic view of the roadmap to value. This figure shows that you begin with the vision; work through planning; and then enter the cyclical world of sprints, reviews, and retrospectives.

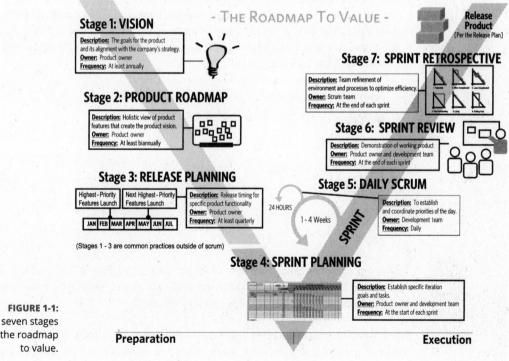

FIGURE 1-1:
The seven stages
in the roadmap
to value.

Scrum overview

The process of scrum is simple and circular, with constant and transparent elements of inspection and adaptation. First, a ruthlessly ordered to-do list — called a *product backlog* — is created and maintained. Then top-priority items are selected for a fixed, regular time period — called a *sprint* — within which the scrum team strives for a predetermined and mutually agreed upon goal.

Figure 1-2 shows an overview of scrum.

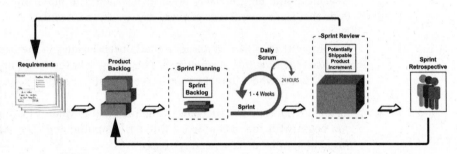

FIGURE 1-2:
A simplified overview of the events and cycles of scrum.

The scrum process allows you to adapt quickly to changing market forces, technological constraints, regulations, new innovations, and almost anything else you can think of. The key is the ongoing process of working on the highest-priority items to completion. Each of the highest-priority items gets fully developed and tested through the following steps:

1. Requirement elaboration
2. Design
3. Development
4. Comprehensive testing
5. Integration
6. Documentation
7. Approval

REMEMBER

The seven steps to fully build the scope of each requirement are performed for every item. Every requirement taken on during a sprint, no matter how small or large, is fully built, tested, and approved or rejected.

When a requirement is accepted and therefore deemed shippable, you know that it works. Hope and guesswork are taken out of the equation and replaced by reality. You build your product increment by increment and showcase these tangible increments to stakeholders for feedback. This feedback generates new requirements that are placed in the product backlog and prioritized against existing known work.

TIP

What's more important: efficiency or effectiveness? Hands down, it's effectiveness. Don't worry about efficiency until you figure out how to be effective. A very efficient development team working on the wrong things is a waste of time. A super-effective development team, however, can easily learn efficiency. Always work on the *right* things first. As economist and management author Peter F. Drucker said, "There is nothing so useless as doing efficiently that which should not be done at all."

The scrum cycle is run again and again. The constant flow of feedback and emphasis on developing only the highest-priority items helps you reflect what your customers are looking for, deliver it to them faster, and deliver it with higher quality.

Scrum teams

No matter what the scope of your scrum project is, your scrum team will have similar characteristics. The sizes of development teams vary somewhat, but the roles remain the same. We discuss the specific roles in detail throughout this book. Figure 1-3 depicts a scrum team.

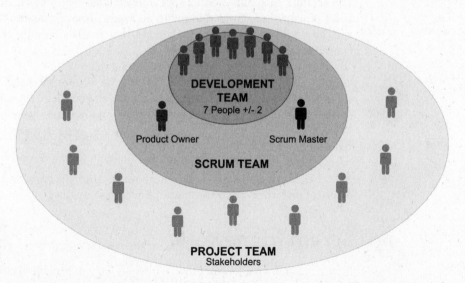

FIGURE 1-3:
A scrum team has the development team at its core.

The heart of a scrum team is the development team — the folks who work together to create the product itself. They work directly with a product owner and scrum master, who align business and development priorities for the organization and eliminate distractions so that the development team can focus on developing a quality result.

Stakeholders aren't scrum roles, but we include them in Figure 1-3 because they affect your project. Stakeholders can be internal or external. Marketing, legal, compliance team members, and especially customers are examples of stakeholders.

The scrum team itself has ultimate accountability. Team members figure out how to achieve their objectives within the environment in which they find themselves.

Governance

Scrum has three roles that are equal in status yet separate and independent in function:

>> **Product owner:** The *what* and the *when* (not *how much*)

>> **Development team:** The *how* and the *how much*

>> **Scrum master:** The *process*

Each role has a defined purpose directly designed to enhance the productivity of the team.

The creators of scrum didn't happen devise these roles by chance, but through years of experience in working with all kinds of project teams. They saw good, bad, and ugly combinations, and found that the best results came from these three roles.

TIP

We prefer that each person in a scrum role be a full-time participant dedicated solely to the scrum team's project. Don't thrash your team members across several projects or use part-time players. How many major-league football teams have part-time players or those who play for several teams? None that are successful.

REMEMBER

In scrum, no single person or role is above another. Everyone is a peer; no one is a boss or underling. *We* is the operative word rather than *I*.

Scrum framework

Scrum is a framework rather than a methodology. It provides clarity of responsibilities through roles, visibility through artifacts, and opportunities for inspection and adaptation through events. Within this structure, scrum is a container for other processes and tools that are appropriate for meeting the specific needs of a team, organization, or product.

A Scrum project has a 3-3-5 framework:

>> Three roles

>> Three artifacts

>> Five events

Each framework element fits within the scrum process, which is iterative and incremental. You incrementally create and improve your product, and you incrementally improve your process with this simple framework, as follows:

>> **Roles**

- Product owner

- Development team

- Scrum master

>> **Artifacts**

- Product backlog

- Sprint backlog

- Product increment

>> **Events**

- Sprint

- Sprint planning

- Daily scrum

- Sprint review

- Sprint retrospective

In the scrum world, *artifacts* are lists of work to be done or work products that have been done and are deemed shippable. Unlike archaeological artifacts, scrum artifacts aren't set in stone. The scrum process requires you to continually review and assess artifacts to make sure that you're digging in the right direction.

Each role, artifact, and event in scrum has a set purpose. You place your project in the scrum framework, moving through the seven stages of the roadmap to value (discussed earlier in this chapter), but the actual tools and techniques for accomplishing your goals are your own. Scrum doesn't tell you how to achieve your goal; it merely provides a framework within which you can clearly see what you're doing.

In concept, scrum is simple, but it can be complicated to implement. Scrum is much like getting into shape physically. In concept, you need to exercise more and take in fewer calories; in practice, the process can be complex.

Following are some common practices that complement scrum (extra elements in italics) and have produced incredible successes. Here, we've switched to a 5-6-7 framework:

» Roles

- Product owner
- Development team
- Scrum master
- *Stakeholders*
- *Scrum mentor*

» Artifacts

- *Vision*
- *Product roadmap*
- Product backlog
- *Release plan*
- Sprint backlog
- Product increment

» Events

- *Project planning*
- *Release planning*
- Sprint
- Sprint planning
- Daily scrum
- Sprint review
- Sprint retrospective

The framework is still simple, but with additional roles, artifacts, and events designed to smooth the process. We discuss these roles, artifacts, and events in detail throughout the book.

The Feedback Feast

One clear advantage of scrum over other project management frameworks is the feedback loop, which tells you early and continuously what's working, what's not working, what's missing, and what's extraordinary.

Feedback is generated regularly from scrum team members, stakeholders, and customers. The process goes something like this:

1. Daily feedback occurs among development team members as they go about developing project requirements.

2. Direct daily interaction occurs between the product owner and the development team for on-the-spot answers and feedback.

3. The product owner provides direct feedback as he or she accepts or rejects every completed requirement.

4. At the end of each sprint, internal stakeholders provide feedback.

5. At the end of every release, feedback is provided by the external marketplace.

You get more from the scrum model than from traditional project management models because scrum emphasizes product development rather than artifact development, delivering tangible, tested products rather than tomes of reports on what's possible. You receive regular feedback along the way, enabling you to incrementally get your product to market as fast as possible.

At the end of the project, which is a series of sprints within a series of market releases, you're not left wondering whether you produced what your customers want; you've been communicating with and receiving feedback from them all along the way. The inspection and adaptation process has been at work on your behalf, and you're delivering what your customers actually asked for.

Agile Roots

To understand scrum, it helps to dip into the broader world of agile techniques, because agile is the umbrella under which scrum resides.

Agile is a descriptor of approaches that align to the values of the Agile Manifesto and the 12 Agile Principles, which we outline in this section. Scrum is one agile approach.

TIP

For a thorough look at agile techniques, see *Agile Project Management For Dummies,* Second Edition, by Mark Layton and Steven Ostermiller (John Wiley & Sons, Inc.).

Three pillars of improvement

The empirical process control model sits securely on three pillars, which are common to agile and scrum:

>> Transparency

>> Inspection

>> Adaptation

Transparency

One distinguishing feature of agile techniques in general and scrum in particular is transparency. When channels of communication are clear and accessible, information is radiated throughout the organization. The entire organization knows what's been done, what's being worked on, and what's left to work on and any impediments blocking the way. Right from the start, you produce real results that are tested and then approved or sent back for adjustments. The lag time between the start date and usable results is now days rather than months.

Transparency isn't just about quickly seeing results. Everyone needs to look through the same lens. A framework (such as scrum) is shared, along with an agreed-on definition of *done.* Both observers and participants can see what's being accomplished and interpret the results in a common language.

Inspection

As you discover in the following chapters, agile projects are broken into the smallest actionable chunks possible (commonly captured as user stories; see Chapter 3). Goals are set within fixed time frames: the sprint, the release, and the project. As each item is accomplished, it's inspected to make sure that it works and does what the customer wants.

These inspections are done by people closest to the job — those who do the work and those who represent the customer. This process eliminates the time lag required for an outside person to complete this task, and it also means that any adjustments can be made quickly because the required knowledge is at hand.

Adaptation

If the inspection shows inaccuracies and/or inefficiencies — that is, if the feature doesn't work right — an adaptation needs to be made. The adaptation should be made as soon as possible and before moving to the next actionable item on the to-do list. In other words, when you move on, you know that everything behind you is functioning properly.

Scrum allows inspections and adaptations to be accomplished immediately at the team and project levels in the form of reviews, retrospectives, and the daily scrum (see Chapters 6 and 7).

One Agile Manifesto

Scrum is a framework, not a by-the-numbers methodology. You still need to think and make choices. Part of the scrum framework's benefit is that it allows you to make the decisions that are best for you, based on the reality in which you find yourself.

In 2001, 17 software and project experts agreed on four main values for their programming methodologies. These values are known as the Agile Manifesto:

We are uncovering better ways of developing software by doing it and helping others do it. Through this work we have come to value:

>> ***Individuals and interactions*** *over processes and tools*

>> ***Working software*** *over comprehensive documentation*

>> ***Customer collaboration*** *over contract negotiation*

>> ***Responding to change*** *over following a plan*

That is, while there is value in the items on the right, we value the items on the left more.

Agile Manifesto © 2001: Kent Beck, Mike Beedle, Arie van Bennekum, Alistair Cockburn, Ward Cunningham, Martin Fowler, James Grenning, Jim Highsmith,

Andrew Hunt, Ron Jeffries, Jon Kern, Brian Marick, Robert C. Martin, Steve Mellor, Ken Schwaber, Jeff Sutherland, Dave Thomas

Even though the Agile Manifesto and principles were written by and for software experts, the values remain valid for whatever scrum project you embark upon. The Global Positioning System (GPS), for example, was designed by and for the military, but that it doesn't mean that you can't benefit from it when you drive to a new part of town.

For more information on the Agile Manifesto and its founders, visit http://agilemanifesto.org.

TIP

Twelve Agile Principles

The Agile Manifesto's founders also agreed on 12 Agile Principles. Within your scrum project, you can use these principles to check that your framework is true to agile goals:

1. Our highest priority is to satisfy the customer through early and continuous delivery of valuable software.

2. Welcome changing requirements, even late in development. Agile processes harness change for the customer's competitive advantage.

3. Deliver working software frequently, from a couple of weeks to a couple of months, with a preference to the shorter timescale.

4. Business people and developers must work together daily throughout the project.

5. Build projects around motivated individuals. Give them the environment and support they need and trust them to get the job done.

6. The most efficient and effective method of conveying information to and within a development team is face-to-face conversation.

7. Working software is the primary measure of progress.

8. Agile processes promote sustainable development. The sponsors, developers, and users should be able to maintain a constant pace indefinitely.

9. Continuous attention to technical excellence and good design enhances agility.

10. Simplicity — the art of maximizing the amount of work not done — is essential.

11. The best architectures, requirements, and designs emerge from self-organizing teams.

12. At regular intervals, the team reflects on how to become more effective, then tunes and adjusts its behavior accordingly.

REMEMBER

The principles don't change, but the tools and techniques to achieve them can.

Some of the principles are easier to implement than others. Consider principle 2. Maybe some parts of your company (or group or family) are open to change and new ideas. For them, scrum is natural, and they're ready to get started. But other parts may be more resistant to change.

Or consider principle 6. Working face-to-face may not be possible in your project. With the Internet and globalization of workforces, you may have team members from Mumbai to Moscow to Miami. You could consider several solutions — such as Skype, Google Hangouts, and teleconferencing — but none of these solutions meets the intention of principle 6, and none is as good as face-to-face communication.

THE MARSHMALLOW CHALLENGE

In 2010, author and speaker Tom Wujec gave a remarkable TED talk called The Marshmallow Challenge that discussed a design exercise devised by designer Peter Skillman. In this exercise, small groups of participants are given 18 minutes to build a free-standing structure with strange, minimal tools: 20 sticks of spaghetti, 1 yard of tape, 1 yard of string, and 1 marshmallow. Wujec began giving this test and studying the results. Most groups struggled to create anything high or reliable. Group members discussed options, planned a final design, and put it together only to find that because they'd left out some crucial aspect, the structure wouldn't stand.

The groups who performed the worst were recent graduates of business schools. The groups who performed the best were kindergarteners, who consistently produced higher and more creative structures.

Wujec said that when business students work on an idea, they believe that only one "correct" solution exists, so they spend much of their time contemplating and planning for that approach. The children, however, started by playing with the tools. They learned what didn't work and changed it; then they figured out what did work and kept it. In other words, they built prototypes all along the way.

A takeaway in the context of scrum is that humans' natural state is inspection and adaptation. We want to do these things, but somewhere along the way, we get trained out of them. We're taught that planning and coming up with one solution is the correct way to do things. But kindergarteners remind us that this way of thinking may be wrong.

Your project is bound to have unique challenges. Don't let a hiccup or a less-than-perfect scenario stop your project cold or cause it to limp along. Part of the fun of using scrum is working through issues to get to results. Stick with the 12 principles, and your projects will get quality results quickly.

Three platinum principles

We've worked with agile and scrum projects for more than a decade, consulted with dozens of companies, businesses, and not-for-profit organizations. We know how well these principles work because we've seen their value as we assisted in their implementation.

Here are three additional principles that have consistently improved the performance of the teams we've helped:

>> Resist formality.

>> Think and act as a team.

>> Visualize rather than write.

These principles can be applied to any project, not just software development. Part of the beauty of agile techniques is that you can use them for anything.

Resist formality

Have you ever seen a knockout presentation and wondered how much time someone spent putting it together? Don't even think about doing that for a scrum project. You can scribble it on a flip chart, stick it on a wall where people will look at it, and then get back to creating value. If discussion is required, walk over to the concerned parties and have the discussion. Each iteration of the design process takes very little time to visualize. Focus your valuable time and effort on the product instead of stylized presentations.

TECHNICAL STUFF

Atos Origin produced independent research showing that the average corporate employee spends 40 percent of his or her working day on internal emails that add no business value whatsoever, which means the real work week doesn't start until Wednesday.

Pageantry is too often mistaken for professionalism and progress. In scrum projects, you're encouraged to communicate immediately, directly, and informally whenever you have a question and to work closely with your team members to increase efficiency and save time.

Avoid these unproductive traps:

- » Fancy, time-consuming presentations
- » Long and/or unfocused meetings
- » Tomes of documentation
- » Excessive effort justifying progress

Emphasize these productivity builders:

- » Be barely sufficient. In all things, the work should be barely sufficient to accomplish the goal. (Don't mistake sufficiency for mediocrity. Sufficient is sufficient; more is wasteful, and problems often arise in that bloat. See Agile Principle 10 earlier in this chapter.)
- » Communicate frequently with all parties to reduce the need for extensive updates.
- » Communicate simply and directly. If you can speak to someone face to face, do so.

Figure out the simplest way to get what you need, always with the goal of delivering the highest-quality product.

TIP

Before long, your projects will evolve a scrum culture. As people become educated in the process and see the improved results, their buy-in for being barely sufficient will increase. So, bear through any initial pushback with education, patience, and consistency.

Think and act as a team

The heart of scrum is working as a team. The scrum team environment can at first be unsettling, however, because U.S. corporate culture encourages the mindset of the individual ("How well can I succeed in this environment so that I stand out and get the next promotion?").

In scrum, the project survives or dies at the team level. By using each individual's talent on a team, you take the project from average to hyperproductive. As Aristotle said, "The whole is greater than the sum of its parts."

How do you create this team culture? The scrum framework itself emphasizes teamwork. Physical space, common goals, and collective ownership all scream "team." Add the following practices to your scrum framework:

>> Eliminate work titles. No one owns areas of development; status is established by skills and contribution.

>> Pair team members to enhance cross-functionality and front-load quality assurance. Then frequently switch the pairings.

>> Always report team metrics, not individual or pairing metrics.

Visualize rather than write

On the whole, people are visual; they think pictorially and remember pictorially. Most kids like pictures — visual illustrations of text. Adults are no different. We're likely to start reading a magazine by flipping through its images and then going back to read any articles that piqued our interest.

Pictures, diagrams, and graphs relay information instantly. Written reports require reader buy-in, which drops as the reports grow.

TECHNICAL STUFF

Twitter was interested in studying the effectiveness of tweets with photos versus those that were text only. It conducted a study using SHIFT Media Manager and came up with some interesting results. Users engaged five times more frequently when tweets included photos as opposed to text-only tweets. And the rate of retweets and replies with photos was doubled. However, the cost per engagement of photo tweets was half that of text-only tweets (Shift Newsroom, January 17, 2014).

When possible, encourage your team to present information visually, even if that means sketching a diagram on a whiteboard. If anybody doesn't understand the diagram, he or she can ask about it. Changes can be made right there and then. Also, with current technology, simple graphs, charts, and models are at your fingertips.

The Five Scrum Values

Scrum is founded on five values that each member of the team uses to guide his or her decision-making:

- >> Commitment
- >> Focus
- >> Openness
- >> Respect
- >> Courage

These values aren't rocket science. Instead, they fall into that familiar category of common sense. Yet they're critical to the successful implementation of scrum, so they deserve discussion here.

In the following sections, we look at each of these values more closely to show how vital they are within scrum projects.

Commitment

Scrum team members must be committed to success, and they must be willing to create realistic goals and stick to them. Everyone must participate. A scrum project is an "all in" situation in which everyone is part of a team, and everyone works together to meet the team's commitments. Fortunately, the scrum model ensures that you have the authority and freedom to do just that.

At the core of scrum is an event called a *sprint*, which we cover in Chapter 5. A sprint requires clear goals set within fixed timeboxes. In this model, you break those goals into the smallest chunks of work possible so that you know what you're getting into. You know what's realistic, so you can set appropriate goals and meet your commitments.

Focus

Part of the magic of scrum is that it's built around the concept of focus. Focus on a few things at a time. You will have a clear role and clear goals within that role. Your job is to use your role to contribute to achieving the goal. Every day, team members know what to focus on for that day to be successful, which is liberating.

You made your goals and commitments earlier. Focus on those goals and nothing else.

Don't worry; contribute your best; be happy.

Openness

Everything in your project, and everyone else's project, is transparent and available for inspection and improvement. The goals and progress of anyone involved in the project — you, your boss, your employees, your in-laws — are open and visible. Gone are the days of six-months-down-the-road surprises.

Fortunately, the basis of scrum is the agile pillars of empiricism: transparency, inspection, and adaptation. Information radiators (big, visible charts) and real-time intelligence allow for unfettered action. Most people aren't used to this level of exposure. But after it catches on in your organization, they won't have things any other way.

Respect

Each team member is selected for his or her strengths. Along with these strengths come weaknesses and opportunities to learn and grow. The golden rule within scrum is that each participant must respect everyone else.

Harmony is created by the synchronization of roles, which creates a development rhythm as the project progresses. If one person is out of tune for a bit, it's in your best interest to help that person, because all team members are held accountable as a team.

People want to do good work; it's in our wiring. If you seek the positive, you'll find the positive. Likewise, if you seek the negative, you'll find the negative. Respect is the burning ember of positivity.

Courage

Scrum is about change and honesty, and every idea you have will get challenged in a scrum model. No procedure is justified because you've always done things a certain way. Say goodbye to procedures you've done by habit and say hello to a process that's built on what the team finds to be successful. Jacob Bronowski could have been speaking about the scrum model when he said

> *It is important that students bring a certain ragamuffin, barefoot irreverence to their studies; they are not here to worship what is known, but to question it.*

Fiefdoms will be challenged. Rules will be tested. Routines will be broken. Improvements will happen. Change can be hard. Change takes courage.

Scrum takes courage.

2

Running a Scrum Project

Chapter **2**

The First Steps

Work expands so as to fill the time available for its completion.
— PARKINSON'S LAW

Scrum is simple in concept yet often difficult in application. Changing 70 years' worth of product development paradigm is challenging. Still, achieving 30 to 40 percent time-to-market increase and 30 to 70 percent cost savings are realistic. Jeff Sutherland, a co-creator of scrum, has documented 1,000 percent performance improvements by using scrum. Given that potential, it's worthwhile to get out of your comfort zone and start dealing with the organizational dysfunctions that are holding you back.

If the number-one trend in IT is converting to scrum and associated agile engineering approaches (such as eXtreme Programming), it's possible for your organization to make the transition. Many companies are making it and making it well. The process just takes an open mind — something that's good for all of us. By the end of this chapter, you'll be up and running with your project and ready to take the next scrum steps.

Getting Your Scrum On

Two factors come into play as you convert to scrum:

>> **The nature of the project:** It's easy to find out whether the nature of a project fits scrum because the fact is that scrum is for everyone. Any project for which you want early, empirical evidence of performance and quality can and should be done with a scrum framework.

>> **The social culture within which the project resides:** Social culture is complex because people are complex. Changing processes can be easy; changing people isn't. Every person and every group of people has idiosyncrasies. As entertaining as these idiosyncrasies are at a barbecue, they can be a hurdle to overcome in teaching new project management techniques.

It's natural for people to resist change, and people resist to different degrees and in different ways. When people understand how the changes will benefit them directly, however, the conversion is faster and easier.

As you see in Parts 3 to 5 of this book, billion-dollar companies benefit from scrum, as do everyday folks. A colleague used scrum to plan, day by day, a recent vacation. He and his wife agreed that because scrum allowed the right combination of structure with freedom, the vacation was the best they'd ever had. (Chapter 17 provides additional examples of using scrum within a family.)

Show me the money

Consider Net Present Value 101: A dollar today is more valuable than a dollar six months from now. The biggest problem in organizations isn't the efficiency of the tactical execution teams; it's poor portfolio management. Executives fail to show the leadership necessary to make the tough prioritization calls, which results in too many projects being pushed down to a lower level of management that lacks the power to fight back. (See Chapter 13 for more on this dynamic.)

This dysfunction is masked by stretching people across multiple projects so that each business unit gets something. Getting everything done takes considerably longer, but the managers of each project are placated by binders of documents telling them how great their products are going to be when they eventually get them. This thrashing between projects comes at a real cost.

Scrum is the opposite. You focus, you produce deliverable tangible results, and then you increment forward. The product backlog (described in detail in Chapter 3) forces you to be effective before worrying about efficiency.

Your organization may be a billion-dollar company or a mom-and-pop store struggling to get a great idea to market. Maybe you're one of a gazillion employees, and you've been given this one project to prove yourself. In each case, disciplined prioritization, increased efficiency, and incremental tested progress can help you survive.

Because of the prioritization within scrum, you're working exclusively on the highest-value features. You're not perfecting a third-tier widget instead of a high-value feature. You're going for the meat every time. As a result, what you produce during each sprint is what's most important, practical, and immediately desirable. In every release, you have something that the marketplace values. That's scrum. That's showing you the money.

REMEMBER

When your back is against the wall, everyone reverts to agile techniques, whether realizing it or not. If your company had 60 days' worth of cash left on hand, nobody would worry about whether a status report has the right cover sheet. Bureaucracy is the luxury of the financially bloated, and it's a luxury that can change overnight in today's economy.

TIP

In our seminars, we teach that it's better to do all of something than a little bit of everything. If you wait for everything to be ready, chances are that nothing will get done. Instead, take those tangible steps of progress that you achieve through scrum, get them out to market, get feedback, and let the revenue flow in.

Fortunately, scrum is built around delivering tested, usable results early and often. You don't wait to see results. You see them after every sprint.

Try this approach for yourself. Ask yourself or your customer, "If we had only one month to deliver value to the marketplace, what would we build, and how?" See how taking this incremental approach brings value to the forefront?

DO SOMETHING BEFORE DOING EVERYTHING

Using the practice of doing something before doing everything, a client agreed to put a product out to market with only one way for the customer to purchase it. Instead of making sure that every credit card on Earth was tied in, that PayPal was set up, and that personal checks could be processed with speed, the client decided to chance raising early funds with only one credit card payment option. The result? Between October and January, he brought in more than $1 million in sales. Now the site can process multiple credit cards, PayPal, and several other payment options — each of which was rolled out one sprint at a time *after* the product was actively generating revenue.

REMEMBER

Scrum may still be a fresh concept to many, but its usage is growing by leaps and bounds. In 2008, we were thrilled to learn that more organizations were using agile techniques than waterfall techniques for software development. By 2012, Forrester estimated at least 80 percent of organizations would be using agile techniques for software development. In May 2012, SimplyHired.com showed 20,000 jobs requiring scrum knowledge, and by May 2013, this had increased to 670,000 jobs. We have crossed the chasm and this growth of agile projects has continued to increase through 2016 according to the annual survey conducted by VersionOne.com.

I want it now

Ever heard that? Three-year-old preschoolers aren't the only people who say it; bosses and colleagues also demand "I want it now," or you may even hear that inner voice within your own head saying it. Scrum makes it more possible to see immediate results. scrum projects regularly see less than a 30–40 percent time-to-market. But how?

The answer is simple: Start development early and thereby end development early. You're creating shippable products from the start. You don't wait for months or years for results that may have passed their technological sell-by date. You quickly plan, create, inspect, adapt, ship, and benefit. In this process, you churn out value early and continuously.

WARNING

In science as in business, the rule isn't survival of the fittest but survival of the fastest. Whoever could crawl into safety fastest missed being snatched up by the predator. In business, innovations are released to market at exponentially increasing speeds. Brands are created and killed overnight. You simply can't afford to be late.

That's not the only reason why you want to experience increased speed to market. As you create your product backlog (the project to-do list), you order and prioritize the items. In prioritization, you take two things into consideration:

>> Items with the highest value

>> Items with the highest risk

Both factors get to the top of the list.

I'm not sure what I want

Most people don't know what they want, at least not until they interact with it. The majority of people, companies, and organizations realize what they want only when they interact with the product or service directly. The gap is the difference between waterfall (seeing it in documents) and scrum (using it).

In your roadmap to value (see Chapter 1), you begin with a vision of what you want your product to be. This vision acts as a beacon for your team, the way that any established destination acts as a beacon. The roadmap allows for the natural progression of decision-making, from large fuzzy generalities down to small specific operationalization of that goal. The vision provides the outer boundary of what can change. If resulting product deviates from the vision, it's a different project.

Scrum enables you to build out a successful business no matter what that business is. For example,

>> Developing a website where people can order organic, allergy-specific restaurant food for home delivery

>> Constructing an Alzheimer's patient residence with individual-specific, on-site monitoring; alerts; and security

>> Selling Grandma's doughnut recipe that you're convinced will lead to the next Krispy Kreme

How these ideas would pan out in reality is yet to be determined. The good news is that you develop the most effective path of progress through the scrum framework. The process of tangible creation, inspection, and adaptation gives you the tools to create the product that's needed.

Is that bug a problem?

Each item that the development team completes is tested and integrated to ensure that it works. The product owner is responsible for either accepting or rejecting each requirement as it's completed. In other words, if something doesn't work, it doesn't make it out of the sprint.

Issues can come up with enterprise integration, load limits, and so on after a product makes it into production, of course. But the feedback cycle is so strong during development that as soon as a defect or process inefficiency is spotted, it can be corrected. The problem is fixed in that sprint or placed back in the product backlog to be prioritized against future work.

Your company's culture

When people see the success and value of scrum, using it becomes easier. Employees discover that scrum improves communication and collaboration, creates *esprit de corps*, has a natural life cycle, develops an honest and transparent environment, and increases ownership and empowerment, all of which affects company culture in a hugely positive way.

The level of resistance to change varies from company culture to culture. The solution, as with so many things, is tangible success. (You'll find no defense against demonstrated success!) Find what the key people need — increased profits, higher product quality, faster delivery, or improved talent retention — and show them how the scrum model delivers.

In any group of people, you'll find the influencers — the ones with clout who can get change rolling. Maybe you're an influencer, or maybe someone else is. Get that person on board (which may mean going to higher management), and your job will be easier.

The Power in the Product Owner

Involvement begets commitment. You want to build a team that can move the gears of change. The key to moving the gears of change is the product owner.

The product owner's primary job is to take care of the business side of the project. This person is responsible for maximizing product value by delivering return on investment (ROI) to the organization. The product owner is one person, not a committee, and is a full-time, dedicated member of the scrum team. This person doesn't own the product but takes ownership of the business-side duties, representing the stakeholders and customers.

Some of the primary responsibilities of the product owner are as follows:

>> Setting the goals and vision for the product, including writing the vision statement

>> Creating and maintaining the product roadmap, which is a broad view of the scope of the product and the initial product backlog

>> Making in-the-moment priority and trade-off decisions

>> Ensuring visibility of the product backlog

>> Optimizing the work done by the development team

>> Taking full ownership of and responsibility for the product backlog

>> Accepting proposed requirements and ordering them by priority in the product backlog

>> Setting release and sprint goals

>> Determining which product backlog items go into the next sprint

>> Handling business aspects of the project, including ROI and business risk, and interfacing with business stakeholders and customers

>> Socialize the vision and the roadmap

>> Being available throughout the day to work directly with development team members, thereby increasing efficiency through clear and immediate communication

>> Accepting or rejecting work results throughout the sprint, ideally the day they are completed

We're often shocked that organizations that plan to pour millions of dollars into a project say they don't have the resources for a dedicated product owner to ensure that the business and technical priorities align and that the product created is the product needed. Yet many of these organizations have a project manager to direct the project. Because the project manager role doesn't exist in scrum (relevant duties are part of the three scrum roles; see Chapter 1), the money for product owners can be taken from there.

Product owners clarify, prioritize, and set an environment for focus. They ensure that the scrum team is effective. The product owner determines what requirements are pursued and when work shifts to those requirements — that is, what and when but not how or how much. How and how much is the responsibility of the development team.

Imagine that your passion is building something. In scrum, you'd be a member of the development team. For you, the product owner is a gift. This person excels in portfolio management because he or she is empowered to make decisions, clarify, prioritize, and fight to ensure that team members focus on one project at a time. Because of effective product owners, development team members are freed from distractions and can spend more of their attention on getting their jobs done.

Both the product owner and the scrum master work to create the best environment possible for the development team to do the highest-quality work it can. The product owner handles and deflects business concerns and noise, and the scrum master ensures that other organizational interruptions don't affect the development team.

The abstraction layer created by the product owner and scrum master doesn't mean less business noise. It means that for the most part, the development team doesn't have to deal with the noise.

On the other hand, development team members can contact stakeholders or other team or nonteam people directly when they need clarification on something they're working on. This model of filtering prioritization but not clarification is like the membrane of a cell that's designed to let certain fluids travel in one direction but not the other.

The result is that the development team is protected from outside interferences but not hindered in their quest for knowledge. These boundaries are important and integral to the successful functioning of the development team.

Why Product Owners Love Scrum

Product owners love scrum for the following reasons:

>> Development and business are aligned and held accountable as a single unit, rather than being at odds as in historical methodologies.

>> Schedules and costs are empirically forecasted, and product owners have daily clarity on progress.

>> After every sprint, product owners know that they'll have the highest-priority items fully functioning and shippable.

>> Customer feedback is early and continuous.

>> The earliest possible tangible measurement on ROI is available — that is, after every sprint.

>> Systematic support is provided for changing business needs, giving the product owner continuing flexibility to adapt to market realities.

>> Product and process waste are reduced through emphasis on prioritized product development, not process artifact development (usually, documents).

REMEMBER

The product owner's number-one characteristic should be *decisiveness*. This person makes tough, pragmatic, and uncomfortable decisions every hour of every day. She needs to be able to create an environment of trust and pivot when changes are needed. The product owner must begin by doing what she thinks is right and then change based on empirical evidence. To be effective, a product owner must be empowered to make tactical decisions without escalating to a higher power.

A scrum product owner's role is much different from a traditional project manager's role. Imagine telling a golfer to hit the ball 400 yards and straight into the hole and also telling him that he'll be hit with his own club if he doesn't succeed. The traditional IT world works that way. With scrum, the golfer hits the ball, assesses the results, and adapts to achieve the goal in the best possible way given where he is, not where he should be.

THE PRODUCT OWNER AGENT OPTION

In today's world, it's not always possible to have an on-site product owner. You may be headquartered in California yet running projects out of a facility in Hyderabad, India. At our company, we've found a controversial but workable solution to be the *product owner agent* role. This role is an on-site person who is responsible for day-to-day communication and decision-making. The agent is the physical representation of the product owner, speaking and acting on behalf of the product owner, who isn't on-site.

Product owner agents aren't scrum. Although we don't recommend product owner agents as a matter of course, we've used them with success in certain situations while the organization matures. The goal is to make the role of the agent temporary, like an apprenticeship, while the person proves his ability to be a true product owner.

With the product owner agent, you're able to provide the quick clarifications and decision-making that scrum requires. Much as a real estate broker takes final responsibility for any real estate agent's decisions and actions, however, the headquartered product owner is responsible for the agent's decisions. The liability remains singular.

Rather than having one foot in each place and getting marginal results, embed a product owner on-site. The up-front cost may seem to be high, but if you consider the increased speed and quality of the result, your true project costs are lowered.

The Company Goal and Strategy: Stage 1

Vision statements aren't part of the scrum model, but vision statements are useful and widely adopted. Companies, not-for-profit organizations, and individuals often use vision statements.

TIP

When we coach clients, we always have them create a vision statement so that their goal is right in front of them. We're looking for a crisp, concise, clear elevator pitch that can be conveyed during the ground-to-fourth-floor ride. We ask them to have their vision statement done before we first meet with them. Then we spend one hour with the people responsible for it, honing it to something we can work with. It doesn't take long to create this invaluable artifact.

Vision statements are so useful that we've made them Stage 1 in our roadmap to value (see Figure 2-1). Think of your vision statement as a destination with a beacon. You may have 100 ways to get to the destination, and it doesn't matter which way you take; the point is to end there. With this beacon of a statement, you always know where you're headed because you have the goal in sight. From this stable, strategic destination, you have limitless tactical flexibility.

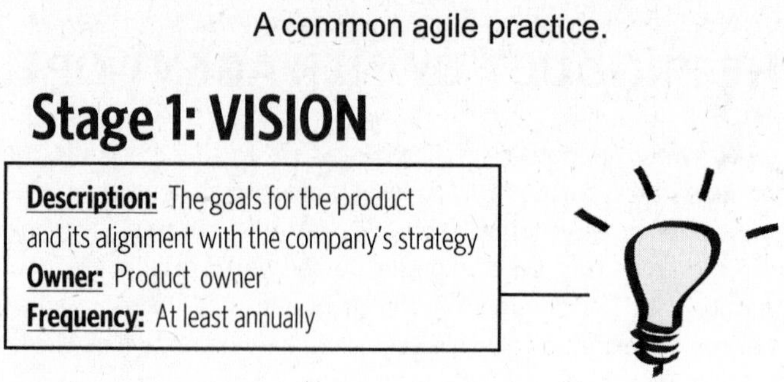

A common agile practice.

Stage 1: VISION

FIGURE 2-1:
The vision statement is Stage 1 of the roadmap to value.

> **Description:** The goals for the product and its alignment with the company's strategy
> **Owner:** Product owner
> **Frequency:** At least annually

A vision statement is

>> Internally focused, with no marketing fluff

>> Fine-tuned to the goals of the marketplace and customer needs

>> Strategic in nature, showing what rather than how

>> Reviewed annually (for multiyear projects)

>> Owned by the product owner

REMEMBER

Your vision statement must be communicated throughout the organization or group of people you're working with. Whether the team is designing a new model of sports car or planning a wedding, everyone needs to clearly understand the goal, which sets expectations and the tone of the project.

Structuring your vision

In his excellent book *Crossing the Chasm* (Collins Business Essentials), Geoffrey Moore recommends an effective method for creating your vision statement. We use this model often, with first-rate results.

The entire statement should be no longer than two or three sentences. Moore recommends this model:

>> For *<target customer>*

>> who *<statement of the need>*

>> the *<product name>*

>> is a *<product category>*

>> that *<product key benefit, compelling reason to buy>*

>> Unlike *<primary competitive alternative>*

- our product *<final statement of product differentiation>*

We recommend adding this conclusion:

>> which supports our strategy to *<company strategy>*

Here are examples of what this format looks like in real life:

>> Tankless water heater

- *For* home owners *who* desire continuous hot water flow and better conservation of energy, *the* Acme Tankless Water Heater *is a* demand, point-of-use, or instantaneous water heater *that* efficiently heats water as you use it. *Unlike* tank-type water heaters, *our product* provides continuous flow at consistent temperatures with lower operating costs at 94 percent efficiency, *which supports our strategy to* provide for tomorrow's generation by reducing the waste of natural resources today.

>> Hawaiian vacation

- *For* my spouse and me, *who* are stressed out of our minds, *the* Hawaii or Bust 2018 vacation *is a* spontaneous, last-minute getaway *that* will remove us from our hectic lives long enough to provide new experiences. *Unlike* family vacations or structured itineraries, *our product* provides complete flexibility without expectations, *which supports our strategy to* make the most of each moment together.

REMEMBER

The vision statement itself is functional, but the addition of business strategy is emotional. Bring purpose to your project in the form of a company strategy that makes people's lives better. It's never your company strategy to make money; it's to do something of such value that it can be monetized.

Finding the crosshair

The vision statement is created and owned by the product owner and is integral to the business side of the project. One mind, however, is just that: one mind. The product owner may own this statement, but she'll surely have better luck creating and refining it by using collective intelligence. To this end, the product owner can choose to receive input from development team members, the scrum master, external or internal stakeholders, and even users themselves. What to do with input is the product owner's choice and the product owner's responsibility.

When product owners are open to input from others, the product owner may become aware of nuances, features, and market angles that one person alone wouldn't think of. The product owner may be wise to take feedback and then carefully filter it through her own understanding of the project.

The Scrum Master

In *The New One Minute Manager* (William Morrow), Kenneth Blanchard and Spencer Johnson describe how some of the most effective managers he studied lacked the technical skills that their employees had. Oddly enough, they also had a lot of time on their hands. If they couldn't do the job themselves, what were these managers good at?

The managers were able to clear the path so that their employees could get the work done, which is the role of the scrum master. Whereas product owner is a directing role, scrum master is an enabling role. The scrum master is responsible for the environment for success.

Scrum master traits

The scrum master's most important trait, after deep expertise in scrum, is clout. Diplomacy, communication skills, and ability to manage up are all good qualities, but the scrum master also needs to have the respect and clout to get difficult situations resolved. Where clout comes from — expertise, longevity, charisma, association — doesn't matter, because it works in the scrum master role.

As a servant leader, the scrum master teaches, encourages, removes tactical impediments, and most importantly, removes strategic impediments so that the tactical ones don't reappear. As with every other role, the scrum master is best full-time and solely dedicated to the scrum master job, especially with new teams, projects, and organizations.

TIP

If the product owner is the quarterback calling the plays and the development team is the running back gaining the yards, the scrum master is a blocker who clears the path. Yet they're all peers with a common goal.

In our experience, developers who double as scrum masters and scrum masters thrashed across multiple teams throw off a team's ability to extrapolate past performance to future capability. This situation introduces availability variation and delivers inferior protection to a development team, which rarely makes sense quantitatively because a minor improvement in a scrum team's velocity (see Chapter 4) often has a huge effect on the bottom line. If your team can schedule its organizational interruptions and is so mature that it can't improve further, contact us; we want to write a book about *you*.

Like every other role, the scrum master should be a full-time role, and the person who holds it should be solely dedicated to that job, especially for new teams, projects, and organizations.

REMEMBER

An ideal development team is three to nine people, so one scrum master improves the performance of up to nine people. Even a minor reduction in performance has a ninefold effect.

In addition to coaching the team on how to play scrum, the scrum master facilitates the events: sprint planning meetings, daily scrums, sprint reviews, and sprint retrospectives.

A scrum team is a bunch of intelligent, engaged people with a high degree of ownership in the work that they're doing. Put these folks in a meeting together, and the creative energy may cause them to explode — or at least go off on a lot of tangents. The scrum master's role is to focus this energy.

The scrum master's influence extends to everyone involved, including stakeholders and product owners. The scrum master is a coach to everyone because everyone needs ongoing education and smooth facilitation in scrum.

WARNING

If you're making decisions as a scrum master, you're not doing the right job. A development team will never become self-organizing if it's not making its own decisions. Scrum masters extract themselves from day-to-day decisions and create a conducive collaboration environment while shielding the team from interference.

As the scrum master shields the development team from external interference, the velocity of the team increases dramatically. Think about how well you work when the door's shut, the phone's off, and everybody's away or asleep versus when you're fielding constant interruptions from colleagues, family members, and even the dog.

Even when outside interference is kept to a minimum, because social density is higher in scrum, it's not unusual for conflict to also be higher. The pressure to get products working in short sprint windows can be wearing, so the scrum master's job entails managing conflict to the right level. Task conflict (being willing to fight for what you think is right) is healthy. Personal conflict (challenging someone personally) is not.

Scrum master as servant leader

The concept of *servant leader* dates to around 500 BCE and was developed by Lao Tzu, who is thought to be the author of the *Tao Te Ching*. Yet this concept is mentioned in every major religion and is popular in modern-day corporate leadership models. That's staying power.

The servant leader puts others first so that they can do their jobs. The leader enables people rather than presenting the solution on a silver plate. If someone says, "I'm hungry," the servant leader doesn't hand him a fish. Rather, the leader asks, "How can I help you so that you're not hungry today, tomorrow, or next year?" The scrum master helps each person build skills and find the solution that works best for that person, whether the answer lies inside or outside the project.

As a servant leader, a scrum master teaches, encourages, removes tactical impediments, and removes strategic impediments so that tactical impediments don't reappear.

Why scrum masters love scrum

Scrum masters love scrum for many reasons, including these:

>> They can focus on having quantifiable impact rather than administrative responsibilities. Rising velocity has a direct tie to additional value that the scrum team can deliver.

>> They coach people rather than serve as check-the-box managers.

>> They get to enable people rather than direct them.

>> They ask questions rather than give answers.

>> They're involved with fewer meetings, and those meetings are shorter.

>> They facilitate building empowered, motivated teams that think for themselves and act with authority.

>> Performance accountability isn't outsourced to them (as in "Hey, Joe, what's the status of the tasks Nancy is working on?"). Instead, accountability is sourced directly to the person who's doing the work.

TIP

A good scrum master motto is "Never lunch alone." Always create and develop relationships. Influence is your currency, so make sure that you create an environment in which you can easily pick up the phone or walk to a person's desk and get results.

THE INTERFERENCE ISSUE

Studies have shown that it takes 15 minutes to get to the right level of concentration for peak productivity — a state that's often called "being in the zone." Yet it takes only a 2.3-second interruption to burst that bubble, so another 15 minutes is required to reestablish focus. A 4.4-second interruption *triples* the number of mistakes made in a sequencing task.

Three types of interference prevail in the workplace:

- **Personal interruptions:** Personal interruptions are email flashes, phone calls from Aunt Martha, and text messages with links to cat videos. Discipline is the solution. Turn off your technology to tune in to your task. Check out the nearby sidebar "The Pomodoro technique."

- **Team interruptions:** Team interruptions are those caused by workmates. The team needs to identify collaboration time versus concentration time and then balance these times based on team dynamics and project needs.

  - *Collaboration time* is time when it's okay to interrupt, talk, and exchange ideas. This time is healthy and productive time, and it should make up the bulk of each team member's day.

  - *Concentration time* can be indicated by physical indicators such as noise-canceling headsets and Do Not Disturb signs. This time helps team members get to a deep level of concentration and crank out product.

- **External interruptions:** External interruptions are the scrum master's domain. These interruptions can happen anytime, all day, and every day. The scrum master's job is to shield team members from these interruptions.

Most interruptions are caused by higher-ups who pass tactical emergencies to the team responsible for creating quality products, which distracts team members from doing the work needed to reach the next goal. This is part of the reason why the scrum master should be a full-time role and why the scrum master should have plenty of organizational clout. Sometimes the scrum master needs to be able to run interference with the higher-ups to prevent current progress from being derailed.

THE POMODORO TECHNIQUE

The Pomodoro technique of time management, developed in the late 1980s by Francesco Cirillo, entails running personal work sprints of 25 minutes (though you can customize them) to get your own stuff done. The technique involves the following steps:

1. Create a to-do list and prioritize the highest-value items.

2. Work on the top-priority item for 25 minutes.

3. Take a five-minute break.

4. Go back to the same highest-priority item until it's completely done and then move to the next-highest-priority item.

5. After you've completed four Pomodoros (in this case, four 25-minute work periods), take a longer break of 15 to 30 minutes to reset your concentration ability.

Repeat these steps throughout the day to ensure that you accomplish your most important tasks.

Common Roles Outside Scrum

Product owner and scrum master are scrum roles created by the founders of scrum and these roles integral to any scrum project. Another role is development team member (see Chapter 4). But like all good things, project management is evolving and growing. Scrum remains a solid framework and foundation. Some common and proven practices can add value.

The following two roles aren't scrum, but we've found that they add enormous value and clarity when approached properly. Consider adding these roles to your project; they may add value to your scrum endeavor.

Stakeholders

Stakeholders are people who affect or are affected by your project. Internal stakeholders are within your company or organization; they could be from the legal, sales, marketing, management, procurement, or any other division of your company. External stakeholders could be investors or users.

REMEMBER

Although scrum prescribes only scrum team members, the role of stakeholder explicitly interfaces with scrum teams, and we prefer to acknowledge this role explicitly so that we can manage it explicitly. The product owner is the business interface for the scrum team, so stakeholders should work with the development team *through* the product owner. Stakeholders may communicate directly with the development team during sprint reviews or when a development team member contacts them directly for clarification, but stakeholders generally work through the product owner.

Two roles deal with stakeholders:

>> If the stakeholders are on the business side (such as customers, sales teams, or marketing), the product owner is responsible.

>> If the stakeholders are on the nonbusiness side (such as vendors or contractors), the scrum master is responsible.

The key to interacting successfully with stakeholders is to recognize and leverage stakeholders' influence while shielding the development team from any interference.

Scrum mentors

As we've said, scrum is a simple framework in concept but complex in practice. The same can be said of golf. Theoretically, you use a stick to whack a motionless white ball into a hole, using the fewest strokes possible. Yet in practice, golf isn't easy. Like scrum, it's a game of nuance. Small factors make an enormous difference in performance.

The mentor, sometimes called a scrum coach, will work alongside the team to help them develop maturity in practicing scrum. The benefit of using a mentor is that mentors are outside of the normal politics and focus on getting the product out the door. They can step back and see objectively watch how the team works. They can not only identify old habits, but also put the brakes on homemade modifications to scrum that are simply ways to let an old dog do its old tricks.

You'll have the greatest ease and success with scrum if you stick to it in its truest form. A scrum mentor's job is to help team members keep good form. Like athletic coaches, they stand aside; see old, unproductive habits; and help you form new habits that make you successful.

SWINGING TO SUCCESS

Years ago, Mark took up golf for business and in the process caught the golf bug. He loved it, worked at it, and improved his game. But he always struggled with consistency. So, he hired a golf coach.

In the first session, the coach teed up a ball, and Mark hit it. Then the coach watched that one swing and said, "I know what your problem is." I Mark was incredulous. How could the coach possibly know what was wrong with Mark's swing by watching him just one time?

Then the coach said, "You used to play baseball, didn't you?" Mark had played baseball for years, in fact, and the coach could tell right away that his golf swing was like his baseball swing. Mark had carried an old habit into the new sport.

When you convert to scrum, you too will carry habits (even ones that you don't realize you have) from a lifetime of managing your projects differently, often from a waterfall methodology.

Chapter **3**

Planning Your Project

William of Ockham, a fourteenth-century logician and Franciscan friar, was quoted as saying, "Entities should not be multiplied unnecessarily." In simpler, modern-day terms, this statement is known as Occam's Razor. (When you have two competing theories that make the same predictions, the simpler one is better.)

In other words, Keep It Simple, Smarty. You can apply this mantra again and again when managing your project with scrum. If something doesn't feel right, it probably isn't.

In this chapter, you see that keeping things simple applies to a technique that we use to enhance scrum projects — called the product roadmap — as well as to decompose your product's features into the smallest requirements possible.

Throughout this book, we point out common practices that scrum trainers and coaches use successfully. Although they're optional, we recommend that you give them a try. They might make your project transition and completion more successful.

The Product Roadmap: Stage 2

In the seven roadmap to value stages we outline in Chapter 1, you begin with the end in mind by creating your vision statement (a common agile practice that works well). The next step is creating a map to help you achieve that vision (see Figure 3-1).

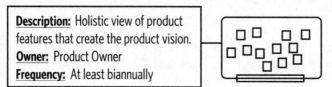

FIGURE 3-1:
The product
roadmap is
Stage 2 in the
roadmap
to value.

Although neither the vision statement nor the product roadmap is a formal aspect of scrum, both elements are common within the agile industry.

Creating a product roadmap is a common-sense way to set off on the journey and align an entire group. If you were to go on a voyage with a crew and passengers, you'd want to know your destination and most likely route before you leave the safety of the harbor. The same holds true with almost any project. Following are the general steps in creating a roadmap:

1. Decide where you want to go (develop the vision).

2. Figure out how to get there (design the product roadmap).

3. Socialize the vision (communicate the plan).

The product roadmap can change, but it gives you something tangible to start with, thereby increasing efficiency. By socializing the roadmap as an artifact of planning or replanning, you can make sure that influencers and stakeholders understand the direction and path. Adjustments to the plan are less costly, and a shared vision contributes to team unification.

Take the long view

The product roadmap is a holistic, high-level view of the features necessary to achieve the product goal that you outlined in your vision statement.

Natural project affinities are established ("If we do this, we should logically do that"), and gaps in features are made readily visible ("Hey, where is . . .?").

The product roadmap is the initial product backlog (your master to-do list), and as the likelihood of product backlog items being developed increases, items are increasingly broken down (progressive elaboration). The product backlog expands to include items that are

>> Small (imminently developable; often referred to as user stories)

>> Midsize (midrange developable; often referred to as epics)

>> Conceptual (clear but lacking details; often referred to as features)

TIP

See the sidebar "Roadmap and backlog terminology" later in this chapter for more information about features, epics, and user stories.

REMEMBER

The product roadmap isn't fixed in stone and fully paved; it's a living, dynamic artifact. We review and update these roadmaps at least twice a year, although this frequency varies depending on the individual project.

Although the vision statement is fully owned by the product owner, the development team needs to be part of the roadmap–building process. Members of the development team are the technological experts who will be doing the work, and they must provide technical constraints and effort estimates. If the development team hasn't been chosen yet, include the functional managers after you create the initial product roadmap. These managers can help identify the skills that will be necessary and get the development team assembled as quickly as possible so that the team can provide high-level effort estimates.

When we begin working with a client, we sit down with the business stakeholders, the product owner, the development team, and the scrum master and create the vision statement and the product roadmap on Day 1. We finish on Day 1 so that the actual development begins on Day 2.

Use simple tools

When creating your product roadmap, use the simplest tools possible. We prefer a whiteboard and sticky notes. Each product feature fits onto a sticky note. This method is simplicity in true working form.

Human brains weren't created in the digital age. Studies have proved that electronics have a dulling effect. In fact, it takes less brain-wave function to watch

TV than it does to watch paint dry. Yet using a simple system like sticky notes is physically and mentally engaging, and using it fosters an environment of change and creativity.

We have helped many clients create a product roadmap by simply placing sticky notes with major requirements on a wall and talking through ideas and issues. For one large project (worth almost half a billion dollars), we put a roadmap together in less than three hours. We start with the highest priority items. As we talk through the vision, stickies are simple to move as the roadmap begins to take shape.

Create your product roadmap

You can use seven easy, common-sense steps to build your product roadmap. Perform these steps on Day 1 of your project; they should take no longer than a few hours. For smaller projects, you'll get the job done over morning coffee. The product owner completes the steps with the rest of the project team (the entire scrum team and the business stakeholders).

Using sticky notes, several colors of flags, and a whiteboard, follow these steps to build your product roadmap:

1. **Write down one product requirement per sticky note.**

   Think of as many product requirements as you can.

2. **If appropriate and synergistic, arrange some requirements in related categories or groups.**

3. **Prioritize the requirements on the roadmap.**

   At the macro level, the highest-priority items are on the left side, and the lowest-priority items are on the right side. At the micro level, the highest-priority requirements are at the top, and the lowest-priority items are at the bottom. The highest-priority items are top-left, and the lowest-priority items are bottom-right.

4. **Identify business dependencies (noted by colored flags on the sticky note).**

5. **Have the development team identify technical dependencies (noted by flags of a different color).**

6. **Have the development team provide order-of-magnitude estimates for the sticky notes.**

7. **Adjust ordering based on dependencies and estimates as appropriate.**

Note the items that prompt the most discussion or concern from the team; these items may be the riskiest or require further breakdown. For estimation methods that your development team can use, check out Chapter 4.

Set your time frame

The nature of your product determines the quantity and timing of your product releases. We suggest a minimum of once per quarter, but the pace of innovation is increasing product releases. We have clients who push to production every day. The most successful social media and Internet firms push twice a day or more.

Ideally, you want to release tested, approved product after every sprint or, better, several times during a sprint (continuous delivery). Occasionally when working with clients, we create high-level product releases (for framing the requirements, not for timeline commitment) so that we can see how those releases align with other product releases, budgetary cycles, holiday cycles, and so on.

Figure 3-2 shows an example of quarterly product releases (common with publicly traded companies). The first release reflects initial release planning and has a level of commitment assigned to it. Everything after that shows how outside influences may affect the project.

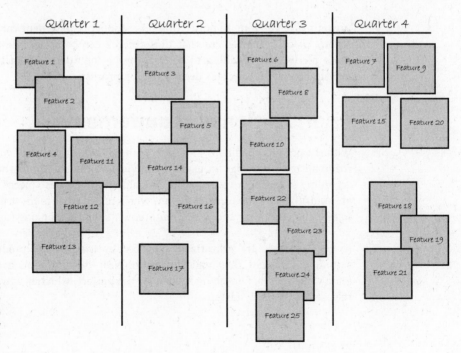

FIGURE 3-2:
An example product roadmap broken down by quarters.

If your time frame is shorter or isn't relevant to your project, consider what your project's time frame is and break it into the initial logical groups, going no farther out than necessary (usually, no more than a year). Follow these steps:

1. **Create the initial groups' worth of features, starting with the highest-priority requirements and moving down.**

2. **Assume at each product release that you will deliver tested, approved, shippable results.**

3. **Above each release, write its conceptual theme.**

4. **Adjust as necessary.**

TIP

The product roadmap and product backlog are excellent for scope control. In traditional project management models, every new idea has to be justified. With scrum, if an idea brings you closer to the project vision, add it to the list. The idea's level of prioritization determines whether it gets completed. Sometimes, only the highest-priority items get done; at other times, every requirement gets done, depending on the budget and the organizational drag on the scrum team.

Breaking Down Requirements

It won't take you long to notice that one product requirement can be broken into several pieces. Chances are that those pieces can be broken down further, and those pieces, we're willing to bet, can be peeled apart too. In this section, we explain how to manage this decomposition process.

Prioritization of requirements

With the product roadmap, you begin with the largest pieces of your project. This roadmap truly provides an eagle's-eye view and is based on what makes sense according to business value and/or risk elimination. These pieces (requirements) are prioritized by the product owner, who decides what is most important to get to that customer first and which requirements logically belong together.

As requirements are prioritized, they become part of the product backlog. In scrum, you work on the smallest set of highest-priority items necessary to generate value, not just anything scoped for the project, which is why scrum projects release functionality faster.

Take two things into consideration as you prioritize: business value and risk. Business value is easy. If a thing has high value, it has high priority. You want to take on the highest-risk requirements first, for four reasons:

>> At the beginning, you have the simplest system to work with. You want to take on your highest-risk developments within the simplest system.

>> You have the greatest amount of money at the beginning. If you're going to take on something that involves high risk, you should do so with the greatest resources at your disposal.

>> Because you have the greatest amount of money, you can fund the development team for the longest time. If you're going to take on a high-risk item, do so with the benefit of the longest runway possible.

>> If you're going to fail, fail early and cheap. If a fundamental flaw exists, you want to know as early as possible. The highest-risk requirements are where the land mines are lurking.

TECHNICAL STUFF

Working with the highest-priority requirements to completion isn't just convenient, but also saves money and is why scrum projects can come in at a 30–70 percent cost savings. If your project runs out of money 80 percent of the way through, you can say without a doubt that you have 80 percent of the highest-priority items completed, functioning, and accepted. The remaining 20 percent? If they were such a low priority, many times you can live without them anyway.

The product roadmap creates your first cut of dependencies. For example, you don't need to worry about having functionality to submit application functionality until you have a website to house that functionality. Critical dependencies are revealed early and help the product owner prioritize the product backlog. Teams begin working on the highest-priority items on Day 2, not Day 120.

REMEMBER

A requirement must earn the right of your investment. Only the highest-priority items deserve your effort to break them into digestible requirements. Everything else can wait. This way, you're always working on only the most important things. Don't waste your time trying to boil the ocean. Learning and adapting is valuable even while building requirements.

Levels of decomposition

In decomposing your requirements into smaller pieces, you want to capture as little detail as possible. In fact, we want you to become expert in doing the bare minimum, progressively elaborating requirements as the likelihood of bringing them into a sprint grows. Gone are the days of spending endless hours working on defining and refining requirements that never see the light of day. Figure 3-3 depicts the layers of requirement decomposition.

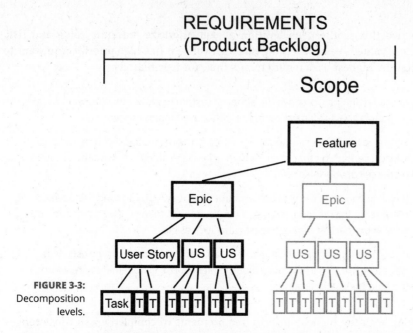

REQUIREMENTS
(Product Backlog)

Scope

Feature

Epic

Epic

User Story | US | US

US | US | US

Task | T | T | T | T | T | T | T | T

T T T T T T T T T

FIGURE 3-3:
Decomposition
levels.

Seven steps of requirement building

Seven steps are involved in building the scope of each requirement. At the end of the seven steps, you know that each requirement works, can be integrated, and has been approved by the product owner. You're tangibly building products to showcase to stakeholders from whom you can garner feedback. This feedback is then used to refine and create new requirements that make the product better reflect stakeholder needs, and the cycle is run again. You incrementally improve the product based on reality.

The seven steps for building each requirement are

1. Requirement elaboration
2. Design
3. Development
4. Comprehensive testing
5. Integration
6. Documentation
7. Approval

ROADMAP AND BACKLOG TERMINOLOGY

The following terms relating to product roadmaps and product backlogs have been developed by scrum experts over the years. They aren't scrum but are part of a collection of common practices that many of us use in the field:

- **Themes:** *Themes* are logical groups of the features that you create in your product roadmap. If a feature is a new capability that a customer will have, a theme is the logical grouping of these features. The functionality that enables a customer to purchase items from a website is an example of a theme. Your product roadmap usually identifies and/or groups features as part of a theme.

- **Features:** *Features* are capabilities that your customers will have that they didn't have before. The functionality that enables a customer to purchase items online via a mobile phone is a feature. Your product roadmap usually consists of feature-level requirements.

- **Epics:** *Epics,* which are a series of actions related to a feature, are the next stage in breaking features into actionable requirements. The functionality that enables a customer to purchase an item via a mobile phone from a shopping cart by using a credit card is an epic. An epic is smaller than a feature (purchasing an item online) but bigger than the credit card integrations that enable an item to be purchased.

  Note: We don't allow requirements larger than epics into a release plan because they aren't specific enough to plan.

- **User stories:** *User stories* are the smallest forms of requirements that can stand on their own. A user story consists of one action of value or one integration of value. Purchasing an item via a mobile phone from a shopping cart by using a Visa card is a user story. Purchasing an item by using a MasterCard is a different integration and a different user story. User stories are small enough to add to sprints and begin developing. We go into user stories in detail in the sections that follow.

- **Tasks:** *Tasks* are the steps needed to implement a user story. During sprint planning, a user story is broken into tasks.

Remember: Requirements are things that users do; *tasks* are what the development team does to make the requirement work.

Your Product Backlog

The product backlog is a true scrum artifact and the master to-do list for the entire project. All scrum projects have product backlogs, which are owned and maintained by the product owner.

The requirements from the product roadmap initially create the product backlog, and the highest-priority ones are broken into user stories on Day 1. (We describe how in "Product backlog refinement" later in this chapter.) Figure 3-4 depicts a sample product backlog.

PRODUCT BACKLOG

Order	ID	Item	Type	Status	Estimate
1	121	As an Administrator, I want to link accounts to profiles, so that customers can access new accounts.	Requirement	Not Started	5
2	113	Update requirements traceability matrix	Overhead	Not Started	2
3	403	As a Customer, I want to transfer money between my active accounts, so that I can adjust each account's balance.	Improvement	Not Started	3
4	97	Refactor Login Class	Maintenance	Not Started	8
5	68	As a Site Visitor, I want to find locations, so that I can use bank services.	Requirement	Not Started	8

FIGURE 3-4: The product backlog is your project's ordered to-do list.

Each item in the product backlog has the following elements:

REMEMBER

>> Specific order number (priority slot in the product backlog)

   Although product backlog items may be similar in priority, they can't be worked on at the same time.

>> Description

>> Estimate of the effort required to complete

>> ID number (optional)

>> Status (optional)

>> Value to the business or product

>> Type of item (optional), which could be a requirement, overhead, maintenance, or improvement (see "The dynamic to-do list" later in this chapter)

REMEMBER

Highest-priority requirements get broken into the smallest actionable requirements possible in the product backlog. A small requirement, however, isn't automatically a high-priority item. Many small requirements have low priority and never see production.

REMEMBER

Anyone can write a product feature or requirement. An idea or concern can be sparked by a business stakeholder, a member of the development team, the scrum master, the product owner, and even the company barista. Ideas are expected from everyone. Only the product owner has the power to accept or reject a requirement into the product backlog, based on whether it supports the vision for the product. The product owner is the full owner of this artifact. If accepted, they will then number, refine, prioritize, and order that new requirement.

The dynamic to-do list

The product backlog never goes away while the project is active. If you have a project, you have a product backlog, which is always changing. As larger requirements are broken into smaller requirements, the backlog changes. As client feedback is received, the backlog changes. As your competitors bring new offerings to market, the backlog changes.

TIP

The product owner not only prioritizes items in the product backlog but also orders them in a logical sequence. This way, the next sprint can be quickly and efficiently organized from these ordered items.

All changes made in the product backlog are made by the product owner. At any point, if anyone (product owner, developer, stakeholder) identifies a new requirement or design idea, it's given to the product owner to be prioritized along with everything else.

In traditional project management frameworks, change is viewed as a reflection of poor planning. If something had to be changed, it was because someone messed up. In scrum, we see change as a sign of growth. As you discover your product more deeply, you will identify changes that need to be made. In scrum, if you're not changing, you're not learning, and that's a problem. It's a lack of change that is a sign of failure. Every day you need to learn something and that causes change. With scrum, change is no longer something you crawl under your desk and hide from. Change is good. Change is life. Change is scrum.

Product backlog refinement

Product backlog refinement is how the scrum team advances its understanding of the items in the product backlog and prepares them for upcoming sprints. Product backlog refinement is a continuous process of breaking down and preparing feedback and responses to change for future development. This process is owned by the product owner and performed with the help of development team members, who ask clarifying questions and provide estimates based on the best information available at that time. The scrum team as a whole spends up to 10 percent of its active sprint time in this process. The scrum master usually facilitates product backlog refinement activities to keep the group focused and on task.

The target outcomes of product backlog refinement are

>> **Clarity:** All developers and the product owner reach a clear consensus on the scope of the product backlog items being discussed.

>> **Acceptance criteria:** All requirements (backlog items) include sufficient acceptance criteria.

>> **Risks identified and mitigated to the best extent possible:** Other known risks should be documented and accepted by the team as necessary.

>> **Sizing:** Requirements are estimated and broken down sufficiently to be accomplished within a sprint.

TECHNICAL STUFF

Acceptance criteria is a term frequently used in scrum practices. It refers to a section on the back of the story card or in project software to communicate to everyone what "done" means for each story. It may include testing criteria and specific examples of how the feature is expected to function when the work is complete.

Backlog refinement should be a regular occurrence, but scrum doesn't prescribe how formal or frequent refinement discussions should be; neither does it prescribe an agenda. Here are suggestions that have worked well for us and our clients:

>> **Format:** The product owner presents one requirement to the team at a time. For each requirement, team members ask questions, challenge assumptions, explore implementation strategies, and use a whiteboard for drawing and clarification until they have consensus on the details and scope of the requirement. Then the development team uses estimation poker or affinity estimating (see Chapter 4) to assign a relative estimation.

For a requirement that moves up in priority, the estimation indicates when the requirement is small enough to fit into a sprint.

>> **Time:** Scrum teams on average spend about 10 percent of a sprint in refining the backlog in preparation for the next sprint.

>> **Frequency:** Backlog refinement is a progressive activity. Requirements get refined gradually, just in time, with those closer to delivery being made ready for sprints. Teams may prefer conducting backlog refinement on one of these schedules:

- Daily, at the end of each day

  This schedule also acts as a demobilization exercise for development team members to transition into going home for the day.

- Daily, at some other agreed-on time

- Once per sprint during a regularly scheduled block of time

- Once per week during a regularly scheduled block of time

- Multiple times per week during a regularly scheduled block of time

- As needed, determined, and scheduled by the team in each sprint

» **Activities:** Backlog refinement activities may consist of the following types of activities:

- Entire team discussions, including whiteboarding, modeling, question-and-answer sessions, and design discussions

- Research of items identified during team discussions

- Interviews of subject-matter experts or stakeholders to gain insights for determining scope and suggested solutions to requirements

- Estimation poker or affinity estimation sessions

As the team discusses and refines the next-highest-priority requirement candidates, use as many of the following questions and guidelines as needed to guide the team through the refinement process. Not all these items apply to every team and/or requirement.

» Breaking down large requirements

- Does the user story satisfy the INVEST criteria (see the "INVEST" sidebar later in this chapter)?

- Can the requirement be completed within one sprint or part of one sprint?

- Is the user story a single action of value or a series of actions?

- Is the scope barely sufficient?

- Has the product owner added technical tasks or other technical details that should be left to the development team to determine?

- Has the scrum team's definition of *done* (see Chapter 4) been considered before determining that the story is sufficiently broken down?

- Is more research required before the team can estimate?

» Clarifying and refining where needed

- Does the development team understand the business intent and/or value of the requirement?

- Have development team members tried paraphrasing the requirement to make sure that everyone is on the same page?

- Is the desired deliverable clear?

- Does an implementation approach make sense from both technical and business perspectives?

- Is the team considering all the work needed to fully complete and deliver the story?

- Does the team know the tasks that will be required?

- Will the team be able to deliver a fully done increment of the product at the end of this sprint?

>> Ensuring adequate acceptance criteria

- If needed, have personas been identified (see "Product Backlog Common Practices" later in this chapter).

- Are the acceptance criteria complete and adequate?

- Have test-oriented development team members stated that the criteria are sufficient?

>> Addressing potential issues and risks

- Can the story stand alone, or are there dependencies?

- What conflicts may arise during implementation?

- What technical debt might this requirement introduce?

>> Assigning high-level estimates

- Has the scrum team decided on a consistent estimation method (see Chapter 4)?

- Has the team agreed on how to reach consensus?

- Have estimations revealed that any of the requirements are still too big?

If estimations bring up additional points that need clarification, use these guidelines to further refine them before reestimating.

TIP

You need to watch a few factors in this process:

>> Only development team members estimate requirements because they're the ones doing the work.

>> The product owner provides immediate clarifications to developers' questions by being actively involved in the refinement discussions.

>> The frequency and duration of refinement activities will vary from team to team, from project to project, and even from sprint to sprint.

Other possible backlog items

When we coach clients in building their product backlog, we encourage them to identify a type of backlog item (refer to Figure 3-4 earlier in this chapter).

We use four types to clarify the nature of the item to be completed. All these items can be done (or not done) at the product owner's discretion:

>> **Requirement:** Basic business requirements make up the bulk of a product backlog. A requirement explains why a feature is being built and what needs to be done.

>> **Maintenance:** Design improvements for the code, such as fundamentally rethinking a login class that can't be tactically tweaked anymore. Maintenance items reduce the technical debt of the project.

>> **Improvements:** Based on results from the sprint retrospective, what can be done differently in the process, such as expand automated testing skills.

>> **Overhead:** Companies often have overhead items that they like to see, such as a requirement traceability matrix, and most companies don't add the matrix into the equation. They assume that it's free, but it costs time and money. We like to make that cost obvious.

Product Backlog Common Practices

Agile techniques are practiced by thousands of companies and organizations throughout the world. As a natural result, common agile practices abound. We incorporate some of these practices into our consulting business and discard others. We recommend that you do the same. No set of universal best practices exists.

User stories

User stories are used to gather customer requirements. *User story* is a common term for requirements small enough to be brought into a sprint and broken into tasks. User stories are one action of value that a user will achieve, such as "As a shopper, I want to be able to scan a product bar code with my phone so that I can compare and find the lowest price of the same product at multiple stores."

Multiple user stories go into every sprint, and each are highest priority at that time. On average, you may have six to ten user stories per sprint. Therefore, at the end of each sprint, if the development team concentrates on completing one requirement at a time (a process called *swarming*, described in Chapter 6), you always have something to show for your work.

We use 3x5 index cards to write user stories. Even with these small cards, because we use a Card ⇨ Conversation ⇨ Confirmation model, we get rich requirement clarity before development starts. User stories aren't the only way to describe what needs to be done, but we've found them to be incredibly effective. Figure 3-5 shows example index-card user stories.

Don't use technical jargon in your user stories. You're writing them with the user in mind. Keep them direct, customer-focused, and simple.

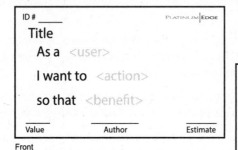

In the Card ⇨ Conversation ⇨ Confirmation model, the product owner uses the 3x5 card as a reminder of the requirement — a reminder that a conversation must take place to refine and clarify it. This model enables the immensely valuable activity of conversing with development team members and answering their questions, supported by an explicit description of what success looks like on the back of the card. Previously, we developed tomes of documents before having a development team as we tried to answer all the questions we thought that team might have — an endeavor in which we invariably failed.

Sometimes, it's easiest to work with *personas:* fictional characters who are amalgams of the target qualities of your clients. A persona might be a 35-year-old single male, professionally employed, who lives in Portland, Oregon, and is looking for his future significant other. Use a persona to ensure that your project meets your target customer's needs.

A user story description is simple yet focused, clearly describing the user, the action, and the benefit. On each card, enter the following lines:

>> An ID number that's the same as in the product backlog and that's assigned by the product owner when she accepts an item into the product backlog

Keep your product ID numbers simple. You don't need to be able to track every item back to its more generic origin; you just need to give it a numerical name, like 123, not like 10.8.A.14. You minimize the amount of work you do by ridding your project of time-wasters so that you can focus on the important things.

>> A shorthand title

>> A description of the user

>> What the user wants to accomplish

>> The reason the user wants to accomplish the task

Critical to the user story is what's written on the flip side of the card — the acceptance criteria. This is how you know that the user story has been successfully implemented. It's phrased as "When I do this. . . this happens.

Figure 3-6 shows an example of a completed card.

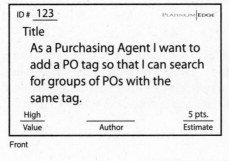

ID # 123   PLATINUM|EDGE

Title

As a Purchasing Agent I want to add a PO tag so that I can search for groups of POs with the same tag.

High		5 pts.
Value	Author	Estimate

Front

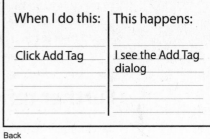

When I do this:	This happens:
Click Add Tag	I see the Add Tag dialog

Back

FIGURE 3-6: A completed index card.

Each user story is written in the first-person point of view ("When *I* do this, *I* get this"). First person puts the author in the shoes of the user or customer.

The person who writes the user story gives it to the product owner to share with the development team. Often, the stakeholder also participates in the conversation phase, sitting down with the product owner and development team to go over every card. This act of direct communication is vital to a thorough understanding of the tasks necessary to achieve the result desired. As a result, communication is clearer and mistakes are fewer, and project quality and delivery speed increase.

INVEST

Bill Wake, an early influencer in the eXtreme Programming (XP) movement, the INVEST mnemonic for user stories. INVEST is an acronym for qualities that you want to look for in your user stories:

- **Independent** (to the best degree possible): The story doesn't need other stories to implement it or for the user to interact with it.

- **Negotiable:** The product owner and the development team must discuss and expand on the story's nuances and details. The value of a user story is in the conversation, not the card.

- **Valuable:** The story shows product value to the customer, not the technical steps (tasks) that the developer uses to enable the story.

- **Estimable:** The story is refined enough for developers to estimate the amount of effort required to create the functionality.

- **Small:** Smaller stories are easier to estimate. A rule of thumb is to bring six to ten user stories into each sprint, so a story should be able to be finished by one or two people during the sprint.

- **Testable:** The story needs to be testable so that the development team knows that the story has been done correctly. "It needs to be fast" or "It needs to be intuitive" isn't testable. "I need to get a response from the application in less than a second" or "I need to complete the action in three clicks or less" is testable.

Further refinement

Development team effort determines whether a requirement needs to be broken down further to progress to the product roadmap, into the release plan, or into the sprint (see Chapter 5 for details). Especially at the beginning, as you find out how to apply user stories within your scrum framework, you may find that the ones you write are too big to fit into a sprint.

Although most user stories have multiple steps, some are bigger than practical and can (and should) be broken into more granular requirements. This process is part of the discovery process and part of the benefit of using user stories.

You may find additional requirements that need to be placed in the product backlog during the user-story elaboration discussion. Excellent! These discoveries help you gain deeper understanding of what the customer and/or user need.

Chapter **4**

The Talent and the Timing

Talent wins games. But teamwork and intelligence wins championships.
— MICHAEL JORDAN

The development team sits at the core of scrum projects. The primary focus of product owner and the scrum master revolves around making sure that the environment is as ideal as possible for the development team to reach maximum productivity. In this chapter, you find out how a development team is organized and therefore able to best contribute to the scrum team.

After you have your team roles, vision, and roadmap in place, the next step is to begin to estimate the amount of work for each requirement. The development team begins by estimating the effort involved in high-level requirements. Here, you create a starting point for future reference. You establish the numerator (product backlog total)/denominator (average velocity) relationship that gives you the estimated number of sprints necessary to complete all, or a target portion of, items in the product backlog. We show you how these high-level estimates can be achieved quickly and accurately.

The Development Team

In Hollywood, actors and singers are referred to as "the talent." They're the ones who get on stage and do the job. Everyone else facilitates this process, because when the talent is successful, everyone is successful. Think of the development team as the talent. Retaining that talent as one of the byproducts of a good scrum implementation.

The development team is the talent responsible for creating and developing the actual product. They drive the how and the how much. In other words, they determine how they will develop the requirements and how many they can do in any one sprint. They are dedicated to one project at a time, cross-functional, self-organizing, and self-managing.

The development team is intentionally size-limited to around six members, plus or minus three. Optimal development team size is small enough to remain nimble and large enough to complete significant work within a sprint. This size allows for a self-sufficient and self-organizing group with a diversity of skills, yet it's not too big and unwieldy. Remember, for each new member, the lines of communication increase geometrically. With more than nine development team members, you can't have a self-organizing team. Under a waterfall model, this issue is masked with a project manager, who is responsible for coordinating all the communication. Scrum doesn't have the overhead cost of too many lines of communication or a project manager.

Although six people, plus or minus three, is a manageable and efficient size, the key factor is self-encapsulation. Is the team able to elaborate the requirements, design them, develop them, test them, integrate them, document them, and have them approved? Have single points of failure been eliminated (that is, at least two people can do any one skill)? Is the total size no more than nine people? If all three answers are yes, you have a good-size, cross-functional development team. Whereas a product owner must be decisive and a scrum master must have clout, a development team member must be versatile, intellectually curious, and predisposed to sharing. No prima donnas are allowed. Development team members' fires are lit with building and creating.

The uniqueness of scrum development teams

In many ways, the scrum development team is the opposite of a traditional team. In scrum, development team members are going to develop cross-functional skills. They're part of the goal-setting process, and, as a team, they have complete control of how they do their development. Additionally, credit is taken as a team.

CREATING A MOTIVATING ENVIRONMENT

Daniel Pink writes about motivation in his excellent book *Drive: The Surprising Truth About What Motivates Us* (Riverhead Books). Here, Pink dispels the myth that the way to motivate people is through more and more money. Surprisingly, Pink found that the higher the monetary incentive, the worse the results. Money is a factor, but only enough to take the subject of money off the table.

As he continued to dig, Pink found three specific factors that produced the environment for the best-quality results, whether at home or work: autonomy, mastery, and purpose. Let your people determine how they will do their work, give them the space and time to master current and new skills, and communicate a sense of purpose in what they're doing.

The scrum framework can enable the environment that Pink discusses. The development team is designed to be self-organizing and autonomous in how it does the work. Cross-functionality and developing new skills are fundamental. Through the vision statement and direct communication with the product owner and stakeholders, the development team members can understand what they're working on and why.

Check out Pink's book or TED talks for more information on his research. You can find his website at www.danpink.com/.

Dedicated teams and cross-functionality

As mentioned previously, development team members are dedicated to one project at a time. No making your development team switch back and forth between projects, which is known as *thrashing*. You want them to focus each day on the current sprint's goal. Whether functional management chooses the team members or someone else does, a diversity of skills is sought after so the team has all the skills they need to be successful (they're self-encapsulated). This leads us to the next point: cross-functionality.

REMEMBER

People don't necessarily start out being cross-functional; they grow into this state. Start with a team of diverse talents and then organically build that team toward being individually cross-functional. Ideally, you want every developer to be able to do everything. This isn't always possible, but you at least want every developer to be able to do more than one thing and for every skill to have more than one person. Becoming cross-functional is a process, but it prevents bottlenecks in work delivery.

Whatever your business or organization, the facts remain: People go on vacation; they get sick; they take on new roles and jobs. One day, they're there next to you, and the next day, they might be somewhere else. In traditional projects, when a key development team member goes on vacation, the project goes on vacation. You're forced into delays as you wait for that person to return or (in the case of attrition) until you recruit and mobilize another person.

In, you strive for cross-functionality in your development team. In this way, you eliminate that single point of failure. If one development team member comes down with the flu or is deeply involved in another task, someone else can take his place and get the job done. Cross-functionality also has these benefits:

>> It allows for diverse input on development for optimal solutions.

>> It enables pair development (which is described later in this section) to ensure higher quality.

>> It's one of the best ways to increase your primary skill. Learning an associative skill exposes you to other ways of thinking about your primary skill.

>> It allows people to work on various things and keeps the work interesting.

Several ways exist to create cross-functional individuals from cross-functional teams:

>> **Don't use titles.** Encourage an equal playing field. We've found that this stimulates junior developers to get up to speed faster, and senior-level skills increase because senior people don't want to be outdone by young, hungry talent. A lack of titles also emphasizes skills over a fixed hierarchy, thereby encouraging skill development. Informal status still exists, but now it's based on skills.

>> **Do use pair programming.** Commonly used in software development practices such as Extreme Programming, pair programming can be used by a development team to develop any type of product. Two developers work together on the same piece of functionality. Developer A is tactically developing (cutting code, for example), while Developer B is free to think strategically about the functionality (scalability, extensibility, risks, and so on). They switch these roles throughout the day. Because these developers are working so tightly together, they can quickly catch errors. In our experience, developers stay more on task and make fewer errors as they're pair programming, and the result is an overall shorter timeline.

>> **Do use shadowing.** Again, two developers are working together, but in this case, only one does the work while the other watches and learns.

Shadowing also increases product quality. Remember, visibility and performance are correlated: Increase visibility, and you generally increase performance. The working developer doesn't want to take a lazy shortcut in front of the learning one, and the learning one will ask those smart "dumb questions." Explaining something improves your own knowledge of it, and vocalizing something uses a different part of your brain and improves functioning. Finally, ownership is reinforced if you're teaching and explaining.

TECHNICAL STUFF

The Hawthorne effect (or Observer effect) is based on studies showing that a worker's productivity increases when someone is watching them. It's named after Hawthorne Works, an electrical company outside Chicago where the first experiments took place.

TECHNICAL STUFF

Rubber duck problem solving, rubber ducking, and *the rubber duckie test* are terms used to describe an interesting phenomenon often used in software engineering. Programmers are told to explain their coding problem *out loud and in detail to a rubber duck.* Most of the time, before the programmer has even finished explaining the problem, the answer comes to them. The same phenomenon occurs when a friend comes to you with a problem. Just the process of vocalizing the issue stimulates a different part of the brain so that answers can dislodge themselves and flow downstream.

PAIR PROGRAMMING

While pair programming at first may seem more expensive — employing two developers for the same job — when looked at holistically, it reduces costs. The development cost may rise, but the quality assurance cost dramatically falls.

It's exponentially cheaper to prevent defects than to rip them out of a deployed system later, as described in these cases:

- If you catch the error on the spot, the cost to fix it is minimal.

- If the bug is found after committing the code, it costs 6.5 times more to remobilize, find, and fix it.

- If the bug escaped through testing and goes out to the production environment, finally being identified several days or weeks later, the mobilization time is much longer, the discovery time is longer, and the cost is about 15 times greater.

- If this same bug makes it into the marketplace and must be corrected by a group that never developed the application — such as the production support group — the cost can be up to 100 times greater.

For every defect, the development team must find the bug, develop code to correct it, and hope that the correction for that specific defect doesn't cause another defect. Remember, for every two defects fixed, another one gets created in the process.

Self-organizing and self-managing

The key word is *ownership*. Self-organizing and self-managing teams develop ownership in what they do. With a scrum development team, whole team ownership is part of what creates such efficiency and success.

We sometimes get asked by clients how we can assure them that they'll get 100 percent from their development team. In response, we ask the clients how they can assure us that a professional sports team will give 100 percent. The answer is that the team gives 100 percent because they would lose if they didn't. The visibility and acknowledgment of their hard work increases drive.

TIP

Visibility and performance are directly correlated. Increase performance by increasing visibility.

One technique sometimes used is to have two (or more) development teams. Synchronize their sprints so that the sprint reviews happen at the same time on the same day. Then invite an executive to come to both sprint reviews randomly for a few minutes and have her ask at least one question before leaving. Each development team knows that its performance will have executive visibility, and all teams want to look good. Historically, they may not have been given credit for the work they did. Now they can produce a product that they can be proud of. They're on stage, getting all the credit. This is hugely motivating and increases drive and buy-in.

Ownership and, therefore, accountability are increased in a scrum development team in the following ways:

>> The development team is directly accountable for the deliverables that they create. This isn't always easy on them because visibility brings intrinsic pressure to perform, but this visibility also creates ownership.

>> Cross-functionality creates ownership because there isn't any my job versus your job. Everything is our job.

>> Because the whole scrum team is held accountable, individual performance is increased. Everyone wins as a team, and everyone contributes to the success of every sprint.

>> The development team actively participates in creating the sprint goals and demonstrating the working functionality during the sprint review.

>> The development team is responsible for tactical status reporting every single day. In less than one minute of administration per day (see the burndown charts in Chapter 5), the organization gets a level of tactical status reporting that it's never had before.

WARNING

Development teams perform best when they're stable. Feed them projects and give them what they need to do their best possible work. Every time you switch members on your team, it takes time to stabilize again. Protect your development team to nurture good dynamics.

TECHNICAL STUFF

Cognitive consistency theory describes humans' tendency to seek out information, beliefs, and stimuli that are consistent with current beliefs and attitudes. In scrum, if development team members have a voice, and if they have buy-in and control, they strive harder to achieve their work-related goals. They try to find consistency between the ownership that they created and their future output.

Co-locating or the nearest thing

Many people have forgotten what it's like to work with a co-located team and to experience the increased production involved. Most people appreciate the concept but may not understand the underlying principles. Here are a few benefits of a co-located team:

>> Increased speed and effectiveness of face-to-face communication, especially through kinetics, voice tonality, facial expressions, and so on.

The value of face-to-face communication shouldn't be underestimated. Albert Mehrabian, PhD, and professor emeritus of psychology at the University of California-Los Angeles, proved the following:

- 55 percent of meaning is conveyed through body language and facial expressions.

- 38 percent of meaning is *paralinguistic* (conveyed by the way we speak).

- 7 percent of meaning is conveyed in the actual words spoken.

These statistics alone are a whopping case for co-locating your development team.

>> Ease of using simple tools for planning and communicating, such as whiteboards and sticky notes.

>> Ease in immediate clarification of questions.

>> Understanding what other members are working on.

>> Ease in supporting other team members in their tasks.

>> Cost savings due to decreased lag times and fewer misunderstandings that lead to defects or wasted work.

REMEMBER

When co-located, your product owner and development team have access to each other all day every day. All sort of banality is exchanged, and it's tempting to think that this might be wasteful. However, we've found that it's during these exchanges when the really good work gets done. Little things aren't actually little; they're differentiators, and they're the things that matter. Quality needs input, and input needs access. When access is high, great things are possible.

TIP

Sometimes, outsourcing is the only viable solution for your company or organization. If this is the case, do it with both feet. Co-locate the entire scrum team. Your development team needs an available product owner, so send one to the outsourcing location to work directly with the remote scrum team. Or develop a local product owner, even if he has to start as a product owner agent (see Chapter 2). The increase in quality and efficiency far outweighs the cost of the product owner.

Getting the Edge on Backlog Estimation

In the product roadmap stage (see Chapter 1), the development team does a high-level estimate of the amount of work entailed in the project. The practical value of this estimation process doesn't come into play until the sprints start (see Chapter 5), but this initial estimation sets a mark from which future estimates may be calculated. The development team does the estimating because only the people who do the work should be estimating the effort of the work.

These backlog estimation techniques aren't requirements of scrum. They're common practices that scrum practitioners have found useful in the field.

The product roadmap is the start of the product backlog. What's on your roadmap is what you will begin developing. So how do you take all those items on your product backlog and with any degree of accuracy estimate the work involved? A few common practices are used depending on the situation. Before we look at these estimating techniques individually, it's important to understand what you're trying to achieve.

Your Definition of Done

If you ask the members of a scrum team what they expect to see when a requirement is done, you get as many answers as there are team members. So before starting a project, scrum teams define what done means with a definition of done. Until you have consensus on this definition, estimations will be based on bad data.

As described in Chapter 3, for each requirement within a sprint, you complete the following stages of development:

>> Requirement elaboration

>> Design

>> Development

>> Comprehensive testing

>> Integration

>> Documentation

>> Approval

This definition of done needs to be specific, refined, and focused on what it means to do these things to completion to achieve the level of quality that you're striving for in your project. Consider which environment the product or service needs to work within and at what level of integration to be considered done. "Works in the development environment," for example, is probably a bad, loose definition of done.

Consider these four factors in your definition of done:

>> **Developed:** The product has been fully developed by the development team.

>> **Tested:** The development team fully tested the product to make sure that it functions in the required environment without any glitches.

>> **Integrated:** The product has been fully integrated within the product as a whole and any related systems.

>> **Documented:** The development team created whatever documentation is needed. Just remember that the goal with all things agile is "barely sufficient."

TIP

When you've come up with your definition of done, write it out on a white poster board and tape it on the wall. You'll always have it right in front of the development team and product owner. We call it *in-your-face documentation*. No cover sheet, no table of contents — simply the lowest-fidelity way that communicates and makes the information the most visible.

In your definition of done, consider not only the development but also the depth of testing and documentation that you might need. You might consider which tests must pass the following:

>> Unit

>> Functional/system

>> Performance/load

>> Security

>> User acceptance

Also consider what documentation you need:

>> Technical

>> User

>> Maintenance

Each of these testing and documentation points may differ between the sprint level and the release level, though we prefer that the sprint-level definition of done include everything necessary to release. You also may have organizationally specific items that you want to include. It's your choice. The point is to have a clear definition of done that's defined by the scrum team for all to work by.

A *release* occurs when a set of marketable features is released outside the scrum team. This could happen several times during a sprint, at the end of each sprint, or after a series of sprints. These requirements may be released into the market and to the users, or they may go to internal or external stakeholders for real-world use and feedback.

A regular sprint entails completing the development, testing, documentation, and approval of items in the sprint backlog. However, before you do a product release, other activities may be needed (such as performance and load testing) that the development team wouldn't have access to in a regular sprint. Therefore, sometimes scrum teams have a release sprint just before the release itself to allow these additional tests to be addressed. The key is at the end of every sprint, the requirements must work and be demonstrable. You can test and tune for scale in the release sprint, but the requirements must work every sprint.

Common Practices for Estimating

Estimating the effort involved in developing product backlog requirements is an ongoing process. (In Chapter 3, we discuss product backlog refinement.) For example, you could do estimations for 30 minutes at 5 every evening before team members go home. This way, at the end of the week, you've covered lots of ground and will be ready for each sprint start. Some teams don't like to develop on Friday afternoon and do product backlog refinement then.

Teams are likely to refine their estimates at three levels as part of the process of breaking the requirements down for sprint-level execution. Depending on your product, you may include more. Your estimate refinement usually goes in this order:

1. Product roadmap
2. Release planning
3. Sprint planning

The development team is responsible for estimating the effort required to fully build the requirements. The scrum master can facilitate the process, and the product owner can provide clarification, but the decision is made by developers doing the actual work.

We use relative estimating in lieu of precise (absolute) estimating, because in many situations, it's much more feasible. If you're asked to look out the window and say how tall the neighboring building is, how precise would be your reply? Very — it's 950 feet. How accurate would be your reply? Not very. Why? Because you honestly have no idea; you gave it a wild guess. But if we ask you to look at two nearby buildings and tell us which one is taller, barring some vision problem, we can guarantee that you'll give us the right answer. Using *relative* sizing is an effective way to overcome the difficulty we humans have in making absolute estimates.

Fibonacci numbers and story points

The Fibonacci sequence is an excellent sizing technique for relative estimating.

With Fibonacci, if something is bigger, you get an idea of how much bigger it is. The last two numbers in the sequence are added to create the next number. Fibonacci numbers look like this:

1, 2, 3, 5, 8, 13, 21, 34, 55, 89, 144, and so on

As the numbering progresses, the distance between the numbers increases. We use this technique to acknowledge the lesser degree of accuracy in predicting larger chunks of work.

A *story point* is the Fibonacci number assigned to an individual requirement (that is, a user story).

Leonardo Pisano Bigollo, also known as Fibonacci, lived near Pisa, Italy, from about 1170 to about 1250. Widely recognized as a brilliant mathematician, he made the Fibonacci sequence famous and instigated the spread in Europe of the Hindu-Arabic numeral system — today, the most common symbolic representation of numbers in the world.

Initial high-level requirements are estimated at the product roadmap level:

>> For scrum teams we work with, the development teams understand that requirements with Fibonacci number estimates from 1 through 8 can be brought into a sprint. This level of refinement usually results in a user story.

>> Requirements with estimates numbered from 13 through 34 are those that you would let into a release but need to be broken down further before you would let them into a sprint. At this level of refinement, we call these epics.

>> Requirements from 55 through 144 are too big for a release but are estimable at the order-of-magnitude product roadmap level. These requirements typically reflect features.

Requirements larger than 144 need to be broken down before the development team can give any semblance of an accurate estimate, so we don't estimate beyond 144. These may represent broader themes.

Whatever the Fibonacci number, only the highest-priority cards get broken down into sprint-level sizes (which we recommend shouldn't be more than an 8). So, if you have a high-priority requirement with a 21 Fibonacci number assigned to it, it needs to be broken into smaller requirements before it can come into a sprint.

With the sizes established, we can apply a few techniques to estimate requirements:

>> When we have shorter lists of requirements, we begin with *estimation poker*.

>> When we have hundreds of requirements, we begin with *affinity estimation* (discussed later in this chapter).

In the estimation process with smaller projects, we have the development team begin as follows. We have the team sit down with their stack of requirements written on 3x5 cards. Then we ask them to pick a requirement that they can all agree has an effort level of 5. This creates a reference point.

We then have them pick another card and, based on the first one being a 5, ask them what number the next one would be. If it's greater than a 5, is it an 8, a 13, or a 21? This process continues until a few representational sizes have been established.

Estimation poker

A popular way to estimate requirements is to use a variation of poker. You need a deck of estimation poker cards like the one shown in Figure 4-1. (You can find them on our website at https://platinumedge.com/store/estimation-poker-cards). You can also download our poker estimation app for iPhone and/or Android by searching for *Platinum Edge Estimation Poker* in your device's app store or make your own deck with index cards and a marker.

FIGURE 4-1: Estimation poker cards for estimating the amount of effort required in each requirement.

Because only the development team decides how much it will take to develop a requirement, only the development team plays estimation poker. The scrum master facilitates, and the product owner reads the requirements and provides requirement details, but neither of those two gives estimates. It goes like this:

1. The product owner reads a targeted requirement to the development team, including acceptance criteria.

2. The development team asks any questions and gets any clarifications they need.

3. Each member of the development team picks from his deck a card with his estimate of the difficulty of the requirement.

REMEMBER

   The estimate is to accomplish the complete definition of done, not just to write code.

   Members don't show anyone else their cards because you don't want others being influenced.

4. After everyone has picked a number, the team members simultaneously show their cards.

   If everyone has the same estimate, nothing is left to discuss. Assign the requirement that estimate and move on to the next requirement.

   If differences exist in estimates, those with the highest and lowest estimates are asked to explain. Further clarification from the product owner is given as needed.

5. With increased knowledge, everyone picks a new number for that requirement by repeating Steps 3 and 4.

We normally do up to three rounds of estimation poker for each requirement to get the core assumptions on the table and clarified, and at that point, we usually have the estimates in a tighter cluster of numbers.

If all developers agree on a single number after three rounds, you're ready to move on to the next requirement. But you won't always have all developers in agreement on a single number after three rounds. At this point, we go on to a consensus-building technique called fist of five.

Fist of five

A fast and efficient method of reaching consensus, fist of five can be used on its own or as an addendum to estimation poker. The purpose of fist of five is to quickly find an estimate that all team members can support (see Figure 4-2).

FIGURE 4-2:
Fist of five is an
efficient way of
finding consensus
in many
situations.

5 = LOVE IT!
4 = Good idea.
3 = Yeah, I can support it.
2 = I have reservations, let's discuss further.
1 = Opposed. Do not move forward.

Perhaps when you tried estimation poker, some team members have given a requirement a 5, and others have given it an 8.

It begins with the scrum master holding up the requirement card in question and saying, for example, "How comfortable would you be with this as an 8?" Each development team member holds up the number of fingers associated with their level of comfort. If everyone is holding up three, four, or five fingers, it's settled.

If some developers are holding up one or two fingers, as in estimation poker, the outliers would be asked to explain, and further information would be garnered if necessary. Fist of five would be performed again. Continue with this process until all team members can give the number at least a 3 (which is, "I don't love it, but I can support it").

With fist of five completed and requirements estimated, you're ready to move to release or sprint planning. They're covered in Chapter 5.

Affinity estimating

Estimation poker and fist of five are effective methods of establishing consensus in small projects. But what if you have several hundred requirements on the product backlog? It could take days to complete. This is where affinity estimating comes into play.

Instead of beginning with Fibonacci numbers, you begin with a more familiar concept: T-shirt sizes (XS, S, M, L, and XL).

With affinity estimating, you first create several areas marked with each size and then place each requirement in one of the size categories. It goes like this:

1. Identify small tables to sort the cards.

   Label a table Clarify, and label other small tables for each of these size categories:

   - Extra-small
   - Small
   - Medium
   - Large
   - Extra-large
   - Epic (too large to fit into the sprint, given that six to ten requirements are the target for each sprint; more on this in Chapter 5)

2. For each size category, give your development team 60 seconds to pick a requirement from the overall stack of requirements and place it on the corresponding table.

   This establishes the *representational anchor* for each size.

3. Each member of the development team grabs a stack of requirements.

4. Each member places each card on the table that they feel reflects its size based on the representational anchor for that size.

   As you can see, these are like T-shirt sizes. Each "size" will eventually correspond to a Fibonacci number:

   - Extra-small equals 1.
   - Small equals 2.
   - Medium equals 3.
   - Large equals 5.
   - Extra-large equals 8.

   Anything larger than an 8 needs to be broken down further before it can come into a sprint.

TIP

Don't let team members linger too long on their stack of requirements. Establish a timebox for them to work within, for example, 20 minutes for 20 cards.

TIP

Timebox is a term that refers to the allotted time for an event or activity. If your sprints last two weeks, the timebox is two weeks.

Figure 4-3 shows what the relationship between size piles and Fibonacci numbers looks like.

FIGURE 4-3:
Affinity estimating
uses T-shirt
sizes for story
sizes and gives
each one a
corresponding
Fibonacci
number.

SIZE	POINTS
XtraSmall (XS)	1 pt
Small (S)	2 pts
Medium (M)	3 pts
Large (L)	5 pts
XtraLarge (XL)	8 pts

FIGURE 4-3: Affinity estimating uses T-shirt sizes for story sizes and gives each one a corresponding Fibonacci number.

5. Have the development team members play something we call *gallery* until all members agree on the sizes for each requirement.

    In gallery, the team members flip through all the cards on all the tables and provide feedback on only the cards that don't appear to be on the right table.

    If one team member wants to move a story from small to medium, for example, check that the original person who placed it there doesn't disagree. If the person disagrees, place that card on a separate Clarify table. Don't get into extensive discussions just yet.

6. Invite the product owner to review for major disagreements:

    - If the product owner sees a requirement on the medium table that she thought would be a small, don't waste any time discussing it. The development team ultimately gets to say the size of the requirement, and a one-size difference isn't worth the time to discuss.

    - If you have greater than one table of difference between where development team members think a card should be placed and where the product owner thought it would be placed, put that card on the Clarify table. The development team may not have understood the product owner's explanation of the requirement.

7. For cards on the Clarify table, play estimation poker (discussed earlier in this chapter).

Within a relatively short amount of time, you've been able to reliably estimate the effort on hundreds of separate requirements. You're ready to plan your first release and/or your first sprint.

Velocity

After you have Fibonacci numbers assigned to your requirements, you have story points to work from.

Chapter 5 shows how to plan both releases and sprints. To plan your first sprint, among those requirements that are between 1 and 8 story points, a scrum team determines a modest number of combined story points to work on. Then, at the end of the sprint, a scrum team looks at the requirements that were done to completion and adds their story points. The result might be 15, 25, or 35 story points. This is the development team's velocity for the first sprint and starting input for a team determining how much it can accomplish in the next sprint.

REMEMBER

Velocity is the combined number of story points that your development team completed in an individual sprint. It's a postsprint fact used for extrapolation, not a presprint goal.

TIP

To accurately determine velocity, you need more than one sprint to find an average. Velocity follows the law of large numbers; the more data points you have, the better. At minimum, you need three data points to establish an optimistic, pessimistic, and most likely extrapolation of how many requirements will be done during the project. After you have these, you can tell stakeholders optimistic, pessimistic, and most likely estimates for how many of the highest-priority requirements on the product backlog can be completed within a project. Giving stakeholders this type of estimation range provides the level of detail they're looking for while allowing some flexibility for the development team as they're still getting into a development rhythm.

In the first few sprints of a project, the team's velocity will usually vary greatly. It becomes more stable as the team gets into a development rhythm. Of course, changes in team members or sprint duration will introduce variability into the team's velocity.

REMEMBER

Velocity isn't a goal; it's a fact used for extrapolation. Higher numbers are not automatically better than lower numbers.

When story points are used, you'll find that some teams are pessimistic in their estimates. Their numbers always come in high. Other teams are optimistic. Their story point total comes in low.

Consider that an optimistic team's velocity is 15 and the estimates for the release total 150 points. It would take them ten sprints to complete the release.

If a pessimistic team's velocity were 30 and the estimates for the release total 300 points, it would take them ten sprints as well.

STORY POINTS AND VELOCITY IN REAL TIME

A real-world example of the value of story points and velocity might appear like this.

Assume the following data:

- Remaining product backlog is 500 story points.
- Your sprint duration (timebox) is one week, Monday through Friday.
- The development team velocity averages 20 story points per sprint.
- Today is Monday, January 8, 2018.
- Your annual development team cost is $100,000 per team member, and you have seven members — that is, $700,000 annually or $13,462 weekly.

Within minutes, you're able to make a solid estimation of the cost and delivery date of the project. Given this data, your project will entail 25 sprints and therefore will take 25 weeks to complete. Your cost will be $336,550, and your completion date will be Friday, June 29, 2018.

What happens if your development team increases its velocity to 25 story points per sprint? Just plug in the numbers. Now you'll need only 20 sprints. Your cost will drop to $269,240 (saving you $67,310), and your final delivery date will be Friday, May 25, 2018. This is the benefit of having a dedicated scrum master who can remove impediments and organizational drag on the team to increase velocity.

TIP

Optimistic or pessimistic doesn't really matter. Teams will generally be consistent one way or the other and therefore balance out in the end. This is the reason you always value a team's velocity against itself, not against other teams. In fact, don't even tell anyone what a team's velocity is. Consider it an extrapolation system, not a performance system.

When you have a clear method of estimating the effort required to complete each requirement, and you have an average velocity established for the development team, you're able to accurately predict the quantity of product that can be created within fixed cost and time constraints. You're harnessing your variables.

Successful scrum teams need to share ownership of outcomes and value authentic transparency between the team and its stakeholders. Progress is visible to everyone.

Chapter 5

Release and Sprint Planning

A complex system that works is invariably found to have evolved from a simple system that worked. A complex system designed from scratch never works and cannot be patched up to make it work. You have to start over with a working simple system.

— JOHN GALL

So far you have a product, a product owner, and a development team. Release and sprint planning is really where the rubber hits the road. As we've mentioned before, with scrum, you'll do more planning than ever before, but it's focused, continuous, results-oriented, and packaged such that you'll wonder how you ever managed projects without it.

In this chapter, you find out how to plan the release of project features in a logical and organized way. The purpose of release planning is to mobilize the wider project team around a specific set of functionality that the organization wants to release to the marketplace. This is when such departments or stakeholders as the marketing department, field support, and customer service get mobilized and prepared to support functionality that end customers are going to be using in the real world.

We also walk you through the scrum event of sprints. Scrum at its core is the sprint cycle. We show you how to use this valuable process and get the best possible results.

REMEMBER

A *sprint* is a fixed timebox within which development is done to produce a working, potentially shippable product. A typical sprint might be one or two weeks in duration but could be as little as a day and as much as a month.

We discuss how prioritizing releases and sprints accelerates time to market and maximizes return on investment (ROI) and explain that by having feedback loops, you create the product that your clients want, with the features they'll actually use.

Release Plan Basics: Stage 3

We began the roadmap to value in Chapter 1 with the bird's-eye basics: your vision statement. This allows you to establish your destination and define the end of the project. The second stage, the product roadmap, provides a holistic view of the features that support the vision. As you narrow your focus and generate more detail, you come into release planning, which is Stage 3 in your roadmap to value (see Figure 5-1). The release planning concept is scrum. However, the release plan artifact is a common practice that many scrum aficionados use with success.

Stage 3: RELEASE PLANNING

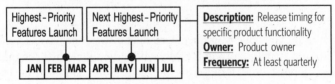

FIGURE 5-1:
Stage 3 of the roadmap to value is the release plan.

(Stages 1 - 3 are common practices outside of scrum)

A *release plan* is a high-level timetable for releasing a set of product requirements. So, you're working down, segmentally, from the big-picture roadmap to the mid-level release plan. (Later in this chapter, we cover the next-smaller size, which is the actual sprint.) The release plan provides a focal point around which the project team can mobilize.

AC + OC > V

Applying a simple formula to your project helps you know when you've achieved the best possible results. In other words, you know to terminate the project as soon as the actual cost (AC) of the project added to the opportunity cost (OC) of not working on other projects is greater than the value (V) you're expecting to get from the future functionality.

As a formula, it looks like this:

$$AC + OC > V$$

This formula helps you determine when it is time to end a project. You'll see how you can achieve the 30–40 percent time savings and 30–70 percent cost saving we've realized so many times by

- Having stable, dedicated teams

- Prioritizing to avoid building features that customers won't use

- Iterating through consistent feedback loops with your customers

REMEMBER

Do the minimum amount possible that still creates a working product. When planning a set of features to release to the market, always ask yourself, "What is the minimum set of features that delivers value to my customer?" This is what is commonly referred to as the *minimum viable product* (MVP).

You should release product to the market as often as you have something of value to offer your customers — the minimum viable product. Your product releases could also come on a regular schedule (for example, four times a year, at the end of each quarter). But with the advances in technology and the need to be quick to market, releases now may be monthly, weekly, or even multiple times a day in some cases.

TIP

Consider the pen-and-pencil rule. You can use a pen to commit to the plan for the first release, but anything beyond this plan is written in pencil. It's just-in-time planning for each release.

A project may have multiple releases. For each release, you start with the goal, which is supported by the next-highest-priority features and requirements. You'll see that this is a pattern you follow at each stage of the roadmap to value. Each release has a release goal, and you commit to only one release at a time. Figure 5-2 depicts a typical release plan with an optional release sprint.

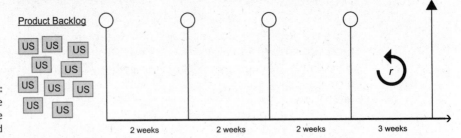

Release Goal: Enable customers to access, view, and transact against their active accounts.
Release Date: March 31, 2021

Product Backlog

US = User Story
r = optional "release" sprint

2 weeks   2 weeks   2 weeks   3 weeks

FIGURE 5-2:
A typical release plan with the release goal and date and an optional release sprint.

TECHNICAL STUFF

The number of sprints within each release can vary depending on the release goal and what's required to complete the requirements to achieve that goal. An option is to use release trains, in which each release has a set time schedule. Releases are set so that everyone knows when to expect them.

At each scheduled release, the product owner decides which of the completed functionalities will be released on that date. This way, organizations and customers know to expect new features on a set schedule. Scrum teams can predictably organize their release plans to cadence.

Scrum is an empirical approach. Each step of the way, you inspect your results and adapt immediately to the changing needs of your customers. These fundamentals enable you to achieve significant cost and time savings while delivering what the client wants. You may have a bird's-eye view of four releases for your project, but you plan in detail only one release at a time. What you learn in the first release may change what you do in the second release.

WARNING

Your organization may be afraid to release software incrementally. You may find it difficult to release completed work before the entire backlog is complete. Sometimes that hesitancy derives from a sense that once the product is released you can't improve it or add to it. Overcome these antipatterns to support more effective and frequent releases.

Prioritize, prioritize, prioritize

You've heard this before when we've talk about scrum, and you'll hear it throughout this book. Identifying the highest-priority requirements, according to business value and risk, and working with only those requirements are key common practices within the agile community.

Think of each release as the next, incremental MVP of your product. When planning each release, ask these questions to identify the highest-priority features:

>> What makes a requirement important for this release?

>> What minimum number of features providing business value to the customer do we need to bring to market?

>> Which requirements present the greatest risk and should be addressed sooner than later?

TECHNICAL STUFF

A famous Standish Group study from 2001 showed on a representational software development project that only 20 percent of the features were used always or often by the customers. Interestingly, 64 percent of features were never or rarely used. With scrum's emphasis on prioritization, only those most important and useful features are developed first. What if your project runs out of funding and you're only 80 percent done? Based on what the Standish study found, you might not have needed the remaining 20 percent anyway. AC + OC > V means the end of the project. Redeploy that capital to a higher and better use.

The following four key reasons are why you want as small a set of features per release as possible:

>> First-mover advantage of speed to market and increased market share

>> Accelerated customer feedback cycle

>> Maximized ROI (a dollar today is literally worth more than a dollar will be worth six months from now)

>> Reduced internal risk from such factors as organizational change and budget poaching

The product owner fully owns the release plan and is the one who prioritizes the requirements in the product backlog and sets the release goal (as shown in the following section). While the product owner decides what the priorities are and when to release completed shippable functionality, she consults stakeholders and the development team to make her decisions. Figure 5-3 applies the 80/20 rule to the value versus effort idea. It's isn't a magic formula, but a helpful way to understand and explain value.

The Pareto Principle (80/20 rule) and the Law of Diminishing Returns

	Imagine a current unstarted project and let's apply the 80/20 rule a few times.	Delivered Business Value	Expended Effort	Value Leverage
Low hanging fruit	80 percent of business value delivered with 20 percent of the effort (a good value by delivering the highest value and best defined stories first)	80%	20%	4:1
Hard or risky but needed	Now taking 80% of the remaining part (20) of business value leaves us with 16% and taking 20% of the remaining effort (80)	16%	16%	1:1
Whoops we feel stuck	We've delivered 96% of the business value so far with only 36% of the effort! Let's do it one more time. 80% of 4% = 3.2 value and 20% of remaining 64% effort = yields 12.8 effort.	3.2%	12.8%	1:4
	We still have over 50% of the estimated effort remaining to gain hardly business delivered value.	99.2%	48.8%	

This illustration isn't intended to be an exact project estimation but rather to demonstrate something scrum professionals experience across projects. If the roadmap to value is followed you will do the most valued stories first.

- More than half of software features don't get used (see the Standish study).
- **Law of diminishing returns** refers to a point at which the level of benefits gained is less than the amount of effort (time, money) expended.

FIGURE 5-3:
Applying the Pareto Principle (80/20 rule) to scrum.

Release goals

Each release plan has an overall business goal called a *release goal.* This goal is created by the product owner and ties directly to the product end goal, which is the product's vision statement. The release goal establishes the midterm boundary around specific functionality that will be released to customers to use in the real world.

Having an explicit release goal expedites the prioritization process: If a requirement doesn't align with the goal, you don't have to worry about that requirement in this release. Any given requirement should earn the right of your investment. Leave it tucked away in the product backlog until it can support a priority goal. Figure 5-4 shows a matrix to help you determine the priority stories.

TIP

Think of the three layers of goal setting as a prioritization filter system. The vision statement is the highest boundary. If a feature doesn't fit the overall vision, it doesn't belong in this project. Don't even put that requirement on the product backlog. The requester needs to go get funding for that idea separately. Don't allow features to be stowaways on your project.

Next comes the release goal. This is the midterm boundary. If a requirement doesn't fit this goal, it stays in the product backlog. Finally, the shortest-term boundary is the sprint goal.

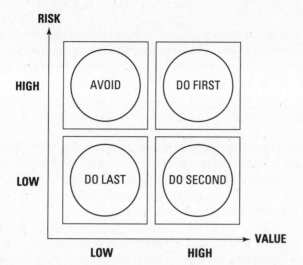

FIGURE 5-4:
Backlog priority
matrix.

REMEMBER

Goals drive the product backlog and the release plan, not the other way around. Every feature and requirement must be thought of in terms of whether it fits the goal. This is *purpose-driven development*. Goals drive what makes the product backlog. Goals drive what gets included in a release. And goals drive what gets included in each sprint.

Release sprints

Sometimes, releasing product features into the marketplace requires completing certain jobs that can't fit within a normal developmental sprint. Ideally, all activities required to release a product to the market are done within a normal sprint. But if the way an organization is set up doesn't allow it, a release sprint may be used to accomplish such purposes as

>> Verifying scaling (for example, load or performance testing)

>> Broader testing activities (for example, focus groups or validating that developed functionality works with live data)

Although we prefer not to have release sprints, simply phrased, a release sprint is for all that other stuff that needs doing to get the product to market.

The release sprint is commonly used at the end of the normal series of sprints within a release. The length of a release sprint may be different from the development sprints in the release. The release sprint length depends on the types of activities and the amount of work required to release the completed product increments from each sprint. The scrum team determines all these factors during release planning.

During a release sprint, no actual development of requirements is done. All development tasks (such as testing, technical documentation, quality assurance, and peer review) are completed during each sprint to satisfy the team's definition of done, which in turn ensures potentially shippable product at the end of each sprint. But before the product can go out to the market, other things (such as focus groups or load and performance testing) may need to be done.

Because the release sprint length and activities are often different from the development sprints, no concept of velocity exists for a release sprint. Development teams estimate to the best of their knowledge the effort and complexity of the tasks for the release sprint. They should all agree and feel comfortable with the release sprint length after it is decided.

The release sprint is a form of antipattern in organizations that can't do scaled testing and organizational support tasks within the sprint. If you don't need it, don't do it.

Including examples already given, uses for release sprints may include the following:

» Conducting focus groups (keep in mind that this isn't to identify new features but to validate what you've done and identify release issues)

» Scaling tests

» Tweaking performance based on scaling test results

» Integrating the product within enterprisewide systems

» Creating documentation such as user manuals

» Finalizing any regulatory requirements

Release plan in practice

To see how a release plan works in the real world, follow these steps:

1. Develop a release goal.

This goal is the target for everything else. The product owner ensures that the goal aligns with the product vision and works with the scrum team to make sure that the entire team feels comfortable with the goal.

2. Identify the target release date.

This date may be influenced by factors outside the control of the scrum team.

3. **Identify the highest-priority requirements (MVP) on the product backlog that support the release goal.**

Priority is a function of value and risk. Tackle the highest value/highest risk items first. See Figure 5-4 for a value matrix.

4. **Refine the requirements estimates as needed.**

Sometimes, issues and/or synergies are discovered when the development team looks at the smaller package of requirements that go into a release plan. The requirements themselves will also be more detailed and broken down (no larger than 34; see Chapter 4) than when the development team originally estimated at the product roadmap level.

5. **Identify the team's velocity.**

If the team is stable and has been working on the same project, established velocity from previous sprints is a great starting point. If the team hasn't established velocity, start modestly until you have run a few sprints and velocity can be ascertained.

6. **Plan a release sprint (if needed).**

Determine as a scrum team whether you'll need one and, if so, how long it will be.

7. **Finalize the release scope.**

Based on velocity, total estimates of requirements and number of sprints within the release timebox, how much functionality can you include? Which is more flexible — the date or the amount of functionality? What adjustments need to be made to the release date or scope of requirements to release as much as you can within your timebox?

Suppose that your velocity is 20, the release timebox is 5 sprints, and the total estimated points for the release is 110. This puts you ten points over what's available in the release. The product owner has a decision to make. Are the requirements that make up the bottom ten points in the release valuable enough to include, or can the release go on without them? Or does the release need to be extended one sprint, and will that be acceptable to the stakeholders and customers?

TIP

One option in release planning is to use the *release train* model. Rather than have releases of varying duration, in this scenario, each release is exactly the same length — six weeks, for example. At the end of each six-week cycle, the completed functionality from each of the sprints is packaged and released. This way, a development rhythm is created, and everyone in the organization can anticipate his workload and schedule moving forward.

Use any of the estimation and consensus-building techniques discussed in Chapter 4 to refine the product backlog items in the release, if requirements still need to be refined and estimated (see the preceding Step 4). If your releases consist of many product backlog items, use affinity estimating (the T-shirt sizing technique discussed in Chapter 4) for release planning.

REMEMBER

As with all scrum documentation, we prefer the simplest tools possible. The entire release plan can be mapped out with your trusty whiteboard and sticky notes. This allows for ease in change and immediate access. As well, it just plain saves time.

Sprinting to Your Goals

Finally, the heart of scrum! Sprints, and their built-in inspect and adapt model, are integral scrum features. It is through the sprint process that you can achieve the three agile pillars of improvement — transparency, inspection, and adaptation — that we discuss in Chapter 1.

By breaking your project into tangible pieces and then using the empirical model of scrum to assess your progress, you can pivot constantly moving forward. This allows you the nimbleness and ease of adaptation so sorely missing in waterfall.

Each scrum team member has the same purpose in the sprints: maximizing effectiveness in delivering potentially shippable product.

Defining sprints

Sprints are the essence of scrum, as we discuss in Chapter 1. They're a consistent timebox for product development by the development team. Each sprint includes the following:

>> Sprint planning, including goal setting

>> Daily scrums

>> Development time, including regular review by the product owner

>> Sprint review

>> Sprint retrospective

The consistent timebox of sprints allows the development team to establish a development rhythm. It also enables scrum teams to extrapolate into the future based on empirical data such as velocity. As soon as one sprint is finished, another begins. A flow of consistent iterative feedback loops is created and thereby creates an ideal environment for production and continuous improvement.

TIP

Imagine that you're a runner. You're consistently training for the 100-yard dash and have become incredibly proficient at it, but suddenly your coach asks you to run a marathon. If you attempt the marathon at your 100-yard-dash pace, you won't finish the marathon. You need to modify your training to adjust for a marathon pace, which will require coaching, schedule, and diet changes over time. All the muscle memory and the type of endurance that your body has developed will need to be relearned to run a different length of race.

Planning sprint length

Because sprint goals don't change during a sprint, the answer to the question "How long should a sprint be?" depends on your project and how long your organization can go without making changes. That is the outer edge. You have no reason to discuss going beyond that in duration. For example, if your organization struggles to go a week without needing changes, don't even entertain the idea of a two-week sprint. You won't be able to maintain the integrity of the stability of the sprint, and stability is a huge driver of performance in scrum. Instead, discuss how much shorter you can make the sprint.

Also, sprint lengths don't change after they begin and ideally don't change throughout a project unless they're being made shorter. If a scrum team changes sprint length during a project, it comes at a significant cost: Their earlier velocity is no longer relevant. Performance is not a straight mathematical line that can be sliced, diced, and reassembled. Just because a scrum team doubles their sprint from one to two weeks doesn't mean that they will automatically accomplish double their historical two-week velocity.

Shorter sprints decrease the amount of time between feedback received from stakeholders, enabling scrum teams to inspect and adapt earlier and more often. Longer sprints have a diminishing return because less of a sense of urgency exists due to the multiple days still available to the team. Weekends and longer sprint meetings can also have a negative effect on efficiency.

The capacity of a development team during a one-week sprint may be higher or lower than half the historical two-week velocity. You don't have any idea until you run a few sprints, and you don't know for sure until you run a lot of sprints.

WARNING

Whereas the cost of changing sprint lengths throughout a project is significant, the cost of changing a sprint goal during a sprint is probably worse. If a sprint goal becomes irrelevant (for example, because of changes of company direction or changes in the market) before the end of a sprint, a product owner may decide to cancel the sprint. But be aware that canceling wastes valuable development resources and is quite traumatic to the scrum team and the organization. Also, the shorter the feedback loop (that is, length of sprint), the less likely a product owner would be to cancel a sprint.

CUMULATIVE FLOW DIAGRAMS

Cumulative flow diagrams (CFDs) provide scrum teams the visibility into the patterns of their output and help them identify possible bottlenecks in their processes.

A burnup chart, shown on the left side of the figure, is a type of CFD that shows the number of requirements that the team was able to complete within a set duration of time. CFDs, shown on the right side of the figure, give a snapshot of how much work is in any given stage of the process so that indicators such as lead, cycle, work, and wait times can be exposed to identify points of inefficiency.

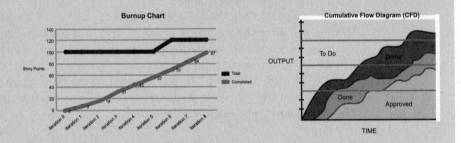

Changing sprint lengths during a project makes performance indicators inconsistent over time. In addition to loss of relevancy of the historical velocity with changing sprint lengths, CFD indicators such as lead, cycle, work, and wait times also become irrelevant.

TECHNICAL STUFF

One things we know from science is that you can't turn off your mind. It's always working. If you can give your development team a small number of problems to solve, and tell them that they'll face those problems tomorrow, they'll think about them consciously at work. Whether they want to or not, they'll also think about them unconsciously when they're away from work. This is the reason why the stability of sprints is so important. After a sprint starts, the developers must have confidence that the scope is stable so that their minds can be fully focused on what needs to be done for this sprint, whether they're at work or away from it. Have you ever had an epiphany while brushing your teeth? That's the dynamic we're talking about here. But you need two elements: a limited number of problems and confidence that you'll face those problems tomorrow. If every day a developer could be working on Project A, Project C, or Project who-knows-what, this won't happen. A developer will mentally engage only when he gets to the office and discovers what's ahead of him in reality. One reason why agile projects are so innovative is that they have this stability and, thus, more of the developer's mind share.

TAKING A QUEUE FROM MATHEMATICS

Queuing theory is the mathematical study of waiting in lines. Studies have found that when customers are waiting in a restaurant for a table, they'll wait twice as long if they are given something satisfying at the start. For example, if they're asked to sit at the bar and offered the ability to order a drink or even given a tasty sample, they'll stick around longer and wait for that busy table to be cleared.

The same principle is working for you in scrum. At the end of each sprint, you have something working and tangible to place in the hands of stakeholders. This "early and often" concept is a known technique for raising customer satisfaction.

With our clients, we've found that the one-week sprint length is a nice rhythm. It gives the development team clear time off, avoids weekend cheating to get more work done than is within the team's capacity, yet is long enough for real progress to be made every week. This shorter feedback cycle also allows scrum teams to inspect and adapt more frequently. For these reasons, scrum teams should always be looking for ways to responsibly shorten their sprint length.

The key is to run sprints that enable your development team to realistically create tangible, tested, and approved product every single sprint. After each sprint, you will have something real to show to stakeholders.

Following the sprint life cycle

Each sprint has the same process: sprint planning, daily scrums, a sprint review, and a sprint retrospective. Sprints are developmental cycles that repeat until your project is complete. Requirements (often in the form of user stories) are developed, tested, integrated, and approved within each sprint. The process continues sprint after sprint. Figure 5-5 depicts a one-week sprint life cycle.

Stage 4: SPRINT PLANNING

FIGURE 5-5:
The one-week sprint life cycle.

Description: Establish specific iteration goals and tasks.
Owner: Product owner and development team
Frequency: At the start of each sprint

TIP

When scrum teams are distributed offshore with team members in faraway time zones (such as the United States and India), arrangements need to be made for all team members to attend each of the sprint meetings. To account for time-zone differences, the domestic team members might join the meeting Sunday night while it's Monday morning for the offshore team members. At the end of the sprint, the domestic team members finish the sprint Friday morning and take the rest of the day off while the offshore team is joining the sprint review and retrospective Friday night. Rotating each sprint might be appreciated on each end so that each team member doesn't always have to work on Sunday nights or Friday nights.

The key is that after each sprint, the scrum team learns new things. Change happens; it's inevitable. Responding and adapting to it should be considered progress, not failure.

Change is easy in scrum because at the end of every cycle what was created was done to completion. When you go into your next sprint and work on items from the product backlog, it doesn't matter whether those items have been on the product backlog for four months, four weeks, or four minutes. Old or new, each product backlog item gets prioritized not by the order in which it was received, but by the order in which it will deliver the highest value to the customer.

DON'T GO CHASING WATERFALLS

TECHNICAL
STUFF

Scrum is different from the traditional waterfall method, in which all items are in a package and that package is matured. So, if changes come in halfway through the project, the impact of those changes is nebulous and woven across multiple requirements. This unknown impact is what made change a dirty word in waterfall.

Some who are new to scrum and hold on to waterfall ways may mistakenly view a sprint as simply a smaller timebox than before for completing tasks, which are part of an overall upfront plan:

- They set multiple sprints up front at the beginning of the project and identify the exact requirements and tasks that will be done during each sprint.
- They hold very brief sprint reviews as status reports about the product backlog, rather than product increment demonstrations.
- They hold brief sprint planning meetings to confirm the original plan.

The increased frequency of review of the original plan seems nice to a team new to agile thinking but completely misses the point and falls short. This is still waterfall.

The sprint life cycle allows for the easy incorporation and adaptation of change based on reality. This is empiricism.

TIP

In our experience, the Monday-to-Friday work week is a natural, biorhythmic time frame. Teams need a weekend break, which fits naturally with life patterns. So, avoid off-kilter sprint patterns of Wednesday to Tuesday or the like.

Planning Your Sprints: Stage 4

The planning of sprints is Stage 4 in the roadmap to value. All the work to be accomplished during that specific sprint is planned here. Each sprint planning session is timeboxed to no more than two hours for each week of the sprint. If you have a one-week sprint timebox, you have a maximum of two hours to plan your sprint, for example.

Sprint goals

A goal is created for each sprint. The product owner initiates the goal discussion, identifying the business value objective that needs to be met. After the team is clear on the goal, the product owner chooses the requirements from the product backlog that best support the goal. As with the release goal, the sprint goal drives the requirements developed, not the other way around.

The sprint goal itself must support the release goal, which supports the vision statement. This goal decomposition and alignment are essential for ensuring that you're doing purpose-driven development.

The development team is critical in creating the sprint goal. Because they're the ones doing the actual work, while the product owner establishes the direction, or the what, the development team establishes the how and how much.

If your development team has an established average velocity, it may be used as input in determining the amount of work they will take on during the sprint.

The development team can also use velocity for stretching, testing its limits, or backing off if they're struggling to achieve the goals set. If they've been achieving 34 story points comfortably, they might push it to 38 or 40. If they've been struggling to achieve 25, they might lower it to 23 while the scrum team figures out organizational drag that can be removed.

Both phases of sprint planning occur in the single sprint planning meeting at the beginning of the sprint. Phase I is where the product owner, with input from the development team and facilitated by the scrum master, determines what needs to be accomplished (the goal). In Phase II, the development team determines how to achieve the sprint goal and develops the actual sprint backlog of supporting tasks.

The sprint planning meeting may not always go smoothly, especially at first. You may slip down rabbit holes, discover tangents, and unearth different estimations of what's possible. This is where a strong and deft facilitator is needed in the form of the scrum master. It's their job to make sure that the session stays on track and the heat stays on low.

Phase I

At the start of Phase I, the sprint goal is created, and the development team must fully understand it, because it will provide the boundaries and direction for the work they will do throughout the sprint. The product owner then selects a portion of the product backlog that supports the goal. This won't necessarily be the final sprint backlog, but is the forecasted functionality that if finished in the sprint, would satisfy the sprint goal. It's what the development team will work from to achieve the sprint goal and determine the actual sprint backlog.

Phase I gives the development team and product owner another opportunity to clarify any existing requirements or identify new ones that are needed to achieve the sprint goal. This would also be the time to give the final size estimation on any clarified requirements and size any new requirements for the sprint. Remember the yardstick: If any requirements are sized higher than an 8, they're too big for a sprint (see Chapter 4).

We like to bring six to ten product backlog items into each sprint. This is usually the right balance of being able to deliver a product increment with substantial functionality as well as litmus that each individual item is sufficiently broken down.

The only requirements discussed in sprint planning should be those estimated between 1 and 8 on the Fibonacci scale. This isn't a scrum rule, but it aligns with our affinity estimating model (see Chapter 4) and has been an effective way for many teams to keep focused on properly refined requirements that can be completed within a sprint. For more on Fibonacci numbers, see Chapter 4.

Phase II

When the goal and the supporting requirements have been determined by the scrum team, the development team breaks down those requirements into individual tasks — how they will turn product backlog items into the product increment. The tasks for each requirement should explicitly satisfy the team's definition of done. For instance, if the definition of done includes integration with system A, at least one task for the requirement should be "integration test with system A."

TIP

Ideally, each task should be able to be completed in one day. This gives the development team a tangible, realistic time target as they break requirements down into tasks. It also sets a benchmark from which the team can be alerted to any development problems. If a task is taking multiple days to develop, an issue might need to be addressed with the task or the developer.

Development teams may choose to estimate the tasks for each requirement in hours if the organization wants that level of visibility. But many teams simply use velocity and complete/not complete of product backlog items to adequately visualize sprint risk.

The development team is forced to be the most detailed here, which helps to sharpen the mind. They can really dig down and look at what needs to be done.

By the end of sprint planning, the development team should be clear on how the chosen sprint backlog items support the sprint goal and how the work to complete those backlog items will be done. This does not mean that all (or any) of the tasks on the sprint backlog get assigned at this time. Rather, each day the development team self-organizes by having each developer pull a task and work on it to completion. (You find more on pull versus push in "Working the sprint backlog" later in this chapter.)

Your Sprint Backlog

The sprint backlog is created in the sprint planning session and is the ordered list of requirements and tasks necessary to achieve the sprint goal.

A sprint backlog might contain the following information:

>> The sprint goal and dates

>> A prioritized list of the requirements (for example, user stories) to be developed in the sprint

>> The estimated effort (that is, story points) required to develop each requirement

>> The tasks required to develop each requirement

>> The hours estimated to complete each task (if needed)

>> A burndown chart to show the status of the work developed in the sprint

The burndown chart benefit

Burndown charts are ways to visually represent progress achieved within the sprint. They depict the amount of work accomplished versus the amount left to go. Figure 5-6 shows an example:

>> The vertical axis represents the work left to be done.

>> The horizontal axis depicts the time still available in the sprint.

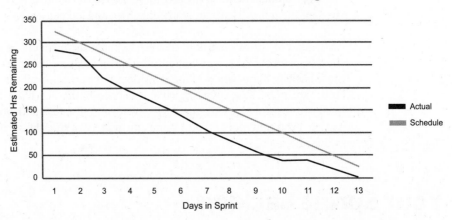

FIGURE 5-6:
Sprint burndown chart.

Your sprints will show a diagonal line from the top-left corner to the bottom-right corner, which represents what an even and consistent burn would look like, though really you won't have a perfectly even burndown.

Some burndown charts also have a line showing the outstanding story points. This allows you to quickly and easily see the status of your sprint from both time and relative estimation perspectives.

You can create your own burndown chart with Microsoft Excel or download the one that's included within the sprint backlog template, which you can download from this page: https://platinumedge.com/blog/anatomy-sprint-backlog.

The burndown chart is generated from the sprint backlog. The sprint backlog should be updated every day, and only the development team can do this. At the end of each day, each developer updates their task (whether on a 3x5 card, on a spreadsheet, or in an electronic tool) by entering the number of *remaining* hours (*not* the number of completed hours) that are left to complete the task. That's it. One number. It takes seconds and the results are invaluable. See Figure 5-7 for a sample sprint backlog.

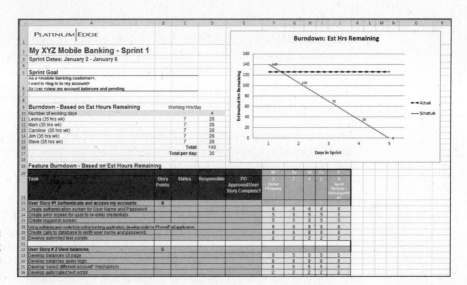

FIGURE 5-7:
A sprint backlog is a key scrum artifact.

The sprint burndown chart is an information radiator that shows anyone who wants to know the status of the sprint. Burndown charts get generated automatically as development team members update the amount of time left on their one active task at the end of each day.

The burndown chart shows the amount of time remaining for the sum of all the requirements on the sprint backlog. Compared with the trend line, it provides a daily level of status detail for a Scrum team that you can't get with traditional project management techniques.

Setting backlog capacity

How much capacity is in a day? If you're looking at the number of hours per day that a development team member is able to devote to her main job — developing! — allow for less than eight. Every organization has a certain amount of overhead. We find that for most organizations, somewhere between five and seven hours is a normal effective workday.

TECHNICAL STUFF

An average of 16 hours per week are wasted on unclear objectives, poor team communication, and ineffective meetings.

How much capacity is really in a sprint? In a one-week sprint, scrum teams will spend up to two hours in sprint planning, up to one hour in sprint review, and up to 45 minutes in a sprint retrospective. That's about four hours in sprint meetings. (Do you have to use all four hours? No. Can you go over the limit for any given meeting? No.)

That accounts for four of the five scrum events (assume that a maximum 15-minute daily scrum won't affect development time), but don't forget product backlog refinement. We find that development teams will on average spend 10 percent of their time each sprint in product backlog refinement activities. This translates to about three to four hours in a one-week sprint.

So, for a one-week sprint, each developer spends between seven and eight hours in sprint events, which takes care of one full workday for an efficient organization and about a day and a half for a less efficient organization.

Is there any buffer in scrum? Sure. Consider that a development team has 165 hours available to them for a sprint. They shouldn't take on 164 hours under the false assumption that everything is going to go exactly according to plan. The buffer varies from team to team, but you should make it transparent.

So capacity for one developer for a one-week sprint would be 18 to 27 hours, depending on the organization's established effective workday. Take this into consideration when identifying a development team's capacity during sprint planning. This is assuming that no paid holidays, vacations, or other time off is planned that will keep developers from developing.

Who said scrum is rudderless? You can't get much more disciplined than this.

What an incredible impact having a dedicated and effective scrum master means to a development team's capacity. By removing the organizational drag (impediments) that keep effective workdays from increasing from five to seven hours, the impact can add up to an additional nine work hours in a one-week sprint per developer. For a development team of seven, that's a potential 63-hour efficiency increase. Scrum masters add value.

What happens if at the end of sprint planning, the development team finds that the number of estimated hours for their tasks from the sprint backlog is more than their capacity? Do they hunker down and work overtime? No, the product owner has a decision to make: which sprint backlog items will be moved back to the product backlog to get the number of hours below the development team's capacity. Sustained overtime leads to poor team morale, poorer quality, and long-term productivity loses.

The value of the iterative planning process is easily visible within sprint planning. By the time the work to be done is outlined and broken down to the task level, you will have done so in a way that minimizes time waste and maximizes business value and ROI. This is because the roadmap to value, from the vision statement all the way down to the sprint level, has enabled continuous prioritization and progressive elaboration of only the most important product backlog items.

Working the sprint backlog

We see development teams get distracted and go off target by making some common mistakes. Follow these practices to counter those mistakes when working with the sprint backlog:

» Make sure that requirements are broken down into tasks that accurately and completely reflect your definition of done (see Chapter 4).

   The product owner should not accept a requirement until it completely satisfies the sprint definition of done.

» The entire development team ideally works on only one requirement at a time and completes that requirement before starting another. This is called *swarming.*

   Swarming can be accomplished by such activities as

   • Each team member working on individual tasks related to the same requirement

   • Pairing two people on one task to ensure quality

   • Team members shadowing each other to increase cross-functionality

   As development teams swarm around one requirement at a time, this ensures cross-functionality and ensures that every sprint will have something tangible accomplished at its end.

» Each requirement must be fully developed, tested, integrated, and accepted by the product owner before the team moves on to the next requirement.

» Don't assign multiple tasks to individual development team members.

   Each day, the development team coordinates priorities and decides who will do what. A developer should only be working on one task at a time until that task is completely done. This is called a *pull mechanism.* Don't fall back into the traditional method of a manager assigning tasks out to team members.

TIP

Swarming on requirements stems from the lean concept of work in progress (WIP) limits. When a development team has a lot of work in progress, it delays taking the actions necessary to finalize that work and rear-loads issue correction. Your WIP limit should ideally be only one requirement at a time for the development team and only one task at a time per developer. The development team usually finds that their tasks get completed sooner than if they had started them all at the same time. Having only one requirement open at a time is also an effective way of exposing process bottlenecks, which can then be addressed and fixed for faster throughput.

PUSH VERSUS PULL

Traditional project management follows the push model of assigning tasks to individuals when they're identified. Each individual manages and focuses solely on the tasks in his personal queue. This queue builds up over time, and attempts are made to redistribute task load across team members to avoid over- or underloading. The trouble with push systems is that it's difficult to know the status of things unless everything is either unstarted or all the way complete. This also tends to contribute to team members operating as silos rather than cross-functional teams.

Pull models, like scrum, maintain all work in a common queue, and items are pulled from the top by individual developers (which assumes proper ordering and prioritization by the product owner). You don't need the redistribution of task load, and it provides a natural pause for developers to evaluate where they can help others on open tasks before pulling a new one. Development teams are also more likely under a pull model to work on backlog items much closer, if not exactly, to the original order of priority than a push system. Bottlenecks are less common, and overall workflow is more predictable.

Push systems encourage individual-centered (silo) goals. Pull systems support collaboration for the sake of achieving product-centered goals.

For example, at the grocery store, you can choose between a push and pull option when you go to check out:

- The push option is chosen by going through a checkout line with a dedicated clerk for that line. The line is "assigned" to you because you chose it and you're standing in it. You're stuck with it unless another line empties, and you get to it before someone else does.

- You can choose the pull system and increase your chances of getting through as quickly as possible. Do this by selecting the self-checkout option, where four to six individual checkout stations are ready for whoever is next in line. Rather than being committed to a single checkout line for the remainder of the checkout experience, you'll be able to take advantage of the next open self-checkout station as soon as it's available.

Prioritizing sprints

Each sprint has its own life cycle, as shown in Figure 5-5 earlier in this chapter. Within each sprint, each requirement has its own prioritization and life cycle, too. Each requirement and task are developed, tested, integrated, and approved before the team moves on to the next-highest-priority item. See Figure 5-8 for a representation.

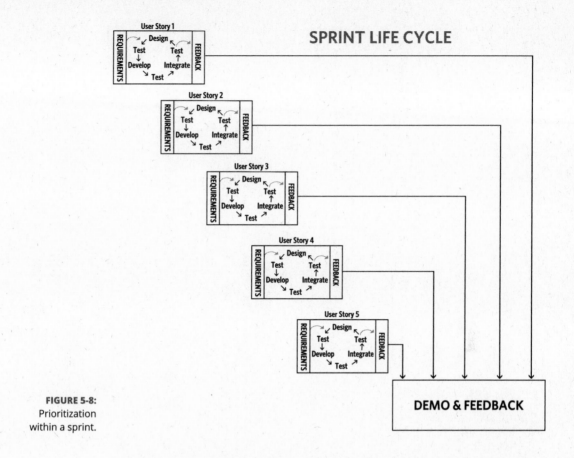

FIGURE 5-8:
Prioritization within a sprint.

The sprint backlog items are prioritized from highest to lowest and developed in that order. The development team works on only one requirement at a time. When that requirement is finished, the team moves on to the next-highest-priority one rather than picking one lower on the list that might be easier or more interesting.

Chapter **6**

Getting the Most Out of Sprints

S prints are the essence of scrum, so it's worth spending an entire chapter on them. You have the gist already: Sprints are fixed timeboxes designed so that your development team can create a development rhythm. They also nurture the inspect-and-adapt premise.

But that's not all that sprints do. In this chapter, we introduce the daily scrum — an invaluable 15 minutes every day that will focus and organize your short-term goals like never before. Facilitated by the scrum master, the daily scrum keeps your project on track as the scrum team deals with impediments and coordinates the day's priorities.

This chapter also exposes you to the sprint review and sprint retrospective. These two meetings take the concepts of inspection and adaptation to new levels. Stakeholders review the product developed and give the product owner immediate feedback; the scrum team itself assesses how the sprint went and incorporates any improvements into the process.

The Daily Scrum: Stage 5

The daily scrum is one of the five scrum events and Stage 5 on the roadmap to value (see Figure 6-1).

REMEMBER

Planning is huge in scrum. You don't set a goal, forget it, and then gather together six months later to see what happened. You inspect and adapt every single day, and even throughout the day.

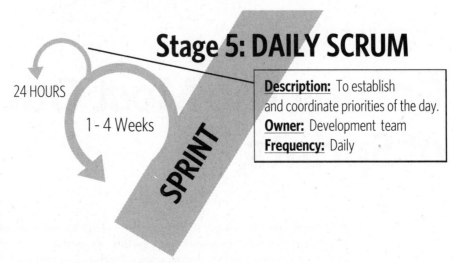

Stage 5: DAILY SCRUM

24 HOURS

1 - 4 Weeks

SPRINT

Description: To establish and coordinate priorities of the day.
Owner: Development team
Frequency: Daily

FIGURE 6-1:
The daily scrum is an integral aspect of the sprint and Stage 5 in the roadmap to value.

Because a development team swarms each day to attack a single requirement, coordination is key. The removal of impediments is also crucial for developers who work closely together to deliver potentially shippable increments within short periods. The daily scrum is how the development team coordinates.

REMEMBER

If you manage your projects by weeks (that is, with weekly project manager status reports that may not get reviewed promptly), you slip by weeks. In scrum, you may still slip but only by a day, because scrum teams manage by day through the sprint backlog, the daily scrum, and daily and direct interaction. We look more closely at this comparison in Chapter 7.

Defining the daily scrum

As its name implies, a daily scrum takes place during each sprint. The timebox is 15 minutes maximum, no matter what the overall length of the sprint is. Meetings in scrum, like artifacts, are barely sufficient. Anything longer than 15 minutes would eat into valuable developing time. Besides, 15 minutes is plenty of time to accomplish everything necessary.

The purpose of the daily scrum is to coordinate the day's sprint activities and identify impediments keeping the development team from accomplishing its sprint goal. Every member of the development team participates, so everyone is dialed into what the entire team is working on. If an impediment comes up during the daily scrum, it's dealt with following the daily scrum. The event is a coordination meeting, not a problem- or complaint-solving meeting.

REMEMBER

The scrum master either removes impediments or facilitates their removal. Some impediments may need to be removed by the product owner or require discussion between a team member and someone outside the team.

Participants in the daily scrum are the development team members and the scrum master. The scrum master ensures that the meeting takes place, and the development team directs it. The product owner should attend (and must attend if specifically asked to do so by the development team). The product owner may provide clarifications on prioritization as needed, and anyone else who's involved and interested can listen in but can't say anything. This way, they can enjoy the daily transparency and be involved in the daily process, but they can't hinder or derail it.

REMEMBER

The daily scrum is how a development team self-organizes and self-manages. Each day, the team decides who will do what and who will help whom. Work isn't dictated by a project manager or some other nondeveloper.

If a daily scrum starts to feel like a status-report meeting or development team members start addressing one person (such as an informal team lead or the scrum master), the meeting has missed the point. A daily scrum should be peer to peer.

The key takeaway from a daily scrum is clarity about what it means to be successful that day. Then the team swarms if necessary to do the highest-priority work. The team finds value in this ceremony only if team members achieve relevant clarity and purpose about the day's goals. Daily scrums offer an opportunity to inspect and adapt in the moment.

REMEMBER

A common misconception about the daily scrum is that it's a time for the development team to report to the product owner or a time for product owners to introduce new requirements or update a sprint goal. Don't let the daily scrum become a business-status-reporting meeting; it's a coordination meeting to enable high performance.

Scheduling a daily scrum

Because a daily scrum lasts only 15 minutes, everyone needs to be on time and ready. You'll find a direct correlation between how late a meeting starts and how loose the focus is after the meeting starts. You may have different ways of encouraging punctuality, such as the following:

>> **Start your daily scrum a half an hour after the normal workday begins.** This schedule gives your development team members time to get coffee, answer emails, discuss the previous evening's antics, and cover anything else in their morning rituals.

>> **Penalize members for being late in a friendly, spirited way.** Have team members pay a certain amount into a celebration fund for each minute they're late or have them sing their college song at full tilt. Get creative and make the penalty uncomfortable enough to stop tardiness.

TIP

A Scrum team in Portland implemented a "$20 or 20 pushups with multiplier" incentive. The first time he was late, a team member paid $20 or did 20 push-ups. The next time he was late, he paid $40 or did 40 pushups, and so on. This penalty was invented by the team members, not imposed on them. It worked for them and was successfully prevented tardiness.

A key disruptor of the daily scrum is distraction. We've worked with some teams whose regular habit is for each member to focus on his or her own laptop screen. Some members even attend via phone while driving to the office. Listen for indicators such as "Can you say that again? I missed it." No electronics should be the rule during the daily scrum.

Conducting a daily scrum

Imagine a scrum team gathering around its sprint backlog or task board at the beginning of the day. Each person can see at a glance the progress made the day before; then each person proactively chooses a new task for the current day. Team members coordinate where help is needed to accomplish a task before the day ends; then they go straight to work.

Each team member should make three statements about how he or she is helping the team achieve its sprint goal:

>> Yesterday, I accomplished . . .

>> Today, I'm going to focus on . . .

>> The things impeding me are . . .

We like to have scrum masters participate beyond facilitation by addressing the impediments that are identified and/or in progress. The scrum master might say after the team members have spoken:

» Yesterday, I removed this impediment.

» Today, I can remove this impediment.

» The impediments I can't remove are . . . , and I'll see whether so-and-so can help me.

As we discuss in Chapter 5, tasks should be broken down so that they can be accomplished in a day or less. Even then, when developers are left to themselves for days on end without coordinating and swarming as a team, they can get bogged down in unnecessary details or problems that could be easily resolved with help.

Daily scrums synchronize a team, and everyone goes to work helping each other do what it takes to get to done. Together they completely own the outcome. Come the next day, the team members are excited to talk about their progress.

Making daily scrums more effective

The following tactics can keep your daily scrum meetings quick and effective:

» Diligently start on time. See "Scheduling a daily scrum" earlier in this chapter for some tips on enforcing punctuality.

» Conduct the meeting standing up. Studies have shown that meetings conducted standing up are 34 percent shorter than those conducted sitting down. No one has a chance to slump in a chair and relax; it's as though everyone is already on the move.

» Focus the meeting on coordination, not problem-solving. Impediments get removed after the daily scrum.

TIP

When impediments are uncovered in the daily scrum, the scrum master can deal with them by hosting an after party immediately following the daily scrum. This event involves only those who need to be involved and is for addressing any issues that came up during the daily scrum.

A backlog of these "team topics" can also be kept so that the topics can be addressed by the team during the after party when appropriate or during the team retrospective. Not all topics raised during the daily standup need to be addressed that day.

>> The scrum master is the meeting facilitator and, as necessary, keeps the meeting on time and on track, and makes sure that only development team members participate. The scrum master's touch should be as light as possible.

>> Cover only immediate issues and priorities in relation to that day in support of the sprint goal.

>> Gather around the task board to ensure context and focus.

>> Don't assign a set speaking order because when people know the order they tend to check out until it's their turn. In some cases, they don't even show up until just before their turn.

TIP

We toss a squeaky dog toy to a random member of the development team when that person should speak. If anyone takes too long, we switch to a timer ball with an alarm. An alternative is to toss a ream of paper (which weighs 5 pounds) and let the person talk for as long as he can hold the paper out to his side. These tactics keep the daily scrum fast, forward-moving, and fun.

>> Don't allow vague statements or rely on team members' memories of what's in the sprint backlog (see the next section, "Team Task Board").

Team Task Board

A *task board* is one way to display the sprint backlog. Although it's common for scrum teams to manage their sprint backlog in digital format, all you really need are some wall or whiteboard space, 3x5 cards, sticky notes, and tape. Figure 6-2 shows a sample task board.

The task board, like the product roadmap, increases engagement and flexibility because it's tangible.

A physical task board is excellent because it's a quick, effective way to show the status of an entire sprint. Keeping the task board within sight of the development team and product owner ensures that everyone instantly knows what's done, what's not done, and everything in between.

Use these basic elements:

>> Top

- The specific sprint goal

- The overall release goal

Release and sprint dates can also be included.

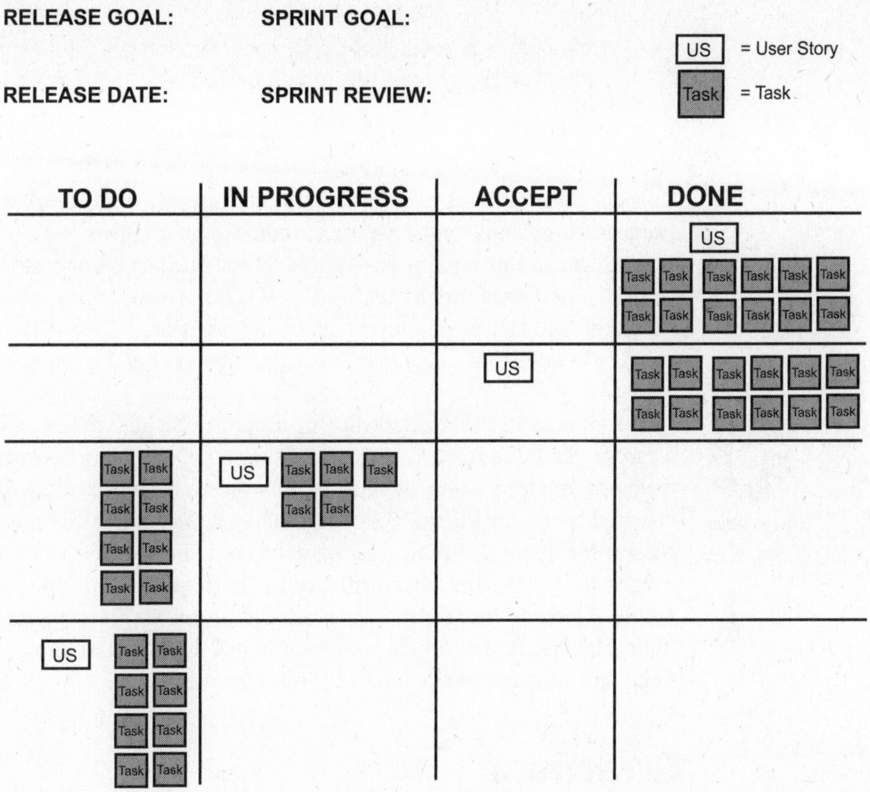

RELEASE GOAL: SPRINT GOAL:

RELEASE DATE: SPRINT REVIEW:

US = User Story
Task = Task

TO DO	IN PROGRESS	ACCEPT	DONE
			US

FIGURE 6-2:
A team task
board.

>> Columns (from left to right)

- *To Do:* Requirements and tasks in the sprint that have yet to be developed

  Developers pull from the top of this list to start a new task. If two developers want to take the same task, they can pair up on it, one developer can shadow the other, or they can decide who can best handle it.

- *In Progress:* The product backlog items and tasks that the development team is working on

  Each task may have different colored dots or stickers to designate ownership or to identify tasks that are blocked by an impediment. Work-in-progress limits, if used, should be displayed in this column. After developers complete a task, they look here to see who they can help. Otherwise, they pull the next task from the To Do column and verify with the team that it's the right task to work on.

- *Accept:* Requirements that are awaiting acceptance by the product owner

  If the requirement is rejected, and enough time is left in the sprint, it goes back to the In Progress column. Otherwise, the requirement gets moved back to the product backlog for consideration in a future sprint (see "Handling unfinished requirements" later in this chapter).

- *Done*: The requirements that the product owner has accepted as complete

Only the development team members can move the requirements from To Do to In Progress to Accept, and only the product owner can move them from Accept to Done. After a requirement is accepted by the product owner and moved to the Done column, the development team moves tasks with it. Otherwise, if a requirement gets rejected, the development team moves tasks back to In Progress to rework them or creates new tasks to address the reason why the requirement was rejected.

REMEMBER

Requirements in the Accept column shouldn't be allowed to pile up. Ideally, when a card is placed in Accept, it should either be placed in Done or rejected for further development the same day. If a delay occurs, the product owner needs to be coached to not letting stories accumulate as they wait to be accepted. You have no reason for delay if the product owner is a dedicated scrum team member who is available at any time for clarification, the requirements have been detailed to a single action or integration, and the requirements have passed the definition of done. It's critical for the development team members to know when their work is done and can swarm the next requirement.

Swarming

In Chapter 5, we introduce the concept of swarming in the context of the sprint backlog. *Swarming* is all development team members working on only one requirement at a time during the sprint. Although this principle isn't specific to scrum, it's such an effective way for teams to execute their sprint backlog that it warrants discussion here.

THE KANBAN BOARD

Kanban is Japanese for *signboard, billboard, signal card,* or *card you can see.* In the 1950s, Toyota formalized this concept to standardize the flow of inventory parts in its production lines. In essence, Kanban boards contain cards that represent single pieces of work. Each card acts as a signal of status and indicates when new work can be pulled in.

This practice helped inspire lean thinking and manufacturing practices, and many agile teams use something like a Kanban board system today. Task boards function much like Kanban boards, in that they provide a visual status (signal) of exactly where each task (piece of work) is in the overall process. This level of visibility makes it easier for development teams to be disciplined and swarming on requirements to get to done.

One of the main benefits of scrum is that development teams start and finish requirements to satisfy their definition of done to produce a potentially shippable product increment within a relatively short timebox. The team revises the process based on lessons learned and repeat that cycle again and again. The goal is to finish, not just start, as many requirements as possible.

Swarming enables teams to enjoy the following benefits:

>> Maximizing chances for success, with the skills and abilities of the entire team focused on a single requirement

>> Completing the cycle of planning, designing, developing, and testing to completion for each requirement

>> Resolving issues and impediments today

>> Dramatically decreasing the introduction of defects into a product through pairing and single-tasking (versus multitasking)

>> Eliminating single points of failure in knowledge, processes, and skill sets

>> Finishing the most important requirements completely and first

When team members see all their fellow developers working on a task, and there are no other tasks left for the same requirement (the user story), it's perfectly natural for them to consider it more productive to start a new requirement than to help other developers on the requirement in progress. This tendency can get out of hand, however, to the point where teams find themselves with multiple requirements started but none of them finished. By shadowing, pairing, researching, or helping in whatever way gets the task to done, development teams avoid this risk.

This process ensures that in every sprint, *something* gets completely developed and is available to show stakeholders. Every sprint produces shippable results. The development team's efforts are focused, teamwork is enhanced, and the iterative process of scrum is put into play.

TIP

Stay focused. Stop starting and start finishing.

Dealing with rejection

If a requirement placed in the Accept column is rejected by the product owner, the developers have two options:

>> **Finish their current tasks and then swarm the rejected requirement:** This option might be better if plenty of time is left in the sprint to complete both the current tasks and the rejected requirement.

>> **Abandon their current tasks to swarm the rejected requirement:** This option might be better if not enough time remains in the sprint to finish both the current tasks and the rejected requirement.

The product owner decides the priority when faced with this decision. Variables other than time left in the sprint may influence the product owner's decision. As the team inspects its learning and adapts throughout a sprint, the rejected story may become less valuable to achieving the sprint goal than the next requirement in progress, so even though time is left in the sprint to do both, the risk of not finishing the in-progress requirement may be higher than the risk of not finishing the rejected requirement.

In any case, attention to priority and close daily coordination with the product owner throughout the sprint keep the entire scrum team (including the product owner) on focus and on task.

REMEMBER

Scrum teams should always push themselves. If development teams accomplish 100 percent of their sprint backlog every time, they may not be pushing themselves to their limit. A high percentage of sprint backlog completion should be the goal, but you shouldn't expect scrum teams to hit 100 percent every time. Scrum masters, like aeronautical engineers, help the scrum team find ways to reduce drag to become more effective and accomplish more in each sprint. As long as teams finish what they start each sprint and increase velocity, they realize the continuous-improvement benefit of scrum.

MULTITASKING AND THRASHING

Recently, Microsoft conducted a study on the effects of multitasking showing that multitasking doesn't work. On average, it takes 15 minutes to get your brain back to the level where it was before you answered that phone call or email. Studies have also shown that an interruption as short as 4.4 seconds triples the number of errors made on subsequent tasks requiring sequencing. Reducing multitasking in your development team gets you a sound head start on achieving the 30 to 40 percent increased product-to-market time we've seen so often.

Thrashing occurs when developers jump back and forth among projects, requirements, and tasks, effectively switching context. Thrashing increases the time required to complete tasks by 30 percent. If you don't have enough people to take on the workload as dedicated, swarming developers, you don't have time to thrash them.

Handling unfinished requirements

Even high-functioning development teams that estimate well, swarm, and stick to a work-in-progress (WIP) limit of one throughout each sprint may end up with incomplete or unstarted requirements left on the sprint backlog at the end of a sprint. This result may be okay if team members swarmed on the higher-priority requirements to completion and have working product increments that can be shipped.

But what does the team do with those remaining requirements?

If a requirement isn't started, or was started and not completed, the product owner puts it back in the product backlog in its entirety (keeping all notes, tasks, and documentation intact, of course) and then reprioritizes it against the rest of the product backlog. The product owner may potentially pull the requirement into a future sprint according to its new priority.

Based on what was completed during the sprint, the unstarted or unfinished requirement may no longer be necessary, or it may not have as high a value as it had before. What was done may be enough; it may be time to move on to a different feature.

Whatever effort was made on the requirement, because it wasn't finished, it isn't included in the team's velocity for that sprint. If the requirement does make it into a future sprint, it needs to be refined, clarified, and reestimated based on the remaining work to be done. You can't bank or cache story points.

An exception may occur when, after working on an unfinished requirement, you find that you can split it. You finish one part of the requirement during the sprint; the other part goes back into the product backlog to be reestimated and reprioritized.

The lesson in all this is swarm to get to done during the sprint.

The Sprint Review: Stage 6

The next stop on our roadmap to value is Stage 6, the sprint review (see Figure 6-3). This scrum event is integral to the inspect-and-adapt process of scrum and takes place at the end of each sprint.

Stage 6: SPRINT REVIEW

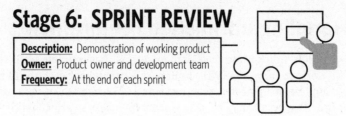

FIGURE 6-3:
The sprint review
is a scrum event
and Stage 6
of the roadmap
to value.

Description: Demonstration of working product
Owner: Product owner and development team
Frequency: At the end of each sprint

The purpose of the sprint review is for the product owner to get organizational feedback on whether the product is moving in the right direction. This review is also a great opportunity for the development team to stand up and show off what it's accomplished. Team members get full credit for what they've achieved and what they haven't.

This meeting at the end of every sprint ensures that the stakeholders are up to date on what was accomplished in the sprint and have a forum for delivering feedback directly to the product owner, with the development team listening in. Also, stakeholders have working, shippable product in their hands.

The sprint review process

The sprint review, which is timeboxed to one hour per week of sprint, takes place at the end of the last day of the sprint. Allow for this time expenditure during the sprint-planning session.

The participants in the sprint review are the entire scrum team and the stakeholders, in these roles:

REMEMBER

>> **Scrum master:** Facilitates the meeting, ensuring that it stays in focus and on time.

>> **Product owner:** Briefly reviews the sprint goal and how well the scrum team met the goal, fills in the stakeholders on what items from the backlog have been completed, and summarizes what's left to go in the release.

The sprint review isn't the time for the product owner to provide feedback on the completed functionality. This event is for the product owner to receive feedback from stakeholders on the direction in which they're taking the product. The product owner accepts or rejects each requirement as it's completed, not at the end of the sprint, and approves the requirements before they're demonstrated to the stakeholders.

>> **Development team members:** Display and explain the completed requirements.

>> **Stakeholders:** Ask questions and provide feedback.

The process begins with the development team preparing for the review. Consider the following guidelines for sprint-review preparation:

>> The development team prepares a sprint review for the minimal amount of time (no more than 20 minutes) to showcase completed requirements.

>> No formal slides should be used in a sprint review. Rather, the development team should spend its time developing the product instead of preparing a presentation.

>> Only the requirements that have been deemed done (according to the definition of done) and approved by the product owner are demonstrated.

>> The development team showcases the shippable functionality of the requirement — that is, how it works in the real world.

WARNING

If you spend your time showing stakeholders what could or should have been done, you're giving a rigged demonstration and haven't done anyone any favors. Stakeholders never expect less; they always expect more. By making it look as though your product increment works when it really doesn't, you increase your workload for the coming sprint, because you'll have to make work what you showed should work, as well all the new work you'll plan for. Demonstrate only working product increments.

Stakeholder feedback

Critical to the success of the sprint review is stakeholder feedback. A constant cycle of communication keeps the project on track and produces what stakeholders want. Although stakeholders can't tell development team members how to develop requirements, they can give feedback to the product owner about the requirements and features they want developed and about how well the implementations serve customers' needs.

This feedback loop also serves another purpose: It keeps the development team involved and, therefore, emotionally engaged in the project.

Feedback is a common theme throughout scrum. Figure 6-4 shows how many layers of feedback are involved in the scrum framework. Each time feedback is received, it gets cycled back into the product backlog and sprint-planning sessions — truly inspection and adaptation.

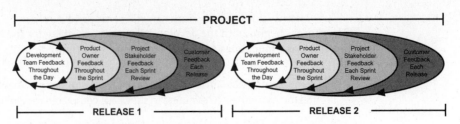

FIGURE 6-4:
Multiple layers of
feedback exist in
a typical scrum
project.

Product increments

The product increment is the final of the three scrum artifacts. (We discuss the product backlog in Chapter 3 and the sprint backlog in Chapter 5.)

Within a single sprint, the product increment is working product deemed done by the product owner and now potentially shippable. It's *potentially* shippable because the product owner may not decide that the product is ready to ship until later. But it's ready to ship as soon as the product owner is ready.

A product increment has been

>> Developed

>> Tested

>> Integrated

>> Documented

During the sprint-review meeting, this product increment is demonstrated to stakeholders. The inspect-and-adapt sprint life cycle continues as feedback is taken and translated into requirements. Then these requirements may be enhanced during product-backlog refinement; they may rise in priority for consideration in future sprints and eventually become new product increments.

The sprint review is about improving the product. The sprint retrospective is how scrum teams can make this continuous improvement happen for their team and process.

The Sprint Retrospective: Stage 7

The seventh and final stage in the roadmap to value is the sprint retrospective (see Figure 6-5). This scrum event takes place after every sprint.

Stage 7: SPRINT RETROSPECTIVE

FIGURE 6-5:
The sprint retrospective, the seventh and final stage in the roadmap to value.

Description: Team refinement of environment and processes to optimize efficiency.
Owner: Scrum team
Frequency: At the end of each sprint

The purpose of the sprint retrospective is to provide an opportunity for the scrum team — scrum master, product owner, and development team members — to assess what went well in the sprint that was just finished and what can be improved. The process is inspection and adaptation one more time, with a focus on the people, processes, and tools that the scrum team uses.

The outcome of the retrospective should be plans of action to continuously improve scrum, people, processes, and tools in every sprint. Although the scrum framework is simple — three roles, three artifacts, and five events (see Chapter 1) — and doesn't require tweaking, each scrum team has quirks and nuances because of their product, organization, and development methods. Through the process of inspection and adaptation, you can aim those individualities toward the project goals.

Because the sprint retrospective asks for input and feedback from all scrum team members, it increases ownership through engagement and a sense of purpose. Team spirit is enhanced, which in turn leads to an increase in productivity and velocity, which is self-management.

REMEMBER

It's critical in sprint retrospectives to create a trusting environment. Each person's view is listened to and respected, and nothing is taken personally. Trust is the key to keeping the retrospective from being a labyrinth of euphemisms or politics. The scrum master plays a pivotal role in creating an environment of trust.

WARNING

The sprint retrospective may unveil problems within the team. An adept scrum master can facilitate the event so that these issues are dealt with in an equitable, low-intensity environment. A sprint retrospective isn't for venting, but for actionable plans for improvement. Be on the lookout for passive-aggressive speech and personal agendas.

The sprint retrospective process

The sprint retrospective takes place at the end of every sprint, after the sprint review and before the next sprint's planning session. For each week of the sprint, 45 minutes is timeboxed for this event, so a two-week sprint has a timeboxed retrospective of 90 minutes.

The entire scrum team participates, and at the team's discretion, other people may be invited (such as customers and stakeholders) if the team believes that these people have valuable insights about needed improvements.

In preparation for the retrospective, everyone should consider how the sprint went and jot down any ideas or concerns. As always, use simple tools such as sticky notes; avoid formal presentations.

Although the scrum master facilitates the meeting, everyone participates at a peer-to-peer level. The purpose of the sprint retrospective is to inspect the sprint that just ended to

>> Identify what went well in the sprint with the processes, tools, and team dynamics.

>> Discuss and discover opportunities for improvement.

>> Define an action plan for implementing the improvement(s).

During the retrospective, remember to emphasize and give equal air time to what went well. It's important to focus on the positive and to identify what's working well so that you can keep doing it. Rejoice as a team in successes. Especially during initial scrum implementation, it's important to recognize the wins — big and small.

TIP

An effective way to keep things positive and avoid isolating people during a retrospective is the sandwich technique. Start with positive, work through negative, and end with more positive.

A retrospective discussion is action-oriented and doesn't focus on justifications. When you hear the word *because*, that's a good indication that the discussion has turned to justifying why someone did something a certain way. Keep moving forward by saying something like "This is what I experienced, and this is what might work better going forward." Don't say "I did it this way because . . ."

The Derby and Larsen process

Esther Derby and Diana Larsen wrote an excellent book called *Agile Team Retrospectives: Making Good Teams Great* (published by Pragmatic Bookshelf). Check it out for more tips and techniques on sprint retrospectives and other agile practices.

In *Agile Team Retrospectives*, Derby and Larsen point out that there is more to finding out what went well and what improvements need to be made than simply asking the same three questions at the end of every sprint. Retrospective facilitation takes preparation and strategy to get maximum participation, candor, and useful data from team members. The Derby and Larsen model for structuring a retrospective consists of answering these questions:

» What do you think went well?

» What would you like to change?

» How should we implement that change?

To maximize retrospective effectiveness, we recommend the Derby and Larsen process:

1. Set the stage.

You want to establish ground rules for productive communication and clarify expectations and purpose from the beginning. Prepare the team for open and honest discussion.

2. Gather data.

Making decisions based on superficial, bad, or incomplete data can do more harm than good. You want to uncover important topics, jog memories, and correlate experiences that need to be addressed. You want to know not only what people think, but also how they feel about it.

3. Generate insights.

Many teams gather data but do nothing with it. Just as the best designs come from self-organizing teams, the best insights come from teams that take time to explore what the data means.

4. Decide what to do.

Only through action can change and adaptation take place. Action requires a plan. Deciding what to do shifts the team's focus to moving forward — to the next sprint.

5. Close the retrospective.

Closing provides the opportunity to scrum the retrospective through activities that evaluate the effectiveness of the retrospective experience and identify ways to improve it. It also encourages expressing appreciation.

TIP

Each aspect of the retrospective can be facilitated by a number of activities that are engaging and provoke individual thought and group discussion. Try doing an Internet search for *Triple Nickels, Five Whys, SMART Goals, Temperature Reading, Team Radar, and Mad Sad Glad,* which are all good activities to use during a retrospective.

TIP

To stimulate discussion in retrospectives, organize activities around specific questions such as the following:

- » What is keeping us from increasing our velocity from 36 to 38?
- » Does everyone have the tools needed to do the job?
- » Do any impediments keep repeating?
- » Is our daily scrum effective in identifying impediments and coordinating daily priorities?
- » Is our team lacking certain skills, and if so, how can we gain them?

Some scrum teams need to be coaxed and prodded to get engaged. They may be hesitant at first to say what they truly feel. Others may want to talk at once and are bursting with ideas and input. A perceptive, proactive scrum master adapts to work with either type of group, or anything in between, to achieve the best results.

TIP

Find only one action to take each sprint. At the beginning, it may be tempting to address all issues the team discusses. Instead, find an action that is both high-impact and easy to implement. Pick the low-hanging fruit.

TIP

The results from the retrospective should be put into the product backlog as improvement items. The scrum team should agree that at least one improvement action goes into every sprint. Bring at least one priority retrospective item into the next sprint, perhaps from the latest retrospective. After all, why wait? The purpose is to inspect and adapt, so don't delay the adaptation part!

Inspection and adaptation

Scrum is about planning the right things at the right time. It's about responding to changing markets and lessons learned. It's about continually learning and assessing, minimizing risk, and maximizing value at every step — each point of work.

The inspecting and adapting perspective provided in the official Scrum Guide (http://scrumguides.org) is a good way to wrap up this chapter. We've added the italics for emphasis:

> Inspections are most beneficial when diligently performed by skilled inspectors *at the point of work.*

The scrum guide goes on to state that adjustments are made as soon as possible. Adjustments occur as soon as an inspector realizes that the work has moved outside the limits and will cause an unacceptable product.

Chapter 7

Inspect and Adapt: How to Correct Your Course

Often during product development, you find your product in a different place from what you expected. In this chapter, we explore how scrum facilitates continuous learning and improvement. We also look at how you can work in the presence of uncertainty instead of hoping that you can plan it away. After all, being agile is being able to learn and adjust as you go — being flexible enough to build the best product with the right features and with the best quality.

Need for Certainty

Management's need for certainty of outcomes may well drive the downward spiral or decay of many projects and great ideas. They could refuse to accept the basic reality of uncertainty, settling for the relative safety of the known at the expense of the better. The power of the empirical approach is being okay with uncertainty until you've learned the information you need to have more certainty about the outcome of your project or goal. For example, six months from now, it will be difficult to know for certain if a needed component being built by another team will be finished on time if the other team won't begin development for three months from now. But two weeks before its expected delivery you can have a much clearer expectation of its readiness.

REMEMBER

Empirical means to learn or verify by means of observation. So, scrum is considered an empirical approach because each step of the way, you inspect your results and adapt immediately to a better outcome.

Figure 7-1 depicts the forecasting tool known as the Cone of Uncertainty. The basic principle is that outcomes are hard to predict across a span of time, but as you arrive closer to your goal, certainty increases.

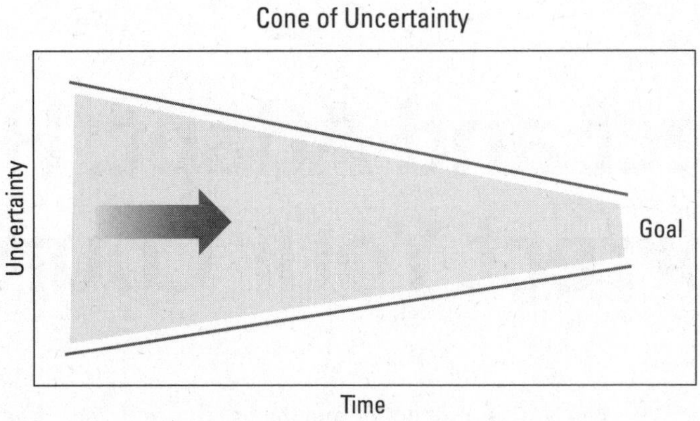

Cone of Uncertainty

FIGURE 7-1:
Cone of
Uncertainty.

[Diagram: A rectangular chart titled "Cone of Uncertainty" with vertical axis labeled "Uncertainty" and horizontal axis labeled "Time." A cone-shaped shaded region narrows from left to right, with an arrow pointing right, ending at a point labeled "Goal."]

Weather forecasters use the Cone of Uncertainty to depict the path of hurricanes over the course of several days. The empirical approach embraces the reality of some uncertainty and provides a framework for managing the associated risks by continually improving and adapting.

The Feedback Loop

In economics, a *feedback loop* is defined as the outcome or results of one process or one cycle used to inform the next. This feedback loop is what feeds the data to the empirical inspection process. Figure 7-2 looks at the feedback process of scrum teams.

TIMING OF DECISIONS

TECHNICAL STUFF

We don't necessarily advocate making all decisions at the last possible moment. A Lean development concept states that because developers are always learning, they should wait until the last possible moment to make decisions. Others argue that there's little value to be gained by waiting. One simple heuristic idea is to put decisions into three buckets:

- Things that are *known*
- Things that are *knowable*
- Things that are *unknowable*

Choosing to delay decisions for the known may bring no value. Likewise, if a decision can't be moved from unknowable to knowable, a delay won't add value. Delaying is appropriate when a thing is knowable. Waiting until more is known about that thing is likely to result in a better decision.

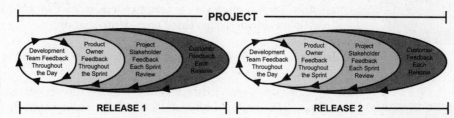

FIGURE 7-2: Feedback process.

The idea behind a feedback loop is that you can continually improve from the information learned from experience if you have a way to apply the lessons learned to future situations. An inherent part of the scrum process is recognizing that the knowledge and experience gained during each sprint need to be reintroduced in later sprints to inform the evolving plan. At the outset of a project, product road-map and sprint plans are always made with the best information available at the time. The plans are accepted by the whole team and socialized throughout stake-holders. Rigid adherence to an exhaustive initial plan can ignore lessons learned during the process and stifle innovations from within the team. Instead, scrum uses customer and team feedback to improve the plan.

You may wonder why you should plan at all if you know that an initial plan is likely to be flawed. You establish a plan as the first step in your learning process. Much as a flight crew files a flight plan based on the expected conditions so that crew members and air traffic controllers know what to expect, product roadmaps lay out the scrum team's preflight expectations. After a flight crew takes off, the members evaluate actual conditions such as weather, winds, and scheduling to adjust the flight plan as needed. Likewise, in scrum, you provide feedback throughout every day, and as you learn more information, you adapt your ideas and plan.

TIP

Feedback loops can be positive (resulting from successes) or negative (resulting from failures). Success can breed success, but failure can inform success if you learn from it. This concept is why we ask both what worked well and what can be improved during each sprint retrospective. It's important to continue to support scrum successes and look for changes that can have a positive effect.

Transparency

Transparency is pervasive in modern society. In everything from open-source software to open collaboration on ideas, transparency is a broadly interpreted term. In Chapter 1, we define why transparency is a basic pillar of improvement. It's important not to miss the critical value of transparency within the inspect-and-adapt process. Without a transparent culture, decisions are made with inaccurate data. Far too often we see organizations value fake good news over truth and end up making decisions based on bad information.

Following are some basic principles of employing transparency in your projects:

>> Just the facts. Display what is fully true to stakeholders specifically by only showing as complete work that is fully done according to your definition of done.

>> Be open and clear about the plan, design, process, and progress.

>> Make all information easily accessible to everyone.

>> Post the roadmap, the release plan, and the definition of done on the wall where everyone involved can see them.

>> Encourage an environment of factual measurements and outcomes.

>> Have potentially awkward conversations early.

TIP

It's common to want to avoid having honest and awkward conversations, but avoiding uncomfortable situations can cause problems. (In fact, whole books and courses have been written to teach people how to deal these situations.) We want you to understand the importance of knowing the hard costs associated with avoiding or delaying awkward moments. The most direct of these costs is time wasted going in the wrong direction and delaying a better course of action. Don't put off having those uncomfortable conversations; have them as soon as you realize that something needs to be addressed.

BEWARE OF OBFUSCATION

Some of the organizations we've trained and coached had a work culture that prevented team transparency. Watch out for antipatterns that force teams to hide reality as a means of self-protection. Additionally, be aware that some outside or contracting organizations have made an art of avoiding factual reporting. As leader, you need to value and trust the specific knowledge of your scrum teams. Enable team success rather than second-guess its progress.

As the chief executive officer of a boutique software development company, David learned this lesson the hard way. While believing in the concepts of autonomous teams, he had a hard time trusting the team's progress when the stakeholders asked for assurances of success. Because the only answer David wanted to hear when he asked the team about product quality or project timing was "Yes, we will be on time," the scrum team wasn't able to ask him for help or clarity because they feared his wrath. The answers, in truth, were available via the scrum artifacts, but David was too busy to look. After realizing that he wasn't creating an environment that enabled the success of the team, he changed. He learned to follow the scrum boards instead of asking for a status report, which enabled him to see the truth and join the team in being successful instead of withdrawing from any potential failure. Then he was able to facilitate awkward conversations with stakeholders as early as possible. His change of approach to ownership was a huge win for his teams. Over time, the teams began to trust him to enable their success again. As a result, team quality and timeliness made a major leap forward. David initially exhibited several familiar antipatterns which hinder the inspect and adapt process.

Antipatterns

The term *antipattern* has been used to describe a well-intentioned solution to a problem that instead causes unintended negative consequences. It's important for an organization that's adopting or maturing its scrum practice to allow scrum to expose antipatterns as part of the inspect–and–adapt process. It's also important not to customize scrum to match a flawed culture or practices. Instead, make changes in the culture to facilitate the success of your scrum practice.

You may be familiar with some of the following antipattern examples that occur in management and software development:

>> **Analysis paralysis:** Being unable to move forward due to continual analysis and unwillingness to accept uncertainty

>> **Smoke and mirrors:** Creating the illusion of further accomplishment, such as overstating quality or completeness

>> **Seagull management:** Swooping in as a leader and making a bunch of noise and then flying away, hoping to have motivated everyone with a sense of urgency but instead causing fear and panic

Scrum teams and agile leaders need to look for the root causes and cultural antipatterns that block the feedback loop. Once the antipatterns are identified, they should be escalated to leadership as an impediment to the scrum process. Removing these cultural impediments needs to be a priority because they may hinder multiple scrum teams within the organization.

External Forces

A team can be affected by things outside the team that affect the team's ability to deliver the product. These forces act like a headwind or crosswind that forces an aircraft off course or behind schedule.

For scrum teams, these forces may be changing regulations, evolving architecture, or reprioritized features. A team may be powerless to change these realities, but scrum exposes the effects of the forces and often exposes alternative courses of action.

One common excuse for saying that scrum can't work in an environment is that external forces make it impossible for scrum to be successful. But scrum can succeed anywhere as long as there are sufficient buy-in and effort from the people involved to make it work. In later chapters, we give you some examples of successful scrum organizations that likely have more constraints than your organization does.

In-Flight Course Correction

In this section, we go back to the analogy of the flight crew and the flight plan to explain the dynamics at play in planning and replanning based on empirical data. A flight crew always plans the details of an upcoming mission based on parameters assigned for that mission. The crew estimates fuel use, time in flight, and execution details based on all known and expected details. On the day of the mission, the crew members gather any updated weather reports and mission changes.

When the aircraft is airborne, members of the flight crew continuously evaluate speeds and headings and compare the plane's actual position with the flight plans. Figure 7-3 shows a planned route and a measured location in flight.

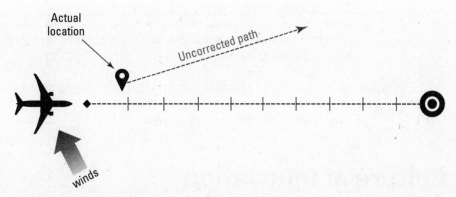

FIGURE 7-3:
Flight path.

Each time crew members measure the location in flight, they evaluate why they're moving away from the plan. They look at the data to determine possible causes for the course adjustment, such as unexpected wind directions or velocities, or a difference between the planned heading and speed and the actual heading and speed. Next, they use the new information to adjust the plan to achieve the mission objectives — all this while going faster than 400 miles per hour. The flight crew repeats this inspect-and-adapt process over and over to ensure a mission's success.

In scrum, sprints serve as perfect times to reevaluate and improve plans. In a transparent organization, new information is welcomed and applied to achieving product success.

WARNING

It is important to avoid the costly overhead of redundant or bureaucratic parallel processes. We've worked with well-intentioned organizations that expend more effort in measuring status and producing status slides than they do in building products, all in the hope of maintaining control or avoiding uncertainty. Creating status reports is an unnecessary parallel activity. An organization that has transformed to being agile and that has fully adopted scrum lets go of these artifacts and embraces the new way.

Testing in the Feedback Loop

In scrum, you test during every sprint, doing things such as code tests, functional tests, and tests for user feedback. Contrast that type of project with a typical waterfall project, in which testing happens only at the end of a project. Finding errors at the last minute causes either heroic and expensive fixes or pushing out the timeline. Like an aircraft whose path goes uncorrected, a product that is not validated ends up way off course.

The feedback received during testing and customer validation as the sprint progresses necessarily informs the daily priority. Corrections in the product are usually made the same day, while they're easiest and least expensive to fix and don't hold up further progress.

REMEMBER

On a scrum team, everyone is responsible for everything. It isn't up to one specialized tester to test everything for everyone else. The entire team owns the outcome, and all members care about quality.

Culture of Innovation

Many companies, from the newest to the oldest, say that they want to be innovative. They likely see the market advantages of creative approaches. Yet the command-and-control structures that they use to manage products and processes impede the innovations they seek. Organizations' fundamental beliefs about purpose determines whether their teams work in a culture of innovation.

The scrum framework functions best in a culture of self-organization, purpose, and innovation. Product and process innovations are encouraged via the inspect-and-adapt model, and the idea of innovation is at the heart of working as a team. Using the feedback loop is a great way to encourage innovation.

Following are some ways that you can create an innovative culture:

>> Empower teams to challenge conventions or constraints.

>> Remove organizational barriers to creativity.

>> Rethink how you motivate.

>> Seek out creative lateral-thinking people.

TECHNICAL STUFF

Psychologist and philosopher Edward de Bono is credited with coining the term *lateral thinking,* which he defined as a mindset of challenging conventions and constraints. A lateral thinker can overcome his previous beliefs about limitations and conventions. A person who engages in lateral thinking doesn't ignore the existence of constraints; instead, he searches for ideas and solutions that aren't immediately obvious.

MOTIVATING CREATIVITY

In his TED talk (www.ted.com/talks/dan_pink_on_motivation#t-1094472), business author Dan Pink challenged previous ideas about how to motivate creativity. Using recent social-sciences research, he laid out a case that challenges the effectiveness of carrot-and-stick or extrinsic reward-based motivators. Intrinsic motivators such as autonomy, mastery, and purpose are more effective for encouraging team members to engage in lateral-thinking tasks.

A popular modern narrative seems to be that engineers and developers are robotic, logic-based or linear thinkers. In our experience, that isn't the case for most highly effective knowledge workers. They're creators with well-honed cognitive skills who can't be replaced by the complex algorithms that they create, and they thrive in a culture of innovation. As we trend toward replacing business functions with automation, we need to make space for lateral thinkers who can go beyond perceived constraints. Without creativity, we get stuck making the same mistakes.

3 Scrum for Industry

Chapter **8**

Software Development

You don't actually do a project; you can only do action steps related to it. When enough of the right action steps have been taken, some situation will have been created that matches your initial picture of the outcome closely enough that you can call it "done."

— DAVID ALLEN

Software development is the context within which scrum's creators formalized agile values and principles and within which the scrum framework was born. Therefore, it's no surprise that scrum is easily applied to this industry.

As technology advances, so do its complexities. New challenges arise, and project management frameworks that endure will be those that allow for and enhance change.

In this chapter, we show you some of the challenges that the software industry faces and describe how scrum helps address them. You see scrum applied in contemporary examples and understand how the framework allows you to be as nimble and fast as this exponentially growing world of technology.

Scrum and Software Development: A Natural Fit

Software development is creative in nature. The sky isn't even the limit, as ideas, concepts, and reality go way beyond that now. Necessarily, the design solutions employed often are as creative as the products they serve.

Given its empirical nature, scrum fits this environment perfectly. Scrum doesn't tell you how to do anything. It simply lets you see clearly (that is, exposes) what you're doing and assess from there.

A huge variety of languages, tools, methods, and platforms exist to solve these complex problems. Scrum doesn't tell you which ones to use. Rather, this framework lets teams self-manage to decide which ways are best for their circumstances. Scrum does this through unfettered transparency, frequent inspection, and immediate adaptation.

The very nature of scrum allows you to find solutions every day, in every sprint, and with every release. Both the product and the process are nurtured for creativity and excellence.

Traditional project management methods and frameworks are predicated on being able to accurately predict the future. They're linear and sequential. They act as a waterfall. (You can read about waterfall approaches in *Agile Project Management For Dummies*, Second Edition by Mark C. Layton and Steven J. Ostermiller [published by John Wiley & Sons, Inc.].) What's important to understand is that technology and design needs have far outgrown this change-averse framework.

Waterfall project management entails progressively maturing a set package of requirements in different stages; completing one stage before moving on to the next, such as designing all requirements for the entire project before doing any development and completing all development work before doing comprehensive testing, which is left to the end. With scrum, these phases are cycled repeatedly throughout a project so that a continuous circle of design, development, testing, integration, and feedback is achieved each day, sprint, and release.

As projects became more complex, the natural boundaries of waterfall became abundantly clear. Multiple phases and long delays existed before coding even began. Early performance was no indicator of later performance because each phase's tasks were fundamentally different; code testing was loaded toward the end of the project, when the team had the least amount of time or money; and customers didn't interact with the product until it was too late to incorporate their feedback. Projects were delayed or never completed, and often they came up short.

WINSTON ROYCE HAD IT RIGHT

In a strange quirk of history, the man mistakenly attributed with introducing the waterfall framework to large software projects emphasized the basic agile and scrum principles: inspect and adapt.

Winston Royce was a computer scientist and a director of the Lockheed Software Technology Center. He published a paper titled "Managing the Development of Large Software Systems," in which he described several methodologies, including waterfall and an early iteration of agile, as shown in this figure.

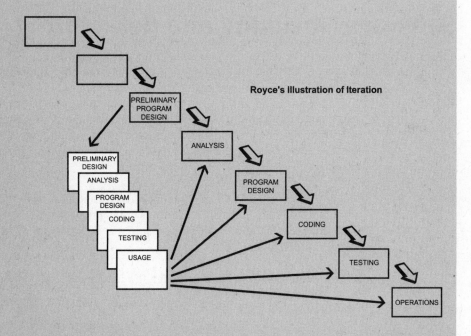

Royce clearly warned about the pitfalls later to be endured with waterfall. It's strange that the very system he's mistakenly credited with inventing is the same system he warned about. He wrote:

"The testing phase which occurs at the end of the development cycle is the first event for which timing, storage, input/output transfers, etc., are experienced as distinguished from analyzed . . .. Yet if these phenomena fail to satisfy the various external constraints, then invariably a major redesign is required. A simple octal patch or redo of some isolated code will not fix these kinds of difficulties. The required design changes are likely to be so disruptive that the software requirements upon which the design is based and which provides the rationale for everything are violated."

(continued)

(continued)

Royce said that leaving testing as a separate phase at the end was "risky and invited failure." He suggested an iterative approach that tested frequently and made adaptations based on the results. Every step linked back to the previous one.

Scrum emerged from the need to find better ways to build software. Keep in mind, however, that the scrum framework can be applied to any project in which you can encapsulate the work and prioritize an item against other items.

Software Flexibility and Refactoring

Scrum works well with software for a variety of reasons. In this section, we look at a few.

As we state in Chapter 4, the cost of fixing defects increases exponentially the later those defects are found. Catching defects early and fixing them is a hassle, but it's doable. When you catch defects later, the accumulated technical debt can be costly.

Building in quality every step of the way to reduce and eliminate defects is a scrum advantage. We state in the sprint sections of Chapter 5 that testing every requirement and its integration with other requirements is integral to the process. Yet mistakes still happen.

Software can be very flexible. Although it's not free to have a developer refactor code, the physical effect is virtual, so in many cases, the work can be done with relative ease.

REMEMBER

Refactoring code is the process of changing the existing code without changing its outward behavior to improve nonfunctional aspects of the system.

Refactoring is inevitable in scrum (in a good way), and you'll do more of it than ever before because you're responding to and embracing change. Fortunately, scrum's empirical approach disciplines teams to continuously inspect and adapt to improve the health and quality of their product. Identifying needs for technical improvements and prioritizing them against new development are part of this ongoing maintenance.

Refactoring code is like maintaining your car. You hear the rattle, see the little red light, or smell something electrical. You know that if you don't do something, those problems are going to get bigger. You can pretend that you have a choice, but you really don't. As in refactoring code, you take the little steps necessary to make sure that your vehicle is running smoothly. Maybe the car simply needs more oil or a bolt tightened. But if you wait, your engine could seize or a part could break, leading to much higher expense and more time wasted.

Refactoring enables you to make a working module that's scalable, extensible, and stable. In today's world, in which the one who's first wins, this type of efficiency in quality control is priceless. Refactor early and often.

Release often and on demand

Deploying new products to the market no longer requires packaging and shipping. Thanks to the Internet, the cloud, automated testing, and continuous integration, you have the flexibility to plan your releases on demand and as often as needed to suit other factors, such as market readiness, customer expectations, and marketing campaigns.

You now have a much higher degree of flexibility in the product that you create and the timing by which you release it to your customer. Money previously allocated to hard-copy product is now diverted to more pressing and profiting needs. The Download Here button makes life easier in many ways. In many cases, such as Software as a Service (SaaS, covered later in this chapter), updates are pushed out automatically, eliminating the downloading step.

With scrum's emphasis on producing shippable product after every sprint, or even within sprints, you have even more flexibility in planning product releases. You don't have to wait until the end of a project to release. You can release incrementally in stages and continuously, with tested, integrated, and approved functionality.

TECHNICAL STUFF

Behemoth tech companies such as Facebook, Amazon, and Google deploy code to production multiple times a day — in the case of Amazon, 3,000 times a day. That's fast!

Customize your release sizes

No matter how often you release, smaller is generally better. As with the flexibility of releasing often and on demand, the size of the product that you release is incredibly flexible with scrum, based on functionality, target dates, and market conditions. Scrum works with everything from one tiny requirement that rounds out a larger, previously released requirement to a huge new generation that's about to be birthed.

Whether you're releasing a single line of code or a full bundle of functionality, the product has been through a thorough process. Quality is the essence of flexibility — and the essence of scrum. Making the cost of change and improvement too high limits quality.

Inspect and adapt as you release

With the ability to customize both the timing and size of your releases, you're able to receive immediate customer feedback. Each time you release product, you're able to assess the results and make any necessary changes. Both analytics and customer service can collect data quickly, and from this input, you can fine-tune future development and enhancements.

With scrum, you inspect and adapt daily, after each sprint, and after every release. These events can happen as often as you like to suit your project. In fact, the more often you release, the more often you can inspect and adapt.

You can even tailor the quantity and focus of feedback. Smaller releases may have more targeted feedback. Larger releases may receive broader evaluation, and from this evaluation, you can set smaller targeted future releases.

REMEMBER

The sprint retrospective (see Chapters 6 and 7) idea of inspecting and adapting your process is important in releases too. You adapt your process at every iteration rather than only once in one sweltering meeting at the end of the project when everyone's relieved that it's over and ready to start on different projects.

Customers have a lot to choose among, because new products hit the market every day. To survive and excel, you must be at least as nimble as, and certainly faster than, the next guy. Scrum provides the framework for just this purpose.

Embracing Change

Although scrum's effectiveness and speed make it a natural fit in many situations, it's different for hierarchically structured organizations. This fact alone can cause problems. Incorporating new ideas and breaking away from old habits can be challenging. Some corporate cultures are open to change; others have more difficulty. It's human nature to find comfort in habits, and it takes effort and energy to break those habits.

To get people in the organization to embrace the change, you must reveal the value of the change to them. When the parties involved clearly understand what's in it for them, they accept the changes more readily. As the parties begin to experience the benefits of early release and adaptation, the conversion will go more quickly.

To help you ease your organization's transition to the scrum model, in the following sections we look at some specific issues.

Development team challenges

In traditional, top-down management cultures, implementing scrum while maintaining status quo won't work. The development team can be frustrated with double work if it isn't solely implementing scrum. Managers can get off kilter moving forward on projects that aren't planned up front and that don't provide the reams of reports and analysis that they're used to.

With scrum, organizations can ease into inspection and adaptation one sprint at a time. It may be difficult to get managers to participate appropriately (as stakeholders) in the first sprint reviews. Equally challenging is getting people to see working software as the new benchmark of success (see the sidebar "Spotify versus Healthcare.gov" later in this chapter).

Scrum is a new way of working for the team and for all its stakeholders and influencers. If the organization perseveres and gives the benefits of scrum time to manifest, however, it sees immediate, practical, quality results. The organization discovers that it has something real to work with after each sprint and that progress accumulates at a logical and rapid pace. Time spent writing reports and managing status has been replaced by time creating real, usable products. Status is clear because it's real.

Business alignment with technology

Traditionally, the business side of an organization and software engineering are separate, and many times, they're at odds. For decades, these groups have operated as silos within the same organization:

>> The business serves the market and the shareholders and is under extreme pressure to deliver value quickly and adapt to a constantly changing marketplace.

>> The technologists want sustainable architecture and foundations with as little technical debt accumulation as possible.

REAL-WORLD CHANGE

Not long ago, we provided scrum training for one of our software clients. The client was working on a research and development project involving new technology and was given a deadline by senior management to complete a comprehensive range of features.

The team initially came up with proof of concept of features and requirements fairly quickly, which won buy-in from management to proceed with the full-scale project. The product backlog was vague, however, and the team spent unbudgeted months developing a demo version for management.

The development process was slow and fraught with technical surprises. The team missed not only the first release date, but also the next several rescheduled release dates. At this point, we trained the team and implemented the scrum framework.

At first, the entire project team held on to traditional practices (up-front design, fixed scope and schedules, and renaming waterfall artifacts and events as scrum). But it pushed ahead; held consistent sprint reviews with stakeholders; and survived a series of tough, uncomfortable conversations about missed deadlines and how the aspects of scrum could help resolve these challenges.

After a few sprint reviews, the clarification of roles (especially getting a dedicated and fully trained product owner), and removal of some impediments, the transparency so inherent in scrum began to shine through. Walls were broken down between the scrum team, stakeholders, and customers (actual users were involved in every sprint review); communication improved; and the project was replanned with a proper vision, roadmap, and product backlog. A release schedule was re-created based on the team's new velocity and product backlog estimates. Long story short, from that point on it took months, not years, to release the minimum viable product (MVP). The new project plan was based on priority, customer feedback, and empirical data (such as velocity).

During initial sprint reviews, the team identified a key stakeholder (a customer who would be using the product) who hadn't been attending the sprint reviews. She was invited, and her involvement provided crucial feedback on the product. As the other stakeholders observed the scrum team's willingness and speed in inspecting and adapting, trust skyrocketed, ownership and collaboration (including stakeholders) improved amazingly.

In the end, the product reflected much more accurately what the customer wanted; extra features were prioritized and left out (something that a stakeholder and the product owner decided, not the development team); an MVP was released in full working order; and the stakeholders were fully engaged and involved with training users on the software. In fact, stakeholders ended up collaborating with the product owner on every aspect of the rollout.

Scrum brings these two sides together. A representative from the business (product owner), a full-fledged member of a scrum team (a peer of the other team members), and stakeholders are involved throughout the sprint and directly provide feedback at the end of every iteration of work (sprint review). You'll never find a more beautiful alignment and facilitation of collaboration and joint ownership. Thanks to scrum, the right people are making the right decisions about the right things at the right times. Finger-pointing is no longer relevant. Progress is exposed at all times to all parties. Inspection and adaptation points exist along the way. Self-organization and self-management mean that everyone is in it together.

Up-front engineering

The propensity of development managers, project managers, and developers to plan everything has deep roots:

>> Most schools still teach up-front engineering (see "The Marshmallow Challenge" in Chapter 1). Fresh out of class, engineers plan first and develop second.

>> Waterfall enforces the "plan all and then develop all" mindset. This process is built around completing one phase, such as designing, before moving to the next, such as developing. In waterfall, up-front engineering is part of the foundation on which everything else rests.

Given this background, you'll find that there's a stigma in changing something after a project starts. But in our mindset, and within the framework of scrum, change is ideal. All changes are learning. You incorporate change every day, after every sprint, and in each release. You find out how to seek out change. In scrum, change is progress.

Also, when management and developers have invested time and energy in planning something, it's hard to drop those plans and potentially suffer sunk costs.

TECHNICAL STUFF

Sunk costs are funds that have been spent on a project and can't be recovered. In waterfall, sunk costs were more common, as projects were planned and funded up front. If they failed along the way, companies had nothing to show for their efforts. With scrum, you have the option of failing fast or incrementally accumulating fully built functionality. Instead of sinking a lot of money into projects up front, you can allocate funds along the way. If the project ends earlier than intended, you lose less money in the form of sunk costs or make a great business decision that maximizes the return of your limited investment. With scrum, your days of catastrophic failure are gone.

If 64 percent of software features are never or rarely used, think of the wasted time, energy, and resources involved in planning, designing, developing, testing, and documenting those features. With scrum, the dominant paradigm of planning everything in advance is dispelled.

We've seen development teams using waterfall spend weeks and months on planning. We've seen scrum teams plan features and systems of the same magnitude in hours.

Because scrum teams understand that they don't know everything up front, they don't plan what they don't know. They assess and adapt along the way as new information is garnered and priorities are reassessed. Because transparency is continuous, management is less likely to overreact.

Emergent architecture

Emergent architecture is the progressive elaboration of the architecture of your application or enterprise based on requirements currently in development to achieve and maintain stability and scalability. The goal is to refactor the architecture based on the reality of working software rather than to develop the entire system based on guesses.

Many programmers see emergent architecture as a sign of failure. They want the entire product to be planned up front, leaving no code (or stone) unturned. But this approach isn't realistic or practical.

You begin with macro-level architecture decisions based on the holistic view of the requirements that you have from the product roadmap. Then, in your first sprint, ask what the requirements and architecture are for this sprint. Let the sprint goal drive the sprint, and if that goal requires code refactoring, don't wait. Your product should work in every sprint. With scrum, you refactor more often, but that's what you want. Requirement change isn't the enemy, and neither is code refactoring.

The beginning of the project is when you know the least. At that point, you shouldn't do detailed planning or build parts of the system that won't be used. You can aptly apply a Lean principle to this scenario: Decide at the last responsible moment. The earlier you make a decision in the project, the higher the risk that the decision will be wrong and the greater likelihood of doing throwaway work. The later you decide, the more information you have to make that decision and the lower your risk of making a mistake.

REMEMBER Refactoring should be built into every requirement estimation. As new requirements come to the top of the list and get refined, architecture emerges in the minds of the development team. As team members estimate and plan, they plan for refactoring.

TIP If your sprints are one week long, you'll be refactoring small batches of architecture. If you wait until the end of the project, as in traditional frameworks, you're refactoring for months or years of architecture. Refactor often. Refactor early.

Scrum Applications in Software

Many technology companies are already using scrum to great success. It allows them to be faster and more flexible to stay competitive.

It's one thing to understand the theory of scrum's success; it's quite another to see scrum in action. Although we can't take you into the field with us, we can bring the field to you in the following sections. In this section, we show you some of the challenges that companies face and describe how scrum's unique adapt-ability comes into play.

Video-game development

This hugely popular, complex area of software development can use scrum with great success for four reasons:

>> **Flexibility:** With scrum, you start with basic features and grow the game into more complexity. This evolution happens organically; therefore, you're always developing what's most important next.

>> **Finding the fun:** Developers can add fun in small, iterative doses. The features that add the most value in terms of fun (a critical element of any game) get added first.

>> **Cost savings:** Most games fail to break even financially. Scrum's cost-saving nature is a company-saver. Even if funding is cut halfway through the project (assuming that minimum play time is met), you still have the most important 50 percent of the features fully functioning and, if not yet marketable, at least reusable.

>> **Regular feedback:** This feedback may come daily, from the product owner, and at each sprint review, from the stakeholders (such as the publisher and marketing).

Gaming is about keeping customers happy and engaged. Feedback within scrum is incorporated quickly, so the result is what users want.

Development stages

For games, technical development generally follows the three stages, shown in Figure 8-1.

>> **Preproduction:** This stage is where artists, directors, and engineers come together to find the fun. The point of this prototyping and proof-of-concept phase is to determine whether the game is a good, fun idea before the company enters production and spends more money.

Especially for mobile games, engineers can prototype without art quickly. For all games during this stage, teams can validate the idea of the game, define it, develop concept art, ensure funding, and assemble a development team.

>> **Production:** The proof of concept is developed by directors, artists, and engineers.

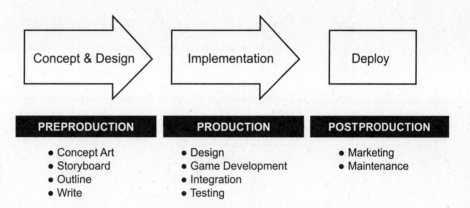

FIGURE 8-1:
The historic flow
of video-game
development.

PREPRODUCTION	PRODUCTION	POSTPRODUCTION
• Concept Art • Storyboard • Outline • Write	• Design • Game Development • Integration • Testing	• Marketing • Maintenance

>> **Postproduction:** Professional testers test the finished product; beta testing follows; and sales, marketing, and support activities begin.

As this process implies, publishers typically engage with studios under traditional waterfall contracts and structures, paying the studio only at certain long-term milestones. This arrangement often implies that the publisher goes long periods without seeing progress.

In a scrum model, game development looks more like Figure 8-2, which shows the ongoing testing necessary for quality assurance. After each task — such as concept art, storyboarding, writing, or prototyping — the task is tested and either moved on or further developed.

With scrum, publishers can identify and kill the nonfun stuff faster and have greater control of quality because they participate regularly in sprint reviews and pay studios incrementally, in line with the delivery of working game increments.

Short sprints maintain a flow of outbound content that attracts and retains consumers. Scrum provides faster delivery of playable games to such stakeholders as publishers and focus groups. This process allows developers to emphasize the fun factor and quickly eliminate the game-play elements that aren't entertaining (which can also save wasted art-creation costs).

WARNING

The definition of *done* may differ between preproduction and production. Be sure to clarify both stages up front. A preproduction sprint's definition of *done* may include different types and levels of documentation and artwork standards from a production sprint's definition.

TIP

Ideally, games can't ship with fewer than ten hours of play time for a single-player game. Although this amount of play time may be the release goal, after every sprint, publishers can review the working software and provide invaluable feedback.

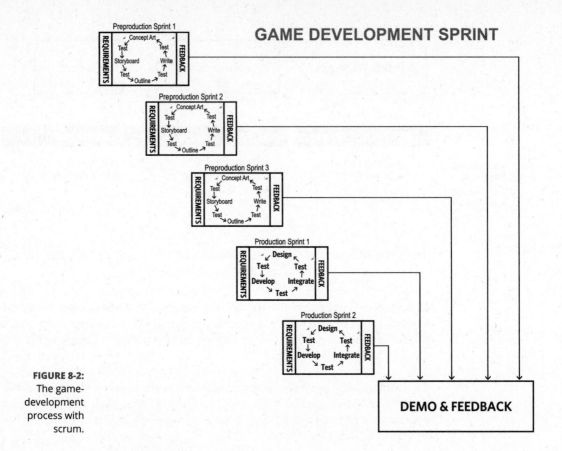

GAME DEVELOPMENT SPRINT

FIGURE 8-2:
The game-development process with scrum.

Marketing

Games have traditionally been sold as retail products, but online and digital distribution are shifting the emphasis from retail to digital delivery. A huge need exists to constantly and quickly update, add, and push content to a game. This capability is the difference between surviving and not surviving. Speed to market is critical.

Game sales are overwhelmingly seasonal, with more than 50 percent of the industry's revenue coming during the Christmas season. This fact is a major factor in the crunch time that many teams face, because the holiday season imposes a hard deadline.

Scrum's priority-driven product backlog ensures that the highest-priority fun will be delivered in minimal crunch time, which not only makes management happy, but also reduces employee burnout.

Art

Art is a significant portion of the development work required in video games. Console and computer games require a lot of art and animation assets, adding up to 40 percent or more of the cost of a game title. Technical and game-play issues late in production are costly.

Art, being the costliest element, is tempting to outsource overseas. But trouble with time zones and communications almost always leads to delays, rework, and customer dissatisfaction with the quality of the finished product.

Scrum allows artists and developers to work on the same team rather than in silos, with the same goals and real-time communication about what works and what doesn't. To optimize collaboration, teams should be onshore and in-house (co-located). Onshore and co-located teams keep delay and rework costs down.

Timeboxed delivery (sprints) of art assets keeps everyone on schedule with deadlines set as a team and a steady flow of deliverables to market, keeping waste to a minimum.

Many large game titles require large development teams, with 15 or more developers, 10 or more artists, and 30 or more members of quality assurance. For a thorough discussion of how scrum scales across larger projects, see Chapter 13.

Services

"As-a-Service" development companies use scrum to get their products out the door quickly and effectively by leveraging the power of the Internet.

SaaS

Software as a Service (SaaS) is a model of distributing software applications that are hosted by a service provider and made available to users over the Internet. No installation on personal computers or devices is needed. Customers usually pay a monthly fee or subscription.

Even mobile apps, which require a download, have quick downloads that can be done on the go, over Wi-Fi, or over a mobile network while roaming. Installation discs, manually entered license keys, and hours of installation steps with your device plugged in are things of the past. The cloud enables scrum teams to inspect and adapt to real live data and redeploy quickly to address feedback.

IaaS

Infrastructure as a Service (IaaS) is a cloud-computing model of providing organizations the outsourced equipment necessary to support IT operations, including hardware, servers, storage, and other networking components. IaaS providers own the equipment and are responsible for sourcing, running, and maintaining it. Clients typically pay per use, based on volume of data or size of equipment. These same products enable other companies to manage their IT departments and operate their infrastructure in a more scrumlike way.

Installing a new database server, for example, used to take weeks or months. The in-house engineer had to procure the equipment and then build, configure, and install it before the database engineers could get started installing the database and migrating data. IaaS solutions now allow this process to be done virtually and completed in minutes.

PaaS

Platform as a Service (PaaS) is a cloud-computing model that provides computing platform and stack (set of software subsystems) solutions. Clients typically pay license fees and/or per-use fees.

With IaaS and PaaS services such as Amazon, IT organizations can spin up a new server in minutes, and it's immediately ready for data and installation.

Customization projects

Some software comes off the shelf; some is customized to meet individual customer needs. How do you handle customization with scrum? Do you need individual teams for each client?

We worked with a client that provides logistics software, which comes with a fair share of customization to work with unique equipment configurations and third-party/legacy software integrations. Before scrum, the project teams that provided the customization service to clients were so far behind the curve that the lead time to get a new client running was costing the company business.

The solution was to invite the customization project teams (which had not yet adopted scrum) to attend the core product scrum team's sprint reviews as stakeholders. This change allowed these stakeholders to anticipate the product well in advance. They provided feedback based on key customer use that allowed the scrum team to engineer the core product in a way that required less customization for each client, as the team saw ways to use certain features and collaborate with other client representatives.

SPOTIFY VERSUS HEALTHCARE.GOV

To understand the effects of agile and scrum-based frameworks within services computing and SaaS, compare two examples: Spotify and Healthcare.gov.

Whatever your political views of the Affordable Care Act, Healthcare.gov was a massive rollout of cloud computing that had myriad problems requiring extensive fixing. Jeff Sutherland, one of the founders of scrum, called the rollout "waterfall gone bad."

Healthcare.gov was an agile project on the front end, but developers missed the second Agile Principle: working software. The people on the front end did their part, but the lack of load and performance testing on the actual hardware rendered the software useless.

Although the plan had dozens of reputable consultancies working on the project, minimal coordination existed among them. The program was rolled out nationwide, but if it had been tested state by state (true to scrum and agile), many of the issues could have been dealt with early and quickly.

Spotify, the online music source, did things differently and saw remarkable success. It embraced scrum and agile so much that all its scrum masters must be agile coaches.

Spotify's competitors are Google, Amazon, and Apple, so Spotify had to be nimbler, faster, and cheaper to even think of competing. The company has locations and scrum teams around the world, and each team is responsible for a single piece of product. But even this setup wasn't fast enough, so the company developed continuous deployment, deploying product several times during a sprint.

When you compare these two huge cloud-computing services, one done through waterfall and the other through scrum, you see the need for delivering, inspecting, and adapting working software frequently.

Chapter **9**

Tangible Goods Production

Even a mistake may turn out to be the one thing necessary to a worthwhile achievement.

— HENRY FORD

G iven the origins of agile and scrum, it's not a far stretch of the imagination to think that they should be used only for developing software. The fact is that nothing could be further from the truth. The 1986 *Harvard Business Review* article "New New Product Development Game," mentioned in Chapters 1 and 8, was written in response to experiences in the manufacturing industries. The article used as case studies hardware, electronics, and automotive products engineered and built by companies such as Fuji-Xerox in 1978, Canon in 1982, and Honda in 1981.

The development and production of tangible goods works beautifully with scrum, and we show you how in this chapter. Situations and products may vary enormously, but the tools and techniques remain the same. By following the framework procedures we've been writing about, you'll easily see how scrum can fit most any project. All you need is a list of requirements that can be prioritized.

The Fall of Waterfall

As we state in Chapter 8, product development is occurring at accelerating speeds and it's not only the software sector that's seeing fundamental shifts in what's developed and how long it takes. Long-term manual manufacturing activities are changing, too. Development cycles in most industries are shorter and faster due to the time and cost savings accrued through technology. Companies such as Apple, whose products are certainly tangible, release next-generation, cutting-edge products multiple times a year.

Some argue that the scrum framework can't be applied to physical products, saying, "We can't be building the tenth floor when we realize that we need to make a change on the fifth floor!" Sometimes, they're right.

People make objections like that one all the time in software development as well. A change in design may be so costly that it can't be realistically implemented, and other options must be considered, including moving forward with no change. Maybe a different database would be preferred, but it's too costly, so the product owner decides to nix the idea and keep going as is.

Scrum is about exposure of reality and making good decisions based on empirical evidence, not about swapping out requirements at a customer's every whim. Whether the industry is developing software manufacturing planes, trains, or automobiles, the scrum foundation applies: organizing a scrum team with appropriate roles, holding frequent inspection and adaptation points, and forcing decisions to happen at the last responsible moment (that is, planning at different levels of detail for the right things at the right time).

REMEMBER

Because of the feedback loop, the customer has input into some business decisions via the product owner. This way, the development team doesn't have to understand all the market and customer nuances needed to make the business decisions. The product owner filters out the noise from all the stakeholders so that the developers spend their time on only the highest-priority requirements. Product owners and developers work as a team to implement the solutions to problems presented by the product owner. When everyone is working toward the same goals, finger-pointing is reduced, and accountability is shared.

Engaged customers are more satisfied customers who end up getting what they want. With scrum, feedback loops are regular, consistent, and as frequent as possible, so customers get what they want at the cost they're willing to pay for it, which keeps customers involved and development teams on track. Impediments can be identified and resolved early, and accountability is taken on by those who do the work *and* those who make decisions, including customers.

Although the following sections of this chapter serve as a field guide for using scrum in specific industries, the scrum roles that make this framework so effective easily morph into new project types.

Construction

Uses for scrum within the vast world of tangible goods are enormous. The speed-to-market increase and cost savings that can be achieved in software is also possible in other areas. Construction and scrum are an excellent example.

Scrum works with any project, provided that you can list and prioritize the work to be done. Obviously, construction projects have these qualities. They also have challenges specific to the industry. Every segment of an industry does. Instead of saying "Oh, scrum won't work with this because of X and Y and Z," say "These are the challenges we face, so let's look at how scrum will solve them and get us faster and cheaper to market."

In the following sections, we outline specific issues in the construction industry and describe how scrum helps solve them. You see how to deal with traditional problems — those that you've been dealing with for your entire construction career — by using scrum.

The best in bids

Competition in the bidding process for construction projects is fierce, and it shows no signs of trending toward easy. Combine this fact with a steady increase in the cost of construction, and you have a formula for cutting corners and potential for skipping essential steps.

None of this is news to anyone in this industry. Your bid may be pristine, providing everything that the client needs at a reasonable price, but you know that your competitors' bids may undercut you by leaving things out that you know the client needs. Scrum can help both you and the client. After all, in the end, the better the client is served, the better the result, the better for your business, and the more potential for referrals.

Scrum provides the following:

>> **Transparency:** Let customers decide where they want their money to go. They can make changes, inspect, and adapt as the project progresses. But they'll be fully informed each step of the way as they participate in regular

sessions of progress review in the sprint review, provide feedback, and ask questions.

>> **Adaptability:** Scrum allows the team to identify course-correcting issues early. Even when you're building to completion, it's better to resolve problems identified by completing a single house than to find out about them when ten houses simultaneously reach the same point of completion. Taking this example a step further, adapting to customer feedback about a non-load-bearing wall that's misplaced is much easier to fix before electrical systems, plumbing, and drywall are installed.

>> **Daily scrum team coordination:** Having an established forum for raising issues limits bottlenecks and prevents small issues from turning into big problems. If Acme Pipe Co. failed to deliver the materials you need, the scrum master is addressing the issue now and ensuring that it doesn't happen again — not at the end of the week, when it comes up in a weekly status reporting meeting.

In Chapter 1, we talk about the three pillars of improvement in agile: transparency, inspection, and adaptation. Although all three pillars serve you well throughout scrum, the transparency issue is clearly (pun intended) key in the bidding and building process.

Scrum roles in construction

In traditional project management, the project-manager role carries huge responsibilities, which are broad, all-inclusive, and often too much for one person to effectively bear alone. The project manager wears so many hats — coordinating among everyone involved — that efficiency and quality can suffer the consequences.

Scrum provides different, clearly designated roles to help the project manager shoulder the burden. Balance is restored as scrum team members take on new responsibilities:

>> The project-manager role disappears.

>> The product owner represents the funding customer and the stakeholders. The product owner could be the person who was traditionally the project manager, or the project architect or engineer, depending on how those roles are implemented in each organization. No matter what the product owner's previous role was, his role in scrum is the same: providing the "what" and the "when" of the product being built.

>> The scrum master role facilitates communication and interactions, removes impediments for the development team, makes sure that each person involved understands the process, and makes sure that the team is set up for members to succeed in their jobs. This role sounds a lot like a foreman or superintendent, doesn't it?

>> The development team consists of the subcontractors, engineers, architects, and individual tradesmen.

Customer involvement

The traditional view holds that change in projects is bad. In scrum, however, change is embraced as a sign of progress. You seek change as clear evidence that you're building a better product more directly in line with what your client wants.

In traditional construction projects (as in so many other fields), you find a tendency to involve customers as little as possible to keep changes to a minimum. Construction companies are still in the change-is-bad mindset. The earlier and more frequently the customer is involved, however, the cheaper changes are and the more likely you are to build something that the customer loves.

At the other extreme, you don't want scope creep. As customers see things take shape, they want to add more features, which builds additional scope into the project. This scope adds costs that may not have been budgeted for. In scrum, you want to reduce costs, not raise them.

Scrum prevents this situation by restricting scope by cost — and, thus, time — rather than by arguments about what a written requirement meant. The customer can have any new requirement that aligns with the vision statement, but each new requirement added is offset by the loss of a lower-priority requirement, unless that lower-priority requirement is funded by additional budget.

Scrum facilitates the customer involvement process by

>> Structuring customer feedback within sprint cycles at natural breaks and milestones in the project, such as inspecting rough electrical or plumbing before hanging drywall to ensure that fixtures are lined up where the customer intended. This practice allows you to make any necessary adjustments before it's too late. The customer inspects completed work at the end of each sprint and provides valuable feedback then.

>> Gaining ownership of the project by making decisions driven by cost and return on investment within these feedback loops.

>> Giving customer change requests visibility throughout the project by showing how those requests will affect the remaining schedule and cost.

In the end, the transparency, inspection, and adaptation process allows better communication. When everyone involved has the information that he or she needs, an environment for excellent decision-making is created.

The subcontractor dilemma

Since the building of the pyramids in Egypt, project managers and subcontractors have struggled to stay coordinated and on track. Issues still arise far too frequently due to the structure within which these valuable parties operate.

The challenges are severalfold. Traditionally, the project process has been difficult to coordinate because subcontractors are numerous and contractors are few. Through a lack of coordination, communication, and therefore ownership of the outcome, as well as human nature, the parties involved focus on their own benefits and outcomes rather than on the whole project.

Each subcontractor is hugely specialized; therefore, a high degree of coordination is needed among subcontractors and the responsible party, stakeholders, and potential users. The waterfall method simply doesn't provide this environment. Fortunately, scrum does.

Here are some ways that scrum facilitates the contractor–subcontractor relationship:

>> Through regular, structured scrum events (daily scrums, sprint reviews, and sprint retrospectives), communication is enhanced, and vital feedback from all parties is encouraged.

>> Sprints and releases are timeboxed and frequent, and each party knows exactly what is expected at each increment.

>> Subcontractors have input into to how much work they can accomplish in a sprint (that is, empirical data from what they accomplished in previous timeboxed sprints). Contractors can give their input on priorities, but the final decisions rest with the people who are doing the work.

>> Subcontractors are given a big-picture perspective of their roles and encouraged to share their knowledge and experience to make the process more efficient (that is, self-organized teams contribute their specific knowledge to come up with the best designs).

>> Contractors receive knowledge and experience from the people who do the work: subcontractors.

>> Subcontractors can bring up inefficiencies and problems early (through sprint retrospectives). This feedback is critical for removing impediments.

>> Supply and procurement issues are easier to coordinate because everyone is looking down the road together through active, in-person discussions (product backlog refinement, daily scrums, and daily feedback from the product owner).

>> Quality is improved through increased coordination.

>> Material flow and staging are easier to coordinate via product backlog refinement and sprint planning, including task planning of requirements.

The key is that disconnected roles and jobs are combined into one communicating, coordinated scrum team. With scrum, you have a living organism. Each part relies on and enhances the others.

TIP

Individual subcontractor teams do well using scrum to organize themselves and their work. But the overall project team is made up of multiple subcontractors. How do you get all these teams to work as one? Well, it may not be realistic to get all teams in the same room every day, but it would be possible to get each foreman in the same room every day to coordinate the day's priorities, identify impediments, and go to work removing them to ensure that the job moves forward unhindered.

Worker safety

Safety concerns for workers are always important, especially now, with the increased number of projects in areas with high traffic volume and large populations. Clear communication of risks and solutions, therefore, is more important than ever. Lives depend on it.

Scrum facilitates increased worker safety through the following means:

>> Safety-compliance regulations are relevant and thorough. Adding these regulations to the definition of done means that documented, validated safety measures can be in place and ready for perusal during audits.

>> Frequent sprint retrospectives allow workers to come forward with safety concerns and solutions. Good scrum masters can facilitate this process to make sure that the appropriate safety subjects come up.

>> Experienced workers can share their expertise in providing solutions.

>> Daily scrums provide a forum for urgent issues.

FLYOVER CONSTRUCTION IN BANGALORE

A Scrum Alliance article titled "A Real-Life Example of Agile, Incremental Delivery of an Infrastructure Project in Bangalore, India" (https://stage-kentico.scrumalliance.org/community/articles/2014/july/real-life-example-of-agile-in-infrastructure-proje) provides an example of the scrum process in action in construction. The project was building a flyover road at a hugely busy intersection in Bangalore, India. Many high-tech companies had major facilities at this intersection.

Normally, a flyover project of this magnitude would take 18 months to complete. In the process, temporary roads would be created on either side of the main thoroughfare while both flyovers were built simultaneously. Naturally, traffic is delayed during construction, as temporary roads are used, and no flyovers are available until both are opened at the end of the project.

This project, however, was conducted with scrum in incremental steps:

- The highest-priority requirement was identified as one side of the flyover for first release. Therefore, a temporary road was constructed and used on one side of the main road. Simultaneously, construction of the flyover on the first side of the road began.

- Upon completion, the first flyover was opened for traffic in both directions, and construction on the opposite flyover began. Although traffic was still delayed, the delay was reduced because at least one flyover was functional. The completion of the first flyover also created a shippable product increment. Swarming was done on that side of the flyover only.

- The same temporary road was used during construction of the second flyover. Time and money were saved because no new road was required. Perhaps a second temporary road could have been planned up front, but the first temporary road was found to be useful during the second phase. Inspection and adaptation eliminated waste.

- When the second flyover was complete, both flyovers were open; traffic was returned to the main thoroughfare, and the temporary road was closed.

The process seems to be simple, doesn't it? Here are some of the results:

- Using incremental delivery of one flyover at a time reduced overall construction time from 18 months to 9 months (a 50 percent time-to-market decrease).

- Traffic congestion was reduced as first one flyover and then the other flyover opened.

- Only one temporary road needed to be constructed.

- As soon as one flyover was operational, risk of failure was reduced. If funding had been cut halfway through, because one side was fully functional (that is, a shippable increment had been created), that cut wouldn't have been a disaster. The highest-risk issues had been dealt with up front.

- Overall efficiency was improved, as there were fewer moving parts at any time.

It's likely that these things are already being done in various ways, just not with scrum terms. Transparency of safety concerns is needed and provides a mechanism to inspect and implement actions to adapt.

Scrum in Home Building

Scrum in home building is real, it's becoming common, and its benefits are just as strong as in other industries. A home can be defined, planned, estimated, and built using the scrum framework.

The first meeting with the builder is to learn about the type of home you're looking for — features such as the number of bedrooms, type of property, and number of garages; the quality of finishes and flooring; the landscaping; the approximate amount you want to spend; and your time frame. This meeting, which takes about an hour, gives the builder high-level understanding of what you're looking for (the vision and roadmap).

Over several weeks after the initial planning meeting, buyers meet with an architect to get more specific details about the plans, such as desired room layouts, floors, basement, lot placement, flooring, and cabinetry. Design elements such as colors, appliances, and fixtures are not yet selected. What does get decided is what's needed to estimate the cost of the house and provide a blueprint and elevation. These higher-risk items that are more difficult and expensive to change later (the product backlog).

From that point, it's expected that the less-risky things will change later, so those decisions are deferred until the last responsible moment. Potential risks are discussed, however, such as surprises that might be found at groundbreaking.

With the blueprint comes a budget, which breaks out the details sufficiently for the builder to factor in profit and for the buyer to see each feature of the house (user stories).

The budget for each feature, such as cabinets, is based on the description given by the buyer to the builder at the beginning of the project. Within that budget, the buyer gets to choose exactly what she wants. At this point, trade-offs can be made or color coordination can take place when the buyer is looking at the actual home rather than pictures in a brochure. Although a certain quality of wood may have sounded great during planning, the buyer may change her mind and choose a less-expensive option, using the savings to add something else or financing less at closing time because of the savings.

Manufacturing

Interestingly, the lines between software and hardware are blurring. Tangible products nowadays have a surprising amount of software within them. The car you may drive, the refrigerator you cool your iced coffee in, and the e-reader that you may be reading this book on are full of code.

TECHNICAL STUFF

Automobiles are now connected to the Internet of Things (IoT) technology and they are becoming increasingly software-driven. A Tesla vehicle connects to your home Wi-Fi and every month or so you download great new features. After an error was found to its charger, Tesla completed a fix for its 29,222 vehicle owners via software update. We are now on the cusp of self-driven cars.

New demands are placed on manufacturing processes that aren't just connecting one widget to another. Complex systems, many of which are software-based, are interlacing and integrating. In fact, software is critical to the success of many manufactured products.

LEAN AND MEAN WITH TOYOTA

In the 1940s, a relatively unknown car company called Toyota devised a plan for producing cars while controlling costs. Rather than employing the standard assembly line procedure, which required huge overhead costs, the company created a just-in-time process.

Rather than producing everything at once, the company built only what it needed at the moment for a project. Just as a supermarket replaces only items that have sold out, Toyota built or procured only the parts that it needed. Because there was no huge inventory, costs were reduced.

As a result, one of scrum's roots is in manufacturing.

These trends are leading to larger, more complex development projects and teams with diverse arrays of talent. They also lead to increased complexity in incorporating product families (not just individual products), increased risk of defects as complexity rises, and a new array of compliance and required standards.

Survival of the fastest to market

One key to winning the race to market share is being the fastest to market, which isn't a new concept. An equally important concept is keeping up with and even leading in innovation — specifically, innovation led by customer needs and desires.

You can be fastest to market only if you're getting customer feedback up front while addressing the highest-priority features and highest risks. Higher quality is built through early testing. Scrum enables early, high-quality release to market. Sounds like a good fit for scrum. This reality is why Tesla and other manufacturers now employ scrum masters and agile coaches.

New technologies are astounding: robotics, artificial intelligence, 3-D printing, and nanotechnology, to name but a few. Each of these technologies introduces new complexities to production. Scrum- and agile-based frameworks are ideal for problem-solving complexity.

Shareholder value

The bureaucracies that are traditional parts of the manufacturing industry emphasize efficiency, cost-cutting, and maximized shareholder value as opposed to added value for customers. This emphasis is their Achilles' heel. Companies that will excel in the future emphasize value to customers.

Scrum and its organic feedback cycle emphasize regular customer-value feedback. After each sprint, you have working, shippable product to show to stakeholders and customers. Even if you can't get feedback during the sprint, scrum allows you to adapt as soon as you receive the feedback.

As stated in the Agile Manifesto, the primary measure of success is a working product in the hands of a customer — the earlier the better, and the more frequently the better. Scrum does both.

Strategic capacity management

In building tangible products, you may not have a final piece of product to place in someone's hands at the end of a one-week sprint. This is fine. Just remember to keep the progression demonstrable and the feedback cycle as short as possible.

The idea is to have regular, frequent feedback from users. The specifics will vary with each product. Work to keep the feedback cycle as short as possible and decrease it when possible.

INTEL'S TRANSITION TO SCRUM

Intel has a long history of waterfall project management, given its manufacturing history. The company decided to test scrum for developing presilicon infrastructure and readiness. The idea was that if scrum worked for that project, Intel could implement it in other manufacturing processes.

Intel hired a scrum coach to help it identify and break old habits, integrate new ones, and generally understand the scrum framework properly. Despite the coaching, however, transition issues arose. Not every senior manager attended the initial scrum meetings, buy-in by important people was slow, and real-world examples of why scrum works weren't being identified.

Eventually, Intel found that best way to get its teams implementing and benefiting from scrum was follow scrum guidelines and avoid customizing scrum to fit their process.

Pat Elwer authored a case study entitled "Agile Project Development at Intel: A Scrum Odyssey (www.collab.net/sites/all/themes/collabnet/_media/pdf/cs/CollabNet_casestudy_Intel.pdf).

In summary, the case study found that the teams discovered that scrum helped the project in four distinct ways:

- A reduced cycle time of 66 percent.
- Their performance remained on schedule with virtually no missed commitments.
- Increased employee morale. Ironically, their lowest-morale team turned into the best-performing team.
- Increased transparency, which has led to identifying impediments and unproductive habits.

After the teams and management bought into the process, the power of scrum soon became apparent.

Hardware Development

Many similarities exist between implementing scrum in software and hardware projects. You may hear that the differences between the two products are so great that scrum can't work with both. That's not true. Anytime you can encapsulate the work to be done and prioritize it against other work, you can use scrum to your immense benefit.

A key element of hardware projects done with scrum is to focus on feedback early and often. You may not have much to work with in the beginning, but keep producing workable increments during each sprint, and what you have to show customers and stakeholders will grow — with their feedback incorporated.

Early identification of high-risk requirements

If you discover defects and problems early, you save time, money, and hassle. In waterfall, testing was left until the end. But why test only at the end when you can test all along the way and find (and resolve) defects early?

Scrum forces timely integration between firmware and software. Scrum breaks down functional silos and gets engineers working together to solve problems rather than coming together later to fix problems.

In the daily scrum (which is no more than 15 minutes), you can coordinate what's been done with what's going to be done and list what impediments are in the way.

TECHNICAL STUFF

Open-source hardware is a gift to scrum and engineering as a whole. As open-source submissions increase, organizations can quickly and creatively implement existing designs, frameworks, and architectures that get their products to market faster.

Live hardware development

In the following sections, we discuss four examples of the scrum framework being used successfully for hardware development. Each situation is unique, but the scrum principles and practices remain the same. For the most part, whatever the project, you can use scrum to develop it faster and with higher quality and ease.

Johns Hopkins CubeSat

The Johns Hopkins University Applied Physics Lab used scrum in its Multi-Mission Bus Demonstrator (MMBD) project for building two CubeSat satellites. The program itself was sponsored by NASA.

Three key elements were identified as being critical to the success of the project:

» **Scrum teams:** These teams were made up of subsystem leads. All team members were co-located and given direct access to the NASA representative (the product owner, who was on-site) for quick decision-making.

» **Emphasis on a working system:** Only one design review was funded, and computer-aided design (CAD) models were used to simulate and manipulate designs. Informal peer reviews were conducted throughout the project, and documentation was minimal.

» **Culture of innovation:** Change was welcomed and incorporated. Daily scrums were held to coordinate and identify the best ways of addressing the highest-priority requirements. Long-term planning was eschewed in favor of responding to reality.

REMEMBER

As in manufacturing, change is inevitable in hardware projects. Accept that fact and turn it into an advantage. Denial will get you nowhere. Fortunately, change in hardware project design and development is workable and practical.

Wikispeed modular car

Wikispeed is an all-volunteer, green, prototype car designer. By forming self-organizing teams and using the scrum framework, the company built a functional prototype car that gets 100 miles per gallon. The teams win races because their car is completely modular. They can swap out components based on how they're running that day, on that track, in that weather. Their competition doesn't have the same ability.

Wikispeed garnered four key takeaways from its scrum experience:

» **Customer feedback:** Teams went to users for regular feedback and tested what they could every week.

» **Sprints and reviews:** Regular sprint cycles were conducted, with meetings at the end cycle of each stating what went right and what went wrong.

» **Transparency:** All team members knew the goals, and anyone could make a suggestion.

» **Peer-to-peer communication:** No one person was the boss; everyone was equal and contributed to achieving the sprint goal each day.

Telefonica Digital

Telefonica Digital began as a hardware manufacturing firm that used waterfall project management. As technology changed, it began to develop more software. As the focus shifted from hardware to software, the company adapted fully to agile and scrum.

When technology and the firm's direction changed again, it went back to producing hardware. Because of its experience with scrum over the years, the company had no desire to go back to traditional project management, so it used the scrum framework for its hardware projects.

The first issue was relocating the facility so that employees could be co-located, because the company understood the value of working in proximity. Telefonica also created a system in which it could easily procure equipment and materials on the day it needed them.

The company used scrum teams and fostered cross-functionality. It tested early and often, even using 3-D printing and prototyping technologies to hasten testing. It used lots of open hardware, which it could use for testing. At times, this process accelerated the hardware team's progress to the point of waiting on the software teams.

Saab jet fighter

Saab Defense is using scrum to develop the JAS 39E Saab Gripen jet fighter. Building this highly complex jet requires more than 1,000 engineers and more than 100 teams. Scrum provides team-level priorities and the transparency needed to expose, inspect, and adapt to changing variables regularly and quickly. Saab scaled scrum across multiple teams and departments. See Chapter 13 for more on scaling scrum.

Why building a complex fighter worked:

>> **Enhanced autonomy:** Teams are given degrees of freedom within a clearly defined framework. The focus on autonomous teams encourages decision-making at the lowest level and reduces bureaucracy (see Chapter 13).

>> **Modular architecture:** Saab used modular architecture to reduce monolithic dependences and focus on flexibility for future changes.

>> **Continuous improvement:** Retrospectives after each sprint and short feedback loops from outside the team enable product and process improvements.

Chapter **10**

Services

There are more than 9,000 billing codes for individual procedures and units of care. But there is not a single billing code for patient adherence or improvement, or for helping patients stay well.

— Clayton M. Christensen, *The Innovator's Prescription: A Disruptive Solution for Health Care*

Scrum within service industries has enormous potential. We rely on health care, education, and public utilities to maintain and enhance our civilized society. Still, there is room for creating lean systems of cost savings and quality improvement. And in many cases, scrum is already being used.

Each sector has specific challenges. Unique sets of circumstances exist that need to be dealt with in a tailored way. Many of the outdated systems of development and maintenance were developed in simpler times. But as the world grows more complex, so does the need for innovative and flexible project frameworks. Scrum is ideal for dealing with new demands. We show you how and with what results.

Health Care and Scrum

Over the past few years, health care has been at the forefront of news. Affordable and accessible health care is often considered to be a basic tenet of a civilized society. Yet soaring costs, pressure to decrease development time without sacrificing quality, wasted spending, and increasing avoidable deaths have led to massive changes in the way Americans pay for and receive medical attention.

In 1970, health care spending in the United States was estimated to be $75 billion. In 2016 spending was $3.3 trillion or $10,348 per person and accounted for 17.9% of the Gross Domestic Product.

Added to this situation is a health care culture in which insurance reimbursements are increasingly linked to customer satisfaction. Health care technology has an expanded and important influence on clinical outcomes and patient satisfaction. New paradigms exist, and new methods for meeting their needs are required. It should come as no surprise that scrum is being used more frequently to address health care issues than ever before.

Some of the highest–priority challenges facing the health care industry are

>> Procedural mistakes during health care delivery are now the third-highest killer in America, just behind heart disease and cancer. A *Forbes* article from 2016 states that more than 500 people die each day from "errors, accidents, and infections" in hospitals.

>> Money is wasted on unnecessary medical tests and treatments. The Institute of Medicine Health claims that a whopping one-third of the billions spent on health care each year is wasted. *The American Journal of Obstetrics and Gynecology* states that elective deliveries alone cost $1 billion annually.

>> New and increasing regulations require speedy and thorough adaptation.

>> The demand to convert to electronic health care records is monumental, yet processes for achieving this conversion are sorely lacking.

>> Research and development on new treatments and medicines need continued funding and innovation.

>> There are concerns that new medical devices and systems have not been thoroughly reviewed for safety risks, and many of them are designed with traditional methods in which design comes first and testing is left for last.

In the following sections, we show you how scrum can help with the preceding issues. Scrum has been used within the health care environment with great success. It starts with administrative buy-in, followed by the implementation of scrum teams and their inherent roles. Then the process begins, following the road–map to value just like any other scrum project. Follow the stages we outline throughout this book, and watch the positive changes unfold.

In general, scrum brings the following benefits to the table:

» **Rapid and regular feedback:** Feedback is crucial for determining what's acceptable and what's not. Feedback is even more important when the development cycle involves adherence to a regulatory framework. Scrum accelerates the point at which internal auditing can happen to ensure better regulatory compliance.

» **Accelerated time to implementation:** Health care is about saving lives, but competitive advantage can be an added benefit.

» **Faster monetization:** Making quality health care profitable enables faster changes that are more likely to stick.

» **Increased talent retention:** Focused workers are proven to receive more job satisfaction and remain engaged longer.

» **Fewer product defects:** Higher visibility leads to higher quality and higher customer satisfaction.

Scrum is needed in the health care industry to help foster changes that support clinical decision-making within highly effective patient care and business administration. Health care struggles to evolve rapidly while also continuing to be compliant with the ever-changing demands of regulatory agencies.

Scrum has helped shorten development time for new administrative and clinical systems and increase quality and efficiency. The current health care environment is in flux between private and publicly funded care. Regulations and laws are being changed and refined. Therefore, a high degree of flexibility and transparency is necessary to survive in these turbulent waters.

Speed to market

Many of the diseases that our parents and grandparents suffered from as children are no longer daily concerns thanks to advances in sanitation and treatments, but new diseases are being discovered and exposed. Aggressive research and progress continue to find cures and prevent chronic and terminal illnesses. But health care professionals want to save more lives and save them faster.

Customer expectations regarding health care and the miracles of science are rising. Payers within the health care system are drilling down to find the best value in the medicines and treatments they're buying.

Pharmaceutical companies are under constant pressure to devise new medicines to keep up with the stiff competition, yet they must do this within a cost-cutting and economizing environment. To compete and succeed, companies in this industry (as in every other industry discussed in this book) must be the fastest, most nimble, and most cost-effective.

Yet the pharmaceutical industry's output has, on the whole, stayed flat. Most pharmaceutical organizations are tackling new situations and technological advances with the same project management frameworks they used in the 1940s. They're surrounded by new ways of doing business, yet they've mostly stayed within traditional management mindsets.

Scrum can offer positive change in the following ways:

» Every experiment begins with a hypothesis. In scrum, this hypothesis is the release goal.

» In testing the hypothesis, premises are found to be true or false. Each premise is a sprint goal. The sprint backlog is broken into tasks and experiments needed to fully explore each premise. The definition of done for the sprint outlines the type of tasks and activities that must be conducted and accepted for a premise to be considered fully tested and explored.

» At the end of each sprint, the team presents its findings to stakeholders, who ask questions and validate the team's sprint conclusions. Stakeholders should include representatives of regulatory teams. If something was missed, the scrum team knows early and can conduct follow-up activities to address the feedback in the next sprint if it's a priority.

» After all premises have been validated, the hypothesis stands or is invalidated. Either way, the hypothesis reaches a releasable conclusion.

» All the actions needed to test the hypothesis are the requirements of the product backlog and are prioritized accordingly.

» For new products and improvements on old ones, scrum allows you to iterate quickly. The mantra "Fail fast, fail cheap" means that you can be as nimble as you like in trying new ideas and processes.

» Self-organizing scrum teams allow developers to come up with the best research and solutions.

» Customer, business, and regulatory involvement throughout the process means continual feedback and direction. For this reason, accountability is shared, and engagement rises.

Reduced mistakes, increased quality

Although current generations have the greatest technology and treatments ever known, we still have room to improve. Incredibly, mistakes during health care delivery in America are now the third-highest killer.

The kind of health care mistakes that cause harm can be such things as complex surgical complications that go unrecognized to more minor errors regarding the doses or types of medications given to patients.

No one knows the exact costs of health care errors because the coding system used to record death data fails to record items such as communication breakdowns, diagnostic errors, and poor judgment, all of which can cost lives. But we know that there are both human and economic costs associated with errors in care. Human deaths in the U.S. are estimated to be more than 300,000 per year and serious harm to be 10 times that high. The economic cost of medical errors can be estimated at $20.8 billion.

A report by the *Journal of Health Care Finance* estimates that these medical errors, if you include lost productivity in the workplace, may total up to $1 trillion annually. In many cases, these errors can result in a device or medicine getting banned forever on a very short notice, resulting in a complete loss to a company that has invested billions of dollars during the development cycle.

The causes of these errors may vary, but the quality assurance built into the scrum framework can ferret out problems and their solutions early. Scrum makes it easy to identify and deal with system inefficiencies, bottlenecks in work flow, communication breakdowns, and lack of timely feedback. The following are some ways scrum can help:

>> As communication increases, inefficiencies become visible. Scrum exposes these inefficiencies through daily scrums and sprint reviews; real solutions can be tried, tested, and adapted.

>> Although licensed physicians are the only people authorized to diagnose patients, self-organized teams (consisting of the entire staff) facilitate the necessary treatment, rather than the command-and-control system of the highest-ranking physician.

>> Feedback is rapid, and adjustments can be quickly implemented and retested.

>> As quality goes up, unnecessary risks and wasted costs go down.

>> As input from all members of staff and key groups is sought and used, buy-in increases, and morale improves. Buy-in or ownership is hugely valuable in health care, in which many people are overworked and burnout can be high.

Cost cutting

Those words alone are enough to pique the interest of any health care administrator. In a sense, every problem and solution we discuss in this chapter helps save costs. Avoidable illnesses and deaths, increased efficiency in care delivery and administrative flow, ease in following regulations, and pretty much anything else you can name can be improved to save costs.

REMEMBER

Cost savings are a hallmark of scrum. Scrum not only helps you increase in speed to market, which accounts for a large part of the savings, but also streamlines processes, removes inefficiencies, and allows you to make better business decisions. The Center for American Progress stated in 2012, "Administrative costs in the U.S. health care system consume an estimated $361 billion annually — 14 percent of all health care expenditures in our nation. At least half of this spending is estimated to be wasteful."

Consider savings in the context of unnecessary care costs. A 2012 study conducted by the Institute of Medicine estimates that in the United States we waste $750 billion annually on unnecessary health care. Causes include inefficient and unnecessary services, overpricing, excessive administration costs, and fraud.

Some of the ways scrum can help cut costs are

>> **Sprint retrospectives:** The sprint retrospectives in scrum routinely ask such questions as

- What about our claims process is unnecessary?
- How can we minimize repeat patient visits?
- What additional steps can we take to reduce patient risks even further?
- Where are the bottlenecks?
- What if form XYZ were electronic?
- What's stopping us from increasing our daily claims processing rate by 20 or 50 percent?

>> **Daily coordination of priorities:** During daily scrums, such questions as these can be asked:

- Is this necessary for this patient today?
- What's in the way of this patient's going home well today?
- How can we remove that obstacle?

>> **Transparency and simplicity:** With scrum, you want to maximize the amount of work not done, especially if it's harmful. Reducing the number of early elective deliveries (37 to 39 weeks as opposed to 40), for example, would eliminate up to 500,000 neonatal intensive-care unit days.

Adhering to regulations

With the changes brought by the Affordable Care Act in 2010 came a flurry of new regulations. These regulations are in place to protect patients and health care providers, and each health care organization needs to find ways to comply. Implementing solutions to address new regulations can be challenging and even tedious, and having fewer resources to work with makes the process more daunting.

Here are some of the ways that scrum helps health care providers understand and abide by new regulations:

>> A product backlog can be created and prioritized by business value and risk mitigation. Then the scrum teams and the organization as a whole have the rationale to make business and resource decisions during complex times of regulation changes.

>> Previously, the technical and business sides of health care solutions may not have seen eye to eye; after all, their mandates were probably different. But as the business side is covered by a product owner and development teams are formed to design solutions, goals suddenly align. Scrum team roles are peer roles. Team members work together to facilitate the right environment for aligning goals and purpose, which is ideal for implementing changes to deal with regulations.

>> Self-organized teams define the best solutions. When new regulations are narrowed down and prioritized, it's easier to pinpoint solutions and implement them quickly.

>> The evolving regulatory requirements can be built into the scrum team's definition of done. This way, product owners and stakeholders can rest assured that they'll be in line when audits and inspections take place.

Scrum isn't an escape hatch for regulations. After all, regulations have the good of the patient in mind. Scrum is a tool for responding to changes by being tactically flexible while remaining strategically stable, thereby making sure that the goal — better health care — is achieved.

RISK AND ISSUE MANAGEMENT

Documentation is critical in risk and issue management for health care implementations for regulatory audit or legal action.

In traditional project management, documenting risks and tracking issues is typically achieved by creating and maintaining a risk and issue log that's based on initial requirements determined at the project kickoff.

As requirements change throughout the course of the implementation, they become hard to manage and often drive cumbersome change management processes.

In scrum, you can build risk management into your process by making it part of your definition of done. The requirement isn't complete until specifically stated risks are identified, mitigated or accepted, and documented.

Scrum's focus on continual review provides better outcomes than traditional project management methodology.

Medical device manufacturing and safety

Like the pharmaceutical industry, the medical device manufacturing industry operates within a highly competitive and cost-conscious environment. Many are beset by traditional project management mindsets. Up-front designing combined with late back-end testing means that defects are detected late and the costs of fixing them rise — assuming that the defects are detected before the product hits the market (see Chapter 4).

With scrum, you can

>> Build product testing into each iteration. Catch defects early, stamp them out, and implement better designs.

>> Co-locate designers with engineers so that they're immediately accessible and can get real-time everyday feedback.

>> Add requirements as the project progresses. Many times, customers don't know exactly what they want at the beginning. After the initial high-priority requirements have been developed, scrum allows customers to see a fuller picture.

>> Inspect and adapt constantly. Build only what's most important, and test and garner feedback regularly and frequently.

>> Get daily signoff with the product owner on work done.

>> Receive feedback from stakeholders at regular sprint reviews. This feedback gets them involved throughout the development process.

>> Coordinate early and often when syncing software and hardware development.

>> Share the definition of done for both teams and include integration and testing throughout each sprint rather than at the end.

GE IMAGING

General Electric's imaging unit found the following ailments in its traditional approach to developing medical devices before implementing scrum:

- **Predictability:** The company was running 12- to 24-month projects, usually with significant delays.

- **Scope creep:** Representatives of the business usually pushed to add features beyond the original scope.

- **Phased approach:** Minimal customer interaction until the first round of testing was a major contributor to delays and soaring project costs.

- **Silo teams:** Artificial barriers existed among functional, technical, and business units of the organization.

Scrum healed these ailments in the following ways:

- Product owners were an integral part of the scrum teams, which significantly broke down silos and aligned priorities across the organization. The whole business began working in unison to release the right product to customers on time.

- Short sprints were held in which actual product increments were completed and demonstrated. The feedback received early steered the project to earlier completion than normal.

- Senior leadership was excited. By observing successes in a joint venture that used scrum, executive leadership saw what scrum could do, and their support accelerated adoption.

- Due to high regulation of the industry, GE built regulatory steps into the definition of done and acceptance criteria. Development teams adjusted to this level of effort when estimating and executing.

By incorporating scrum into the medical-device manufacturing process, GE brought costs down and reduced time to market. Most important, the company reduced defects, which resulted in fewer reputational and regulatory risks. The chance that a product would harm a person went down because the product was tested and integrated so many times.

Education and Scrum

Throughout this book, we emphasize the fact that scrum can be used in a variety of industries — all of them, in fact. Scrum is a framework for developing products, not a software-specific tool.

Education is one such industry. Children are the future, as their children will be after them. Educating young people and ensuring that they have the ability to come up with creative, innovation solutions and decisions themselves should be the top priority of every culture.

Public education was created in a different landscape — that of basic education for workers. The need was simple, as the work world was simple. Today, however, complexity has grown exponentially, as have students' choices of jobs and roles in the world.

Because of this change in the work landscape, education needs to prepare children to participate effectively in work. Many teachers are still trained to prepare and deliver material in the old way, but a better way exists.

Scrum in the classroom helps children adapt creatively and flexibly to change, prioritize projects and ideas, and come up with new solutions. Technology and media are changing so rapidly that the information that children receive is always in flux. With scrum, they learn how to turn change into an advantage.

Challenges in education

Education faces different challenges today than ever before. Curriculum is expanding in scope, underperforming students require more attention, and classroom sizes are increasing. Despite this appearance of chaos, progress can be made with scrum.

In many respects, teachers inherently use scrum, but they use terms that may not be known to those outside the profession, such as objectives, scaffolding, minilessons, modalities of learning, and reflection.

Teachers already set goals for each lesson. They use the standards as the goal and set objectives for the lesson, as some standards require multiple steps. These multiple steps are called *scaffolding*. Teachers break the lesson into iterations so that students can be successful and accomplish each necessary aspect. Along the way, they use formative and summative assessments to gauge and modify learning. Students and teachers alike reflect at the end of each lesson, as in a retrospective.

Next, teachers are trained to use collaborative learning models and do projects that engage students and get their buy-in.

Increasing curriculum scope

Curriculum requirements for teachers have been expanding for decades. More information must be covered, and teachers can be overwhelmed trying to keep up. These curriculum pressures come from four sources: school systems, governments, parents, and students.

Many topics and experiences used to be taught in the home by parents. School was for basics. Today, school systems cover subjects never before imagined in the classroom. A few that were introduced in the past decade are listed:

» Bullying prevention

» Antiharassment policies

» Body-mass-index evaluation (obesity monitoring)

» Financial literacy

» Entrepreneurial skills development

» Health and wellness programs

Nothing is wrong with these additional programs. In fact, they serve a great purpose. But teachers are being asked to include some of these topics, along with many other new ones, along with the old standards of reading, writing, and arithmetic. However, they've been given no more hours in the day for teaching and often work with limited resources and funding.

Students themselves arrive with a host of experiences and knowledge that would have been science fiction a few decades ago. They're often computer-literate by their early years and have been exposed to adult themes and messages through television, films, and music. Although the teaching techniques we mention previously are inherently scrum, the spectrum of what's being taught has grown. But the overarching goal of education remains the same: well-educated students.

Effective prioritization and inspection-and-adaptation methods are essential for administering this growing curriculum effectively. Teachers reprioritize as they carefully plan each day and empower students to be self-organizing and self-managing. Rather than follow a rigid plan outlined at the beginning of the year, they regularly conduct assessments and adjust their schedules, sometimes spending more time than planned on a subject to help a struggling class and sometimes spending less time than planned when a class understands a concept faster than expected.

Teachers are also recognizing the value of refactoring. In the old days, you took a test, you got a grade, and that was it. As educators have learned from experience, adaptations have been made to allow students to learn from their mistakes and be rewarded for their learning. Continual-feedback loops allow for learning, followed by an assessment (pretest or quiz), with feedback and more learning followed by the final assessment. The grade isn't the only goal. Students are starting to understand and appreciate what they learn by using these same events as used in scrum.

Moving low-performing students upward

Teachers are hugely instrumental in moving students through learning blocks. Sometimes, however, teachers work from a structured curriculum that requires them to move on with new topics and subjects even though not all their students may have full comprehension. Although they may want to spend more valuable one-on-one time with each student, they simply can't afford the time without preventing the overall curriculum from moving forward.

Therefore, the individual attention needed to help low- or moderate-scoring students sometimes isn't available due to lack of time. Teachers need to keep progressing in their curriculum. Large class sizes can add to this conundrum.

As a result, low-performing students arrive in the next year's class without fully understanding the previous year's material, or they're held back and taught the same material again without new learning techniques. Evaluations are done, but teaching doesn't necessarily circle back to weaker areas of understanding.

Success in elevating individual students comes through collaboration among schools, teachers, parents, and students. If the scrum framework were applied for each student, with team members consisting of such participants as the teacher, the student, the counselor, a school administrator, and a tutor, this team could set iterative goals leading to an end goal, with regular feedback loops, all the while inspecting and adapting progress and the process to fit the student's needs.

Increasing student-to-teacher ratios

Classes are getting bigger, and individual teacher-student attention is dropping. It's a tall order to manage an entire class and the increasing curriculum and to provide student- and subject-specific teaching.

REMEMBER

Teachers spend time building relationships, modifying a lesson, executing lessons, and helping students one on one. Finding time is the most important challenge of education. As funding decreases, but teaching methods and systems stay the same, it's inevitable that education in the classroom will suffer. Scrum can help leverage teachers' time and increase adaptability.

Scrum in the classroom

Scrum works in education like anywhere else. As scrum is based on goals and vision, setting focused learning goals allows students to adapt their learning styles to their speed of learning. By focusing on one learning goal at a time, students can master each subject and level before moving on. With scrum, teachers can emphasize high-priority learning items that students focus on.

Scrum remains effective in large classes because smaller scrum teams can be formed for projects. Within limits based on the ages and natures of individual groups of students, these teams can be self-organizing and self-directed to reach educational goals.

Inspection and adaptation work remarkably well in learning environments. Studies have shown that students who have lesson plans to adapt to and can work specific areas in which they struggle achieve better comprehension. Iterative teaching models have been introduced to the classroom with remarkable results in the following ways:

>> The teacher outlines the unit or project for all the students, and groups are formed (sprint planning).

>> The teacher executes daily teaching and guides group work-learning tasks, setting a time goal too (sprint).

>> The student and teacher assess student performance at the end of the timebox (sprint review).

>> If students perform above a preset cutoff level, they move to new material. If they perform below this level, a sprint retrospective is conducted.

>> Using feedback received at the sprint review, problem topics for each student are identified.

>> New teams are formed to maximize the teacher's ability to help students by leveraging the challenges that each student is facing. These teams work together in increasing their understanding of the topic.

>> Material for these new groups is revised (product backlog refinement). Students come up with ideas about ways to better learn the subject material.

>> Another sprint is run.

>> Student performance is assessed.

This process is repeated, incrementally improving student performance.

In studies, student performance showed significant improvement. Students also made fewer mistakes, and had more confidence, and spent less time figuring out the problems.

Student scrum teams don't have to be shifted; they can be kept stable. That way, cross-functional teams can be created, made up of students who have higher skills in some areas than others. Subsequent sprints use the same techniques as in pair programming and shadowing. By learning from other students, each student gains new skills, and advanced students expand their skill sets.

State and national standards dictate certain requirements for demonstrating mastery of subjects (that is, the definition of done), but each school or teacher can enhance the state or national definition of done to suit specific circumstances. What students learn and how they show that they've learned it are vital elements of the overall success of the sprint. Success will vary according to the situation, but the definition of done should be made clear to everyone, especially the students.

An example approach using scrum

How does the scrum-in-the-classroom concept work?

Kids love it. They become active participants with the whiteboards and sticky notes and the responsibility of making sure that each bit is in its proper place.

Following is how one teacher approaches scrum in the classroom:

1. Set up a project of one to five days' duration.

   This project is effectively a sprint. The teacher has the original plan but gets class buy-in through listing requirements. If the project is to understand the periodic table of the elements, for example, requirements could be sections of the table. Tasks might be the individual elements themselves.

2. Scrum teams of students are formed, and team members decide who fills the scrum roles.

   These teams have a high degree of autonomy.

3. A project backlog is created, often using a task board.

   The kids write down the requirements. The teacher serves as a scrum master and keeps everyone focused.

4. Sticky notes on a whiteboard, wall, or blackboard are used to get children involved with ordering and prioritizing the requirements.

Children love the sense of accomplishment that comes from seeing things move from the to-do stage to the doing stage to the done stage.

5. Each project session begins with a daily scrum.

   The students are using scrum language, such as daily scrums, scrum master, and sprint reviews.

6. At the end of each sprint, both the review and retrospective are conducted.

   Buy-in increases, and when appropriate, the students can contribute to goals for new projects.

Children enjoy the hands-on process and progress. They quickly see progress and are amazingly flexible in adapting. In short, kids naturally think in terms of the iterative process (see Chapter 1). Scrum is just a formalized way of dealing with natural brain wiring.

eduScrum

In Alphen aan de Rijn in the Netherlands, scrum is being used in a high school and secondary educational college. The program is called eduScrum, and educators who use it are experiencing amazing results.

Teachers and students use scrum in all subjects, forming scrum teams with all the roles intact. Three teacher scrum masters lead the charge, each facilitating the process in his or her class. The scrum masters also conduct daily scrums on the projects, as well as sprint reviews and retrospectives.

The school collected data on the results of this process with 230 students, ranging in age from 12 to 17. The results were impressive. In the Netherlands, test scores fall in a range of 1 to 10. A score of 5.5 is fine, but students strive for 6.7 or better. The students who participated in scrum teams consistently outperformed those who didn't by 0.8 to 1.7 points — significant increases in terms of percentages.

Half the students said that they understood the subject material better, had more fun (hugely important for learning), could work harder and faster, and felt that they were learning in a smarter way.

Teachers also noticed greater engagement from their students and a more positive experience. Interestingly, corporations and organizations often report improved employee morale when they incorporate scrum.

TIP

An interesting side effect of scrum in schools was that the students reported just plain having more fun with classes and learning. This made them more eager to go to school and participate. And those shy, quiet types? They flourished as their skills and contributions were noticed in the reviews and retrospectives.

The team atmosphere also improved. Well over half the students learned to cooperate better and developed trust in their team members. They were open to giving and receiving feedback, and teachers noticed a more relaxed atmosphere.

Blueprint

Blueprint High School in Chandler, Arizona, is a not-for-profit organization that creates and implements special-education options. Leaders at the school decided that having a high school diploma wasn't enough to prepare students for the twenty-first century. Students also needed skills in collaboration, creativity, accountability, critical thinking, and teamwork. Interestingly, scrum naturally fosters all these qualities.

Blueprint's scrum roles were flexible based on the individual team context. Sometimes, the teacher was the product owner or scrum master; at other times, students took on these roles. As team members matured and garnered more experience, they automatically took over the role of product owner. The teachers simply identified the type of projects to be completed; then the students took over by developing their own goals, implementation, and reviews. Collaboration and teamwork skills took off.

The success of scrum in the high school led Blueprint to spread the idea into its elementary school with similar results. Although Blueprint didn't conduct the type of quantitative study that eduScrum did, it experienced many positive anecdotal outcomes, including greater student engagement, more fun, greater empathy, independent thinking, and a more positive educational experience. One teacher said that her kids would even come in if they were ill because they didn't want to miss a single day of school, which is wholehearted buy-in from students.

Military and Law Enforcement

Many agile and scrum experts appreciate Agile Principles and the scrum framework because of their experience in the military. Military organizations are mistakenly perceived to value strong centralized decision-making. Military strategists, however, have long known that centralized decision-making leads to defeat on the battlefield. A commander can't possibly see all parts of the battlefield or communicate fast enough to understand a chaotic, rapidly changing situation or exploit fleeting opportunities. Wise commanders understand that they must empower those at all levels to make timely decisions.

In 1871, German military strategist Helmuth von Moltke (the Elder) sagely observed, "No battle plan survives contact with the enemy." Today, his approach to decentralized decision-making is known to the military as Mission Command.

The doctrine of Mission Command allows leaders to make agile decisions and adapt under conditions of uncertainty. The principles are practiced by most Western military organizations, including the U.S. Marine Corps and the U.S. Army. The U.S. Army operates the Mission Command Center of Excellence to train leaders in the methods of decentralized decision-making.

Traditional military organizations have huge command-and-control structures. More military leaders are seeing that all command and control may not be the ideal approach after all, however.

In 2007, General David Petraeus enabled small, cross-functional teams to make agile decisions that exemplified the counterinsurgency on the ground in Baghdad. "Security of the population, especially in Baghdad, and in partnership with the Iraqi security forces, will be the focus of the military effort," Petraeus said.

Special operations forces, also called special forces, are uniquely trained to be adaptable, self-reliant, and able to operate in uncertainty. In the U.S., *special forces* refer to notable teams like the Green Berets and Navy Seals.

In many ways, agile teams are analogous to special-forces teams. Both types of teams are small, highly trained, highly professional, cohesive, and cross-functional. Special-forces teams are small and cross-functional, so they can adapt to situations that arise. Cross-functionality means that every member of the team can do more than one thing; ideally, everyone on the team can do every skill necessary.

Like agile teams, special-forces teams are stable and long-lived. Through hard-earned experience, their members know how to work together and trust one another, and they pitch in to do whatever is needed to accomplish the mission. That mission may require fluency in a foreign language, building relationships with local villagers, or even skilled use of deadly force if necessary. The mission may call for any combination of those things, yet carrying out the mission may involve something completely different. Special-forces teams know how to learn and adapt.

Another similarity is that both agile and special-forces teams create a sense of mutual accountability. In high-stakes situations, whether in business or on the battlefield, the desire to not let down a team member is more important than any deadline.

Like scrum sprints, missions for military teams are normally broken down to be accomplished quickly, within weeks at the longest. Longer missions wear out soldiers, deplete supplies, and require significant ongoing support. You find an exponential correlation between the length of a mission and the cost and rate of failure. Short missions provide better focus, team morale, and success.

One of many examples in which a military commander succeeded by changing his command-and-control approach is Admiral Nelson at Trafalgar. Instead of requiring strict adherence to signal flags hoisted on his flagship, Nelson delegated substantial authority to ship captains, saying, "In case signals can neither be seen or perfectly understood, no captain can do very wrong if he places his ship alongside that of the enemy."

SCRUM AND THE FBI

Cyberattacks of all sorts, from credit card hacking to government and military security threats, are increasing around the world. Military and cyberwarfare experts agree that controlling this expanding threat is a major concern. Cyberthreat deterrence programs that can adapt to the ever-changing nature of these sophisticated challenges are needed — and needed fast. In many cases, it's an issue of national security.

The FBI has been increasingly active in finding solutions for responding to these cyber-attacks on a national and criminal level. Leadership knows that using old techniques for handling these uber-modern threats isn't enough. New ways of applying technology, shaping their workforce, and collaborating with partners are required.

Not surprisingly, they're approaching this conundrum with scrum.

After the 9/11 terrorist attacks, the FBI began to work on streamlining its flow of information and coordination with all relevant entities. After a couple of false starts, it developed the Sentinel program: a comprehensive software case management system. The goal is to replace a current system consisting of a mixture of digital and paper information flow with a purely digital one.

For ten years, the project was conducted using the FBI's prescribed waterfall methods, including extensive up-front design and fixed requirements. A new CIO, Chad Fulgham, started requiring incremental delivery from the contracted developers. Here are some of the symptoms of the waterfall process used up to that point:

- Only 4 of 18 workflows were live, but with defects.

- Less than 1 percent of the 14,000+ forms were created in the new system.

- Cost to date was $405 million, with an estimated $350 million more to go over six years.

- All delivered functionality was considered optional throughout the organization.

In three months using scrum, with 5% of budget and 80% less staff, scrum did what waterfall couldn't do in 10 years. Overall, excess staff was cut by more than 50 percent, user stories were created, and 21 two-week sprints were scheduled — an 85 percent decrease in projected schedule.

Chapter **11**

Publishing: A Shifting Landscape

History will be kind to me, for I intend to write it.

— WINSTON CHURCHILL

In any disruptive environment, quick and pivoting innovation tactics are needed. Publishing and the news media are going through massive changes before our eyes. Traditional products and readers are changing, and no one knows where the change will end.

Publishing houses and news organizations need to continue monetizing current products and finding new sources of revenue. Trying a new form of native advertising, for example (such as ads intermingled in a feed of news articles), calls for quick turnaround time and quick response to customer feedback. Promoting a new book through an author's existing social media channels or developing new revenue-generating ideas for customer feedback require a disciplined feedback cycle, focused development, and close interaction with customers.

Scrum can handle this type of shifting landscape smoothly. When the goalposts keep moving, it doesn't make sense to aim for where they used to be. We don't know how publishing and news will continue to evolve, so we can inspect and adapt along the way. Those in publishing who are most successful are doing just that.

A Changing Landscape in Publishing

Enormous rates of change are occurring. Brick-and-mortar bookstores are suffering, and readers have shifted ways of finding books and authors. Even libraries are receiving less funding, and much of their shelf space is being converted to computers and other media.

On top of this, readers can now choose between reading on desktops, mobile platforms, and less and less, traditional hardback and paperback books. Now, different forms of media are competing against each other for the same content.

In this new publishing environment, traditional revenue models are changing for advertising and subscriptions so new models are needed that can take advantage of this new digital world. But publishers are still discovering those models.

The music industry experienced a similar seismic shift. Traditional album buying flew out the door when iTunes flew in. Free and often illegal music downloads stirred up a fresh debate on copyright law (enriching scores of lawyers along the way), and avenues for music today are dramatically different from those 10 and 20 years ago. But new songs and albums are created all the time, and musical life goes on. It just looks different.

The same can be said of publishing. For some organizations, massive industry changes are terrifying; for others, opportunity is recognized, flexibility is sought, and inspection and adaptation are seen as paramount. Some publishers say that because of the rapidity of change, they're not sure which data they should use to form their decisions. The sand is shifting under their feet.

Scrum can help the publishing industry flourish. The very qualities that so many people in the industry find unsettling — rapid change, shifting consumer needs and desires, and uncertain sources of revenue — are the ones in which scrum excels.

Inspecting, adapting, and refactoring

Inspection, adaptation, and refactoring are the heart of scrum, and they fit the world of publishing. Like each industry we cover in this book, publishing has its own set of challenges and scrum solutions.

Changing readers

What readers expect from a book, magazine article, or newspaper feed is changing. Immediate information and instant gratification are the norm. Unless the author is already a huge best seller with a wide following, most readers won't sit down to finish a 1,000-page tome.

Incorporating rapid feedback from readers, via short articles, blogs, and analytical tracking tools for reader click-through rates and responses, a flood of data can be accessed. News media, publishers, and individual authors can quickly see what readers are responding to and adjust accordingly.

Not only does this rapid feedback cycle mean better content, but it also means faster monetization. As you inspect and adapt on the go, you're able to follow those paths that lead to more clicks and hits, and therefore incorporate more revenue streams through advertising and sales.

Changing writers

Hugh Howey broke more than one mold with his *New York Times* best-selling novel *Wool*. He published the original short story on Amazon for 99 cents a copy and received such overwhelming positive response that he kept on writing.

Howey wrote and self-published five serial stories, getting feedback from readers with each one, and combined them to create the book *Wool Omnibus* (self-published by Broad Reach Publishing). It landed on the *Times* best-seller list and created a sweet seven-figure revenue stream for him.

Serial stories are produced in sprints. Feedback comes from readers and potential book buyers. Some authors use self-publishing where each detail could be inspected and adapted along the way. The entire success story was an unintentional variation of scrum.

After self-publishing and reaching the best-seller list, Howey signed a contract with a traditional publishing firm, Simon & Schuster. In yet another mold-shattering move, he sold only the print rights to the publisher, keeping all digital rights and proceeds for himself.

Changing products

What and how people read are in flux. Graphic novels, manga, and interactive serials combine with novels, articles, and blogs to create a wide net within which authors place their work. Add e-readers, smartphone apps, and steadily decreasing hard copy numbers, and you have a changing world.

No author or reader is untouched by this literary revolution. T.S. Eliot's classic epic poem *The Waste Land* has its own iPad app, but it isn't just a copied-and-pasted edition of the text. The app incorporates these features:

>> A filmed performance of the poem by Fiona Shaw

>> Audio readings by T.S. Eliot and actors such as Alec Guinness and Viggo Mortensen

>> Interactive notes to help the reader with cultural references and poetic nuances

>> Videos of literary experts providing insight on the masterpiece

>> Original manuscript pages that show the reader how the poem developed under the guidance of Ezra Pound

The publishers (Faber and Touch Press) aren't sitting on the sidelines lamenting the good old days. They're jumping right in and producing great art in new ways.

For publishers and authors alike, scrum's feedback cycle allows for fast input and, therefore, accelerated time to market, creating products that customers want and will pay for. Those who embrace this change and incorporate agile frameworks (such as scrum) that allow for it are excelling in this new environment.

"Survival of the fastest to change" is the mantra. See change as an opportunity, and you'll come out on top.

Applying scrum

As in software, publishing content can be easily and frequently inspected, adapted, and refactored until it's ready for publication. For short works, the process is easier, but it can be adapted to all sizes and lengths.

Creating content for YouTube, for example, is a natural for inspection and adaptation. Post content, and with analytics, you can see an amazing array of data, such as how many people saw it, did they subscribe to your channel, how long they stayed, and what links they followed.

For longer pieces, the process works as well. Mark's first book, *Agile Project Management For Dummies* (published by John Wiley & Sons, Inc):

1. Mark established the vision for the book (a field guide that people who were doing scrum could use as a reference).

2. He established a roadmap: the book outline.

3. He broke the outline into book sections (releases). Each chapter became its own sprint.

4. He started with Chapter 1, writing it according to Wiley's *For Dummies* development standards.

   After he sent Chapter 1 to the Wiley editor, he was told that she hated it and why (feedback, feedback, feedback).

5. He implemented that feedback in Chapter 1, identified the lessons learned, and used what he learned to write Chapter 2.

    He sent Chapter 2 to the Wiley editor and was told that she didn't much like it and why (feedback, feedback, feedback).

6. He improved Chapter 2 and used what he learned to write Chapter 3. That time, when he sent Chapter 3 to the Wiley editor, she told him, "It's okay, but it would be better if you . . ." (feedback, feedback, feedback).

    This cycle continued until Mark and the editor synced up with Chapter 5.

Had he written all 20 chapters and sent them all to Wiley at once, and the editor said she hated them, the book would not be in the marketplace today.

THE SCRUM IN *SCRUM FOR DUMMIES*

With the experience garnered from his last book tucked firmly under his belt, Mark applied what he learned in his approach to writing the first edition of this book. There's truly scrum in *Scrum For Dummies*.

He set up the book as a virtual task board. His sticky notes were virtual, and the columns from left to right were

- A product backlog listing all the chapters, front and back matter, and anything else relevant

- To do

- Doing

- Done

Each chapter included tasks such as research, write, edit (feedback!), revise, review, and approval. In some cases, multiple tasks were created (such as for multiple edits).

Requirements were chapters. Tasks were chapter activities. The publishing team members (development team) swarmed each section and chapter and then moved to the next. There were daily scrums in which each party outlined what he was doing and raised any impediments. Each weekly sprint was followed by a review and retrospective, in which team members worked out what could be done better.

The clarity was amazing. All members of the authoring team knew what they were supposed to be doing and by when.

News Media and Scrum

The news media has experienced a seismic shift all its own. Print has gone online, advertising changes with every new medium (such as print, radio, TV, online, social, and mobile), and readers' news-gathering experience has metamorphosed. For example, many people no longer get a daily newspaper delivered to their homes.

But in scrum, change is good. At least, scrum helps you harness change for improvement.

What the industry is experiencing is disruption. Clayton Christensen coined the concept of "disruptive innovation," which can be described as what happens when a new product or service enters an existing market and relentlessly gains share until it uproots well established rivals.

The biggest challenges for traditional print media organizations are finding ways to monetize their current product offerings and going digital. Print and digital are different beasts. Smart media companies that have both a print and digital presence have separated the two sides of their businesses to allow them to do what they do best. The digital side of these companies, as pointed out in Chapter 7, implement scrum. But what about the traditional sides?

Brady Mortensen, a newsroom veteran and senior director (product owner) of publishing systems at Deseret Digital Media, said,

> In reality, news organizations have probably been practicing a lot of scrum techniques for many years without realizing it. Daily scrum meetings are not uncommon. With local TV stations or daily papers, the "sprint" length is one day, and the end product is a collection of newscasts and a paper. There is also a usable product created at the end of each cycle. Newsrooms live and die by these practices. What would help traditional news organizations is to recognize that what they already do is scrum-like, but to embrace the techniques even more.

The companies that are flourishing in this new environment are those that have proved to be nimble — and especially those that have adopted scrum to identify their highest-risk areas at regular intervals and pivot (inspection and adaptation).

Organizations such as *The Washington Post*, *The Chicago Tribune*, and National Public Radio use aspects of scrum in their newsrooms. Some specific techniques are as follows.

» ***Chicago Tribune:*** Teams begin by asking who the users are, what they need, and what features can be included to fulfill those needs. Teams then prioritize features in piles labeled Must, Want, Nice, and Meh. The teams toss out the bottom two piles and work from feature to feature. When the deadline arrives, iteration stops.

The assigning editor is usually the product owner. The development team consists of journalists, designers, photographers, editors, and others related to developing content.

Scrum reduces the number of meetings, which can be overwhelming, especially in digital media.

» **NPR:** NPR uses a two-week sprint cycle, with a two-hour-long sprint planning meeting at the start.

Stand-up daily scrums last for 15 minutes. Teams coordinate who's working on what stories, and impediments are identified and removed.

» ***Washington Post:*** The paper has a specific agile technique for developing content for its live-blogging platform.

The team begins with a vision: What is the effect it wants to have on the user?

In the daily scrum meetings, the team decide what they are working on for that day. Journalists pair up for work, which is a process *The Post* had used since long before scrum was implemented. Two journalists sit at the same desk and finish the project. This intensifies the work and limits distractions.

The goal is to go live with the news as soon as possible, and then get feedback from the users and the group. Based on the feedback, the team adapts and adjusts for the next cycle.

Defining done for content

Using scrum to develop nonsoftware products and services, such as content for publication, is quite similar to using scrum for software. The definition of done for content development teams should clearly outline what it means to consider content ready for prime time.

Going back to our roadmap to value, a publishing scrum team should have a vision statement that states what readers' needs are, how the publication meets the needs of those readers and is differentiated in its market and industry, and how the vision ties in to the corporate strategy. (For more on vision statements, see Chapter 2.)

The roadmap reflects this vision by outlining the areas of editorial emphasis to be covered by the publication, including any seasonal considerations. The product backlog is a prioritized and ordered list of proposed features, series, and stories to be researched, developed, edited, and published.

The vision is the framework for defining what it means to have done content, one story or article at a time. The definition of done might look something like this:

With each article, we have succeeded in fulfilling our vision to [statement of how the need is met and differentiated] after we have

Addressed the who, what, when, where, and why in the lead. Those elements are not buried.

Ensured balance, making sure that both sides of an issue are represented.

Ensured that search engine optimization standards and requirements are met in article elements such as headline, tags, and body.

Cited at least one source for each side of the issue.

Checked twice for accuracy to avoid embellishing and bias.

Prepared accompanying content for social media posts.

Verified that line edits and copyedits are completed.

A newsroom in which these criteria are front and center for content curators, editors, and producers to see at all times provides consistency and clarity on what is expected and what success looks like.

The news-media scrum team

A content team director for a major regional news site identified the following scrum implementation. This team's role was to curate, edit, and post daily content to the site. Scrum is still applied, but the team wasn't developing code. The site's adoption of scrum covered the following issues:

>> What is the product? (News content customers want to read)

>> What is the product backlog? (Potential news stories and associated media posts, which were constantly changing)

>> What is the release? (Continuous delivery; content is delivered as soon as it is edited and approved)

>> What is the sprint duration? (The 24-hour news cycle)

>> When is sprint planning? (First thing every morning; backlog stories that have received editing approval are discussed)

>> When is the sprint review? (End of each day or before sprint planning each morning, which includes a review of the articles published and resulting analytics for inspection and adaptation for the next sprint's articles)

>> Who is on the development team? (Content curators, reporters, photographers, editors, graphic artists, and videographers)

>> Who is the product owner? (The managing editor)

>> Who is the scrum master? (A member of the development team who understands and has experience with scrum, and has the organizational clout to remove impediments for the team)

>> Who does backlog refinement, and when? (The entire development team and the product owner throughout each day, curating and evaluating proposed stories, including breaking news)

When these basic questions are asked and answered, the broader picture comes to light. Each role, artifact, and event can be identified and assigned.

Sprint flexibility

Daily sprints in a news organization often provide the flexibility needed for daily news feeds. You can't plan the news five days from now, but you can plan a day of story time — most of the time. Breaking and unexpected news stories can be dealt with during the sprint by direct communication among team members.

Media with longer content cycles, such as magazines (online and/or in print form), can have longer sprint cycles for content. Each feature — a section, article, chapter, or other segment — can be broken into requirements and tasks when appropriate.

4

Scrum for Business Functions

Optimize project portfolio performance.

Scale scrum across 1,000+ person project teams.

Fund projects incrementally and profitably.

Maximize business development and customer service teams.

Enhance IT and maintenance value and efficiency.

» **Enabling and securing IT tools**

» **Retaining and training talent**

» **Improve operational value**

» **Innovative maintenance and Support**

Chapter **12**

IT Management and Operations

Any sufficiently advanced technology is equivalent to magic.
— SIR ARTHUR C. CLARKE

I n Chapter 8, we discuss scrum in the software development industry, providing examples of scrum's power in this arena. Some people assume that information technology (IT) and software are one and the same, but that assumption is way off the mark.

Software development has to do with the creation of software applications that run on computer systems and electronic devices. Information technology is all about computer and telecommunications systems for storing, sending, and retrieving information.

Not every organization has a software development division, but it's rare indeed to find an organization that can survive without a staff of IT professionals devoted to the smooth flow and security of information.

IT operations can vary widely from one organization to another. Roles and responsibilities may differ, and even within an individual group, the type of work done may vary from day to day and quarter to quarter. Further, IT is experiencing rapid changes as technology continues to evolve and possibilities race ahead.

In any growing field, challenges abound. When the system gets overwhelmed and services get interrupted, mission-critical work may be delayed or even stopped, resulting in increased costs, wasted resources, loss of revenue, and even loss of customers. The backlog of an IT team can fill up so fast they can't keep up.

In this chapter, we look at IT management and operations, and describe how scrum provides time- and cost-saving solutions for modern challenges.

Big Data and Large-Scale Migration

The sheer scale of data is astounding, and even as we write this chapter, it's getting bigger. Trying to get your head around the size of Big Data is much like trying to picture a huge mathematical phenomenon such as the speed of the expanding universe. Big Data is so big that it goes beyond what most people can imagine.

The following numbers are just a few examples of how big Big Data can be:

>> Walmart conducts 1 million transactions per hour, feeding databases of more than 2.5 petabytes (about 167 times the size of the data in all the books in the Library of Congress).

>> Facebook houses more than 40 billion photographs.

>> eBay handles 50 petabytes of information every day.

>> Decoding the human genome requires analyzing 3 billion base pairs. The first time, the process took ten years; now it takes one week.

>> Cisco estimates that in 2016, the annual run rate for global Internet traffic was 1.2 zettabytes (ZB) per year or 96 exabytes (EB) per month. Annual global Internet traffic is expected to reach 3.3ZB per year, or 278EB per month, by 2021.

The importance of Big Data can't be overstated. Much of this data is highly personal and sensitive, and it can affect lives as well as bottom lines. The challenge is to gather, manage, and interpret data quickly, effectively, and correctly. Also, possible future uses for this data must be considered in the design of storage and retrieval processes. This data needs to become useful intelligence, not just data.

A significant challenge is that 80 percent of this data is unstructured (such as emails, blogs, spreadsheets, text documents, images, video, voice, and search logs). This unstructured segment is growing faster than structured data. In other words, the majority of data is a huge mess.

HOW MUCH IS A ZETTABYTE?

TECHNICAL STUFF

A zettabyte is billion gigabytes, or 10^{21} bytes of digital information. Here is the scale of data sizes:

- 1 byte is the equivalent of a single digital character of text (such as the letter *a*).
- 1KB is a kilobyte, or roughly 1,000 bytes of digital information.
- 1MB is a megabyte, or 1 million (1000^2) bytes of digital information.
- 1GB is a gigabyte, or 1 billion (1000^3) bytes of digital information.
- 1TB is a terabyte, or 1 trillion (1000^4) bytes of digital information.
- 1PB is a petabyte, or 1 quadrillion (1000^5) bytes of digital information.
- 1EB is an exabyte, or 1 quintillion (1000^6) bytes of digital information.
- 1ZB is a zettabyte, or 1 sextillion (1000^7) bytes of digital information.

Data security and protecting privacy are more important than ever; at the same time, security is more difficult to ensure than ever. Traditional data management frameworks and processes aren't capable of processing this quantity. Speed, flexibility, and instant feedback are needed. Six months is too long to hope that a new, untested system works. And chances are that in six months, the requirements will have changed, or a new gap will be identified.

To deal with this tsunami of data, many firms and organizations are moving to the cloud. Many organizations have their own in-house clouds or virtualized environments. (See Chapter 8 for details on cloud computing.)

Data warehouse project management

Data warehouse projects are traditionally thought to be difficult to manage. Although each segment or phase of the project may have a discernible beginning and end, the data warehouse itself is never finished; it's continually growing and changing.

REMEMBER

A data warehouse isn't some barbed-wire-fenced building on the outskirts of town. Rather, it's a process or framework for handling data within a firm or organization, or a knowledge-based applications architecture that facilitates strategic and tactical decision-making.

LARGE DATA MIGRATION

An example of successful implementation of scrum is a multibillion-dollar energy company with operations in the United States and Brazil. Frequent mergers and acquisitions created a need for timely, accurate integration of data. Senior management needed reports created on the new entities and their new products and customers. Specifically, management focused on energy-efficiency projects to keep a strong hold on that customer segment.

Data existed in multiple formats across multiple applications, including budget and financial data in spreadsheets, a customer relationship management (CRM) tool, and data from a variety of cloud-based customer surveys.

The scrum integration process went this way:

1. Roles were established.

   Stakeholders were identified as end users. The product owner represented the stakeholders and sponsors. The project manager became the scrum master. The development team was represented by the data architect, system architect, and an ETL (extract, transform, load) architect/resource.

2. The stakeholders and product owner determined the highest-priority starting point: budget data.

3. ETL was the scope of the initial project chunk. As data became available, the product owner worked with stakeholders to identify reports that could be implemented incrementally and plugged them into the product backlog for prioritization in upcoming sprints.

4. Sprint 1 was executed. Budget data was loaded into the data warehouse. The data was verified with sample reports.

5. Sprint 2 was executed. CRM data was loaded into the data warehouse. Sample reports were used to validate the data.

   After the second sprint, stakeholders identified new requirements in the budget data after comparing it with the loaded CRM data. These requirements were added to the product backlog and prioritized.

6. Sprint 3 was executed. Survey data was loaded and validated with sample reports.

   During the third sprint, new data sources were discovered and loaded.

7. Sprint 4 was executed. Integration of all three data sources was verified with sample reports.

8. In the remaining sprints, reports were written according to priority.

In a matter of months, not years, the entire database migration was finished. The data warehouse was fully functional, and a process was in place for managing new data and changes along the way. Part of the reason for the success of this project was how business and development teams worked together toward a common goal.

The process was quicker to market because it didn't entail the waterfall approach of loading all possible data from all possible sources and then testing. Rather, the highest-priority data was implemented first in phases and inspected and adapted along the way. New findings were incorporated in the next sprint, and the next-highest-priority data was implemented next.

A further complexity is that continuous merger and acquisition activity creates enterprisewide data-integration issues. New assets and groups are acquired or spun off, and corresponding data and processes need to be managed. Maintaining diverse legacy applications that don't integrate well can be costlier than conversion projects.

Enterprise resource planning

Enterprise resource planning (ERP) is a suite of integrated and dynamic software applications that organizations and corporations use to gather, manage, interpret, and integrate business processes, including planning, purchasing, manufacturing, inventory, marketing, sales, distribution, finance, and human resources.

Implementing an ERP system usually means doing simultaneous development across various functional areas (such as marketing, sales, inventory, and purchasing) to conduct a specific business transaction. Implementation involves the design and configuration of many modules simultaneously. These modules, while being developed individually, must also be designed for cross-functional application. During design of the sales module, for example, careful consideration is given to both upstream and downstream processes.

Think about how sales fits in the overall end-to-end process. You start with inventory, and subsequently, you need to be able to bill your orders. Therefore, the sales module must seamlessly integrate with your inventory module and your finance module (and your inventory module must integrate with your manufacturing and purchasing modules, which must integrate with your finance modules, and so on).

Unfortunately, designing and building these individual modules traditionally takes years before the integrated testing phase begins. By this time, any gaps between modules require even more time to identify and fix. One small gap between sales and finance can result in months of extra work. Commonly, this fix may not integrate perfectly with another module somewhere else in the process. When everyone works in silos until the integrated testing phase, early detection of gaps and misfits is difficult.

Traditionally, ERP providers handled this interdependency by locking in a specific development sequence. In fact, even parameters that weren't going to be used needed to be configured in the order defined by the ERP provider.

Now, with scaled scrum teams (see Chapter 13), you can do that customization in parallel, with each scrum team focusing on a specific functional area and using automated integration testing to ensure that the business transaction works across the modules. Following agile techniques allows integration testing to occur every day (from the first day) as opposed to months or years into the project.

Although these modular interdependencies may seem to be liabilities, they make it easier to divide the work into chunks that fit separate scrum teams running synchronized sprints. Product backlog prioritization is set at program level, and incremental requirement changes are minimized. Sprint backlog prioritization also falls in line. You maintain the flexibility of scrum and dramatically accelerate the pace of implementation. (We dive into this vertical slicing model in Chapter 13.)

ERP systems architecture is increasingly becoming oriented toward Software as a Service (SaaS; see Chapter 8), which means that monolith components are more modular than they used to be for client installations.

Also, the tasks required to configure ERP systems are usually repetitive, so cadence and estimation can be established early and provide accurate sizing and timing predictions.

In Chapter 13, we talk about scaling scrum across multiple teams. To tackle more of an ERP implementation project at once to speed delivery, multiple teams may work on each business-function component at the same time. Effective use of scaled scrum enables multiple scrum teams to structure their definition of done to include integration, regression, performance, security, and regression testing at the sprint level rather than release. Alignment of definition of done is required because ERP systems are difficult to correct when conflicts are introduced into production. Teams learn to be disciplined in their definition of done.

We've also found that scrum works well with these types of projects when they focus on delivering business intelligence for the organization. Visual reports of data have a clear business-focused requirement for users. The work of preparing the data (such as aggregation and manipulation) makes up the tasks supporting the delivery of a report to the specified user (such as an executive or manager).

CONVERTING LEGACY SYSTEMS

A not-for-profit client of ours took on a massive project of converting several legacy systems to a new ERP solution. Historically, this job would have been a nightmare. Apt description would have been hammering a square peg into a round hole or herding cats. But even those euphemisms are easy challenges compared with combining diverse data management systems.

The roadmap that the client set up indicated an 18-month project life. The vision was an end-to-end solution for the company's management of global real estate resources. The company took the following steps:

1. One team secured an open space that it organized as a scrum team room, complete with a full wall dedicated to a task board. Another team set up shop next door, within earshot for easy collaboration.

2. With the help of the stakeholders, the product owner determined the first minimum viable product (MVP) — a set of the most common processes relating to leasing activities. Users could benefit from these common processes right away.

3. The release was planned, including a few sprints, with the new MVP as the goal. The team went to work.

4. Developers were added to the team to set up third-party integrations.

5. Shadowing and pairing were used immediately, as the system was new to everyone. Team members wanted to achieve cross-functionality as quickly as possible.

   The team also invited a member of the traditional deployment team to join full-time. He sat with the scrum team and learned the configuration steps during the sprints. When it came time to deploy to production, deployment came off without a hitch thanks to shared knowledge and up-front testing.

6. The team moved on to integrate new features of the roadmap, while customers enjoyed the benefits of the recently developed leasing features.

Much that was learned from this first release was incorporated into future releases for different aspects of the new system, such as planning, building, operations, and maintenance. Through the scrum process, the team got something in front of the customer quickly and could move forward comfortably on the next-highest-priority features.

Multiyear ERP implementations used to be common, but organizations can't wait that long in today's fast-paced market. Organizations need solutions faster and cheaper. Customers want to see a return on their investment as quickly as possible, with improved customer satisfaction.

Iterating, inspecting, and adapting through scrum make shortened implementations possible.

The Service-versus-Control Conundrum

The value of an IT group is staggering. This group keeps information coursing throughout an organization as the technology systems it manages become more sophisticated and complex. Further complicating the job of an IT group is the easy availability of other software applications and cloud resources, and an increased trend in employees bringing their own devices to work (BYOD) or bringing in outside applications (BYOA).

TECHNICAL STUFF

BYOD means *bring your own device*, specifically referring to the use of outside phones, laptops, and tablets not supported by IT. *BYOA* stands for *bring your own application* and refers to procuring and bringing software tools and subscriptions.

BYOD and BYOA are widespread. A recent survey by Syntonic found that 60% of companies over 100 employees have a BYOD friendly policy. If employees don't feel that they have the tools they need from IT, it's natural for them to seek solutions elsewhere, especially when those solutions are so readily available through SaaS and mobile apps. This loss of control becomes a significant concern for IT teams when nonsupported devices and applications create security risks or interfere with enterprise-approved solutions.

The fact is, a balance can be achieved between providing employees the tools they need to do their jobs and maintaining control and security. Following are some examples of how you can use scrum to manage common issues in IT:

>> IT can't control the personal devices and apps that employees use, but it can control data access. Use scrum to develop apps that securely access the data. The scrum framework narrows the features so that the MVP is quickly identified and implemented.

>> Have IT members participate as stakeholders in other scrum teams' sprint reviews so that IT knows firsthand what development teams are working on and what tools they're using. Questions can be asked on the spot, and needs can be addressed in an informed manner.

>> Invite department representatives to IT sprint review meetings to get their feedback on the IT roadmap. They can learn what's important to the organization for developing products. In this way, the business comes into alignment with IT.

Treat the problem, not the symptom, by giving employees the tools they need, when they need them, in the way they need them. Scrum helps you do this.

Security challenges

You may have heard some of these terms: *bots, worms, malware, phishing,* and *security breach.* For some people, the Internet is fertile ground for malicious activities. Major data breaches are making the headlines far too regularly. Following are just a few examples of companies and organizations that recently experienced compromised customer information:

» August 2017: Equifax (143 million people affected)

» June 2017: Republican National Committee (200 million people affected)

» February 2017: PayPal/TIO (1.6 million people affected)

» October 2016: Uber (57 million people affected)

» February 2015: Anthem healthcare (78.8 million people affected)

Too often, security is an afterthought. Managers sometimes view it as nice to have and say, "We'll deal with it when it becomes a problem." Security risks are increasing and need to be addressed earlier rather than later. Following are some common ways that scrum can help expose security-related issues and facilitate improvements in the way they're handled:

» Refine your definition of done. At both release and sprint level, the definition of done is critical. Decide on security requirements that should be met at each timebox. By adding a security task to each requirement to address your definition of done, costs of mitigating security risk can be spread out over the life of the project. Make security a high priority from the first appropriate spot.

» As a scrum team member in any role if security isn't as high a priority as you feel it should be, address it at the next retrospective. The business stakeholders and/or product owner may need to be trained about the issues. Identify the issues and place them in the product backlog.

» Have IT team members attend project team sprint reviews and provide security feedback.

» Automate security testing as much as possible. Consider automating penetration testing, cross-site scripting, and vulnerability scanning.

» Consider establishing a security guild within the organization that promotes awareness and skill development on security common practices and technologies throughout the organization.

The Retiring-Boomer Gap

The entry-level employees taking the place of retiring Baby Boomers have a different generational mindset than their predecessors. Personal growth and ambition are often higher values than staying with the same firm for an entire career. This means that those long-term employees you could always count on to be there will be fewer and fewer, which can present operational challenges. The following agile practices can help you retain and grow newer employees:

>> Create a mentoring program for those who are about to retire and their younger replacements. This program increases the efficiency in transfer of knowledge as well as increases buy-in and loyalty.

>> Give new IT employees projects and responsibilities outside their comfort zone. Give them training and new things to learn to increase mental and emotional engagement. Guilds (see the nearby sidebar) facilitate this process by providing pools of experts in each area. Senior- and junior-level developers enhance their skills by working together.

>> Create cross-functionality activities such as pairing and shadowing (see Chapter 4).

TIP

These activities can also help longer-term employees keep growing. People on their way out of organizations sometimes resist change, as they just want to finish those last years before they retire. Guilds can provide a means to tap their expertise and immense value. Get these employees out of their comfort zones by organizing workshops, lunch-and-learn sessions, and other types of training.

Encourage new people to grow and then empower them with the means to do so. Where boredom and routine can motivate people to leave for greener pastures, challenges, opportunities for growth and recognition, and a sense of purpose help people stay and commit.

Profit-and-Loss Potential

The business value of IT is immense. Its value needs to be communicated and demonstrated regularly to the rest of the organization. Sometimes, however, this value is overlooked in the face of problems that piggyback on technology. A huge opportunity lies in communicating clearly the value that IT brings to everyone involved — even if these benefits are only in the form of risks mitigated.

REMEMBER

The key question to ask is, "Does this task or activity improve our organization's core priorities?" If so, keep it in and prioritize. If not, figure out how to eliminate that function and focus on mission-critical tasks.

Increasing visibility to the organization (through such artifacts as IT's prioritized product backlog and increments demonstrated at sprint reviews) gives insight to the entire organization of how IT works to remove bottlenecks in information and communications flow and provides the tools to enhance productivity. When the entire organization understands the value that IT brings, interactions between IT and other departments become more collaborative and IT's solutions become clear enablers of corporate strategy.

Just like a scrum team increasing its velocity from 25 to 27, all it takes is a small operational cost percentage savings to make a big bottom-line improvement over time.

Energy efficiency is a hot button these days and is one such example of how saving a little bit amounts to a lot over time. A wide array of tools is becoming available to help save costs on energy. Through better monitoring and application of energy-saving products, a few percentage points in cost can be saved; this allows IT to bring in more profits.

IBM estimates that IT and energy costs combined account for up to 75 percent of operational costs and up to 60 percent of capital expenditures in an organization.

It's estimated that a 25,000-square-foot data center uses more than $4 million in energy each year. While this number won't be eliminated at once, by using incremental steps to inspect and adapt, costs can be decreased gradually and appropriately. A small percentage savings out of $4 million isn't bad.

Innovation versus Stability

Organizations rely on IT operations for stability, performance, and uptime, yet IT must always be innovating, which implies the need to change quickly and often. Stability and change conflict. This conflict is solved by tightening collaboration between operations and development teams. Rather than developing new technology and throwing it over the fence for operations to support, and vice versa, the operations side of the business builds sandboxes, or sets of standards within which development teams can build.

Every time development teams make code changes in the process of innovation, they can breathe easy knowing that those code changes are made within the set of standards agreed on between operations and development. Changes in database structures or designs within operational standards avert the risks inherent in the same changes made in development silos with little or no collaboration with operations.

These standards are incorporated into a team's definition of done. IT can rest assured that within each sprint, the teams are staying in the sandbox with each requirement. When changes in the sandbox need to be made, development and operations consult and establish the new boundaries.

The need for improved coordination is key, especially in software development, which is where DevOps comes in.

DevOps

Development and operations (DevOps) is a growing solution to a gap in developing software applications. Figure 12-1 shows how DevOps addresses coordination challenges.

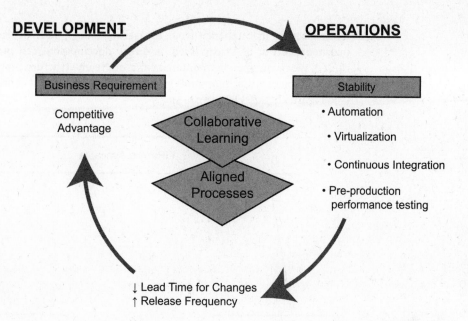

FIGURE 12-1:
DevOps balancing a business requirement against stability.

Traditional IT tasks are being shifted to DevOps team members, which not only offloads tasks from IT, but also enables development teams with DevOps team members to take their product development further to production with fewer IT dependencies. Virtualized data centers make this practice increasingly possible because IT manages the platform, which makes creating new virtualized environments possible by someone with DevOps capabilities on a project scrum team.

IT dependencies can now be done within the scrum team. Higher quality and faster speed to finish are achieved within the sprints.

Maintenance

After an application is deployed, maintenance teams provide support. This support can be in the form of responding to support inquiries, fixing defects, and implementing minor enhancements to address functionality gaps in production.

When scrum teams focus on project work, whether software or IT, triaging operational issues is disruptive. Project and maintenance work are quite different. They require different types of work and effort by developers, which also involves a different cadence. If a project scrum team maintains operational or maintenance responsibilities, development of new functionality is interrupted frequently, affecting release schedules that are of business value and functionality to the customer. (See Chapter 13 for more about the cost of delay from thrashing a development team.)

By separating maintenance from the scrum teams' new development efforts, maintenance can be streamlined, and new development can progress uninterrupted. We recommend a maintenance scrum team structure that separates these two functions so that interruptions are minimized without increasing overhead (see Figure 12-2 and Figure 12-3).

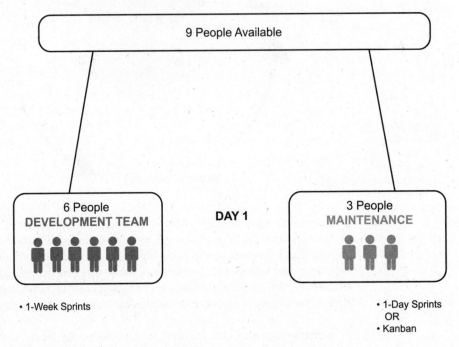

FIGURE 12-2:
A common practice for separating maintenance from the project development team in scrum.

Kanban within a scrum structure

We introduce the kanban concept in Chapter 6. Some scrum and agile teams use a Kanban board to visualize their workflow. Here's how the process in Figures 12-2 and 12-3 works:

>> At the start of a new release cycle, split out a small subset of the development team with enough skill and knowledge to effectively maintain the product into a maintenance team.

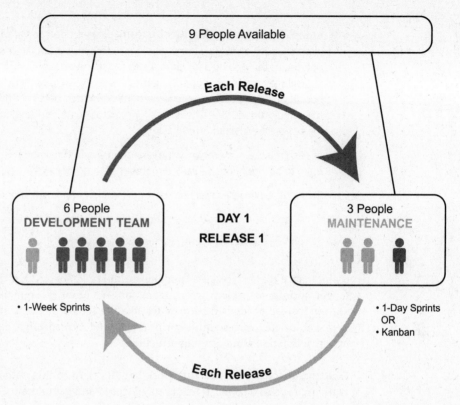

9 People Available

Each Release

6 People
DEVELOPMENT TEAM

DAY 1
RELEASE 1

3 People
MAINTENANCE

• 1-Week Sprints

• 1-Day Sprints
OR
• Kanban

Each Release

FIGURE 12-3:
Team members
are rotated
among teams at
reasonable
intervals to
ensure cross-
pollination
of knowledge
and cross-
functionality
of skills.

As shown in Figure 12-2, if you have a nine-person development team, you can take three developers and form a separate maintenance scrum team, leaving six developers to do new product development work in the existing scrum team. Your team size may vary. Fewer or more than three maintenance team members may be needed. (Although the existing scrum team is now smaller, it will no longer be thrashing between new product development and maintenance work. Fewer people doesn't mean less output. Actually, because thrashing has been eliminated, the team should be able to significantly increase its output.)

» The maintenance team runs one-day sprints or kanban to respond to rapidly changing requirements (often changing daily). Each morning, the team triages and plans the priorities for the day. It executes the work planned throughout the day. At the end of the day, the team reviews what it accomplished and clears that work for release. (Release can happen at any time and doesn't need to happen daily.)

» Maintenance teams can be smaller than new development teams. The product owner and scrum master for the maintenance team are often the same as for the project team. Thrashing is minimal, if it occurs at all, because both are working on a single application.

- » At each project team release (or if a team releases often and at reasonable intervals, such as 90 days), one member of the project team transitions to the operations team to be a full-time dedicated member, providing the necessary knowledge transfer for supporting the release. Again, thrashing is minimized because it's done at release level, and the team members continue to work on the same product. (See Chapter 13 for more about minimizing thrashing to maximize stability and profitability.)

- » At each release, a member of the operations team transitions to the project team to be a full-time dedicated member of that team.

- » Everyone eventually does both new development and operational work.

- » Cross-pollination of product and domain knowledge is a key benefit.

- » Cross-functionality builds through rotations as well.

Maintenance teams typically run daily sprints or kanban rather than one week or longer sprints, as project scrum teams do. We often recommend running daily sprints instead of kanban because we like the forced product and process touch points associated with scrum's sprint review and retrospective, but kanban can be effective if done within a scrum structure.

Kanban's practice of visualizing workflow fits right in line with scrum. Limiting work in progress also helps teams stay focused and get to done.

Managing flow and estimating based on lead time (elapsed time from the request to delivery) and cycle time (elapsed time from the start of work to delivery) are also useful for teams using kanban. Scrum teams may find lead and cycle time useful in their planning and communicating with stakeholders as well.

REMEMBER

Lead time is the amount of time between receiving a request and delivering the finished product. *Cycle time* is the time between when the product gets started and when it's delivered. Therefore, lead time is what the stakeholder often cares about.

Teams using kanban are also aware of the theory of constraints, meaning that the team's system is limited by several constraints. In scrum, velocity is a constraint, and the scrum master continually looks for ways to remove organizational drag to increase velocity, thus reducing it as a constraint.

Kanban falls short in its lack of a forced feedback mechanism. It's very easy for teams using kanban to avoid this feedback loop and perpetually communicate among themselves and with stakeholders by saying, "Yeah, we have work in progress, and we're making progress." The Kanban board is visible, but the inspect and adapt efforts for both the product and the process may not be effective. Scrum provides structure for that process to kanban.

In the context of one-day sprints, if you're concerned about the overhead of daily sprints, don't be. A one-day sprint is one fifth of a one-week sprint. The time cost works out to be incredibly efficient and minimal. Here's the breakdown in minutes:

>> Daily sprint planning rounds up to 25 minutes maximum. Be sure to involve the stakeholders who requested the requirement as needed to help clarify anything the development team needs to understand about the requirements.

>> Daily sprint review becomes 15 minutes maximum.

>> Daily sprint retrospective is 10 minutes maximum. Be sure to inspect and adapt every single day, even if you have an emergency and everyone just wants to go home.

>> Also do retrospectives at macro levels, in sync with the development team's sprint retrospective, as this practice allows for larger-scale inspection.

>> Daily scrums won't be necessary because your sprint planning in the morning takes care of coordination and synchronizing priorities. Impediments need to be addressed as they arise throughout the day, however, so the scrum master needs to be vigilant and to proactively follow up on known or potential impediments throughout the day.

The key to one-day sprints is splitting the requests so that they fit in a day, which takes practice. In the beginning, our teams did one-week batch releases. When they first transitioned to their new one-day cadence, the number of fixes completed by week's end decreased. Customer satisfaction still increased, however, because customers went from waiting a week to getting something every day. Waiting and satisfaction are opposing dynamics.

Chapter **13**
Portfolio Management

There is nothing so useless as doing efficiently that which should not be done at all.

— PETER DRUCKER

Portfolio management is the simultaneous coordination, integration, management, prioritization, and control of several projects at the same time across the entire product or organization.

The number-one issue in portfolio management is a failure of leadership to prioritize projects properly and allocate talent appropriately. This failure of leadership is masked by thrashing or moving people across several projects at the same time. Communication fails, priorities get dropped, and the squeaky-wheel syndrome takes over (the loudest stakeholder gets the most attention and resources).

You have only one way to handle the situation of having more projects than you have talent: Prioritize effectiveness over efficiency. If an organization is highly efficient but is working on the wrong features, how effective will that organization be? It's far more critical to be effective. Work on only the highest-prioritized projects and the highest-prioritized features of those projects. Profitability flows from this model.

In this chapter, we go through the main challenges in portfolio management and discuss the scrum solutions that are available. We look at how Lean Startup is a natural fit for scrum and how to scale large multi-team projects with scrum.

Four key challenges, when they're not handled effectively, prevent good portfolio management:

>> People allocation and prioritization

>> Dependencies and fragmentation

>> Disconnect between projects and business objectives

>> Displaced accountability

People allocation and prioritization

Above all else, not having enough time, money, or people is the biggest constraint on portfolio management. Lack of resources forces leaders to prioritize effectively, to reduce organizational drag (such as thrashing) on talent, or to push the burden down to a level that doesn't have the clout to fight back. Unfortunately, many leaders choose the latter. Often, squeaky-wheel syndrome reigns, and the loudest stakeholder voice is the one that directs the action. Corporate strategy, not whims or the loudest voice, should drive prioritization.

Prioritizing effectively means choosing only those projects that are highest-value and highest-risk and feeding them to stable teams one a time. If you have only one scrum team, feed it one project at a time. If you have five teams, feed each team only one project at a time. If one project is too big for one team, have as many teams as needed swarm around the highest-priority project until it's done; then feed the teams the next project.

WARNING

Racing in reverse is a concept that we teach regarding spending too much time on the wrong things. If you're not effective, you're racing in reverse. If you're pushing people to work more, put in overtime, and pump out beyond their means, you *increase* the number of defects, which increases future work and cost. You can see Mark's webinar on this topic at https://platinumedge.com/blog/video-mark-laytons-racing-reverse-presentation.

The project prioritization conundrum can be addressed by asking one question: If this project isn't high-priority enough to have dedicated talent, is it necessary right now? If the answer is no, the best thing to do is finish the highest priority projects first and then ask this question again.

A HIERARCHY OF THRASHING

No matter what thrashing looks in your organization, apply scrum to minimize the impact of it. Just remember — the more stable your team, the higher your profitability. Following are descriptions of the various faces of thrashing:

Team is stable for project duration: Here the project is stable with no thrashing because the team is focused for the entire project until $AC + OC > V$ (see Chapter 5). This is the most efficient structure. It will quickly produce the best quality possible and maximizes profitability.

Team is stable for release duration: The team is focused on project A until they have something releasable to customers. They then switch to project B until they have something releasable for customers, then they switch to project C, and so on. This is worse than project stability.

Team is stable for sprint duration: The team is focused on project A for the entire sprint. They then switch to project B for a same-duration sprint, then switch to project C, and so on. This is worse than release stability.

Team is stable for the day's duration: The team spends Monday working on project A. They then switch to project B on Tuesday, project C on Wednesday, and so on. This is worse than sprint stability.

Team is stable for blocks of hours: The team spends every morning working on project A, the afternoon on project B, and so on. This is worse than day stability.

Minute-by-minute team thrashing: This is the most common portfolio management approach. Individual team members get started working on project A; 45 minutes later, an emergency occurs on project B, which takes them until lunch. After lunch, they attempt to restart project A, but something comes up on project C that takes the afternoon. On the next day, they are back to square one with project A because of mental remobilization time. The process continues until a project close to an influential executive is so late that the team is forced to spend their evenings and weekends working on just that project. This is the worst-case scenario.

(continued)

(continued)

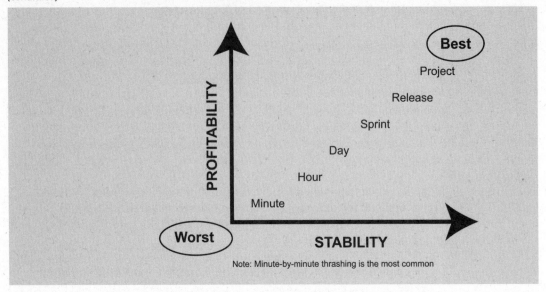

Best Project
Release
Sprint
Day
Hour
Minute

Worst | **STABILITY**

Note: Minute-by-minute thrashing is the most common

Dependencies and fragmentation

With projects running simultaneously, bottlenecks from dependency issues arise, as do delays because of integration difficulties. In traditional project management, people, money, and equipment are shared. It's not uncommon for managers to allocate each person across multiple projects (50 percent here, 40 percent there, and the last 10 percent for some other project) just to feel as thought they're using every ounce of power available and making the organization as efficient as possible.

REMEMBER

People lose a minimum of 30 percent of time in the cognitive mobilization–demobilization associated with task switching. Having employees divide their time among multiple projects is detrimental to their productivity.

Historically, project managers end up trying to do everything at the same time because they're under pressure from business owners to deliver across several areas. They end up racing after different goals without separating and prioritizing what needs to be done first. Dependency issues tie the projects in knots because the core dependent project wasn't executed first.

Disconnect between projects and business objectives

Most projects begin in line with business objectives, but as time passes, managers continue to brainstorm product ideas and hypothesize all the directions the product could take. Unfortunately, without consistent feedback loops with customers and stakeholders, and without daily coordination with the development team, the scope creeps in many directions. The more time that has passed since the initial planning, the more the common understanding of what the objectives are breaks down until the original objectives become unknown.

This scope creep reflects the lack-of-prioritization issue at the core of the problem. With scrum, prioritization and reprioritization happen continuously throughout the project at the roadmap, release, sprint, and daily-scrum levels. The product backlog always has the next-highest-priority items ready to go, and products are released in order of priority.

Displaced accountability

Being the bearer of bad news to management is no one's favorite task. Even when a team knows that its project is awry, members may hesitate to tell senior management because of the perceived negative effect on their careers. Unfortunately, the longer a team waits to deliver bad news, the worse the problems become.

Although early and frequent communication of impediments and problems is the scrum style, traditional project management supports a "tell me when it's done" mindset; business owners often don't know that their project has gone astray until it's too late to correct it.

Accountability needs to be in the right place, not assigned to a middleman project manager who's not doing the work of product creation. Scrum's transparency removes this issue. The product owner has ownership of the business objectives and priorities, and the development team owns how to implement those goals and how much it can commit to achieving. Team members share their solutions with the product owner every day of each sprint and to the stakeholders at the end of each sprint.

The product owner doesn't answer for the developers, and the developers don't answer for the product owner. Each person answers for himself or herself. Scrum provides the opportunity for appropriately placed accountability, transparency, and ownership.

Scrum solutions

Scrum conserves resources for business owners by placing high-risk and high-priority items first. The approach is "if you fail, fail early, fail fast." If business owners don't think that a project will come to fruition as they want it to, they have the opportunity to pull the plug early and save precious resources and time.

When the actual cost (AC) and opportunity cost (OC) outweigh the value of the project (V), it's time to move on. Effective portfolio managers use the equation shown in Chapter 5, AC + OC > V, as a termination trigger.

With the scrum framework, a portfolio manager can determine within a few sprints whether a project is viable. The project moves forward speedily and efficiently, or it's removed from the backlog and the talent are freed for higher-priority projects. Less stigma is involved in having a project fail because the costs of failure have been dramatically reduced.

Chapter 5 discusses work-in-progress limits for development teams. Those same limits apply to portfolio management. You can have as many projects open as you have scrum teams. A stable team can swarm on a requirement, a release, and a project until it's done and then take on the next-highest-priority project. If you have multiple teams, great. Align skills with projects. Because teams are dedicated and stable, they get projects done serially faster than if talent is thrashed among projects. *All* projects complete under a dedicated team model before *any* project completes under a thrashed model.

Figure 13-1 illustrates the difference between running serial projects (dedicated teams) and parallel projects (thrashing teams).

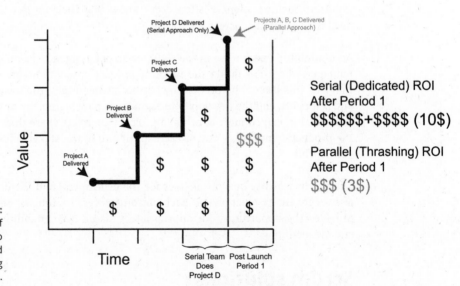

FIGURE 13-1: Financial cost of delay due to thrashing instead of dedicating teams.

In this example, a portfolio has three projects, each running in succession (that is, serially). Assume that one unit of value can be produced in one unit of time and each project can produce one unit of value ($) when it's complete.

The cost of thrashing the team is at least 30 percent more time to finish each project — say, 33 percent for this scenario. Over three projects (99 percent), that's roughly the equivalent of a whole project's length by thrashing the teams around.

Going only one unit of time past deployment of the serial projects, the parallel projects return $$$ (3$ — one $ for each project deployed) at the end of that period. The serial projects return $$$$$$+$$$$ (10$, which is more than three times the return on investment [ROI]).

Stop thrashing. Run one project at a time through one team at a time. When you dedicate teams, everyone gets projects earlier and gets an earlier, higher ROI.

As executives start prioritizing to eliminate thrashing, the feedback loop of sprint reviews ensures that stakeholders (including executives) are brought into direct alignment with the scrum team's work. Through communicating the highest-priority items, they can ensure that they get what they want, and developers avoid the squeaky-wheel syndrome.

Goals are kept in alignment, and strategies and tactics are prioritized. Constant communication means that problems and impediments are brought up early so that solutions can be applied or directions changed. Creative innovation and experimentation can be encouraged without fear of undue waste.

REMEMBER

Don't underestimate the cost of delaying delivered value. Delaying delivery is like paying a high rate of interest over a long time because the organization is unable to prioritize the portfolio. Have these mature and potentially difficult conversations up front to avoid large debt payments in the future.

Lean Startup

Forming your own startup company is no small endeavor. You have all the normal challenges associated with starting a business venture, including use of personal funds to finance the endeavor and planning for success. Startups have certain portfolio advantages over larger established organizations and huge potential to bring value. Their small size increases their agility, and decisions can be made quickly without the weight of corporate bureaucracy. Still, making tough decisions early and getting minimum viable product out the door faster than everyone else is critical for entrepreneurial survival.

Lean Startup is scrum for startups.

Typically in the waterfall method, many startups begin with an idea, spend time and money developing that idea into a formal multiyear business plan, and hope that it's what the customer wants. Many times, startups fail before they have a chance to show the client the product. Recent data shows that 80 percent of new businesses fail within the first 18 months.

REMEMBER

In one sense, an 80 percent failure rate is terrible. Those odds aren't betting odds. On the other hand, all those potential competitors are being swept away on the tide of ineffectiveness. With Lean Startup, new businesses can expand on their advantages and avoid unnecessary pitfalls.

In traditional project frameworks, the client is often left out of initial planning and prioritizing conversations, which misses the opportunity to collaborate and tailor the project. One size doesn't fit all, and the user could remain unsatisfied and unengaged.

With Lean Startup, the same inspect-and-adapt approach used with the scrum framework is applied from the beginning. The feedback loop is critical. Sprint planning, sprint reviews, and sprint retrospectives allow constant inspection and adaptation at the startup level.

REMEMBER

With Lean Startup, you don't have to wait months or years for valuable prototypes to be made. With the prioritization process of highest value and risk, you have products to place in stakeholders' and customers' hands within weeks. The feedback you gain, you can immediately use for future iterations.

You can also address critical yet often-overlooked questions such as these:

>> Should this product be created?

>> Does the product work at its most basic level?

>> Is the product economically viable?

Before you commit huge sums of money, basic questions and answers can be brought to light. "Fail early, fail cheap" is a form of success.

TECHNICAL STUFF

Pivoting is part of the Lean Startup world. You pivot when you inspect and adapt and then adjust your course based on information you gleaned from the feedback loop.

The prioritization process is driven by reality, not hope. As features are developed and feedback is gained, that data is immediately incorporated into new iterations (sprints) and requirements.

The Lean Startup model follows the pattern build, measure, and learn, which is essentially the scrum model:

>> **Build:** The sprint cycle creates the product increment supporting the release goal (minimum viable product [MVP]).

>> **Measure:** The feedback is received in both the sprint review and the sprint retrospective.

>> **Learn:** New requirements are added to the product backlog as a result of customer feedback, intitiating the plan of action for the improvements learned from the retrospective.

DROPBOX

Dropbox, a file-storage and file-sharing application, was once a product that people didn't think they needed. The company used the MVP concept to get people to use its product early in its development. How do you sell something that people don't know they need? Henry Ford once said "If I had asked people what they wanted, they would have said faster horses." Lean Startup is a great agile tool for enabling entrepreneurial innovation.

Because developing Dropbox involved extensive integrations with computer platforms and operating systems, developing a full prototype wasn't feasible, given the complexity of the engineering necessary. Dropbox solved this dilemma by creating a video targeted to technologically savvy early adopters, showing why they needed the product and how easy it was to use. The company knew that it needed feedback as early as possible, and that feedback needed to come from the people who would give the developers the most knowledgeable feedback. Taking a Lean Startup approach allowed Dropbox to drive early traffic and grow its waiting list from 5,000 to 75,000. Literally overnight, the company had validation that its product was what the market wanted. The video was the first MVP and captivated the audience for the next MVP, which was the highest-valued file-storage and file-sharing features.

The Dropbox MVP was an opportunity to demonstrate to customers what they didn't know that they needed, and to quickly and inexpensively validate or nullify their hypothesis of the market demand.

Scaling Scrum for Large Portfolios

Scrum in essence was designed for decomposed projects (projects broken down to achievable goals) that could be started and finished quickly. A scrum team consists of about six developers, a scrum master, and a product owner. A natural limit exists on what a team of this size can accomplish. Some projects are large enough to require more than one standard scrum team.

Scaling scrum occurs when multiple scrum teams are working on a project or portfolio of projects that have some level of affinity. Microsoft Office is one example. One team may have worked on Word, another on Excel, and a third on PowerPoint. All the teams had to be integrated and working together effectively for Office to be sold as one package, however. Many projects are so large that they require multiple teams and projects. Scrum has the ability to meet this need.

REMEMBER

Whenever multiple teams work toward a single release package, an enterprise-level scrum model is required to ensure effective coordination, communication, integration, and removal of impediments.

A Vertical Slicing Overview

Vertical slicing is a form of scaling scrum in which several scrum teams are established to achieve the program goal. Each scrum team works in synchronized sprints of the same length on a separate portion or module of the overall product, and those modules get integrated by an integration scrum team after each sprint. The integration scrum team lags the development scrum teams by one sprint and is its own scrum team, with its own dedicated development team members, product owner, and scrum master.

Figure 13-2 illustrates how each team's features feed into the integration team's backlog for architectural and system-level coordination.

The integration scrum team handles all system-level development work for the integration of functionality produced by the teams that feed into it and provides architectural oversight to unify the teams.

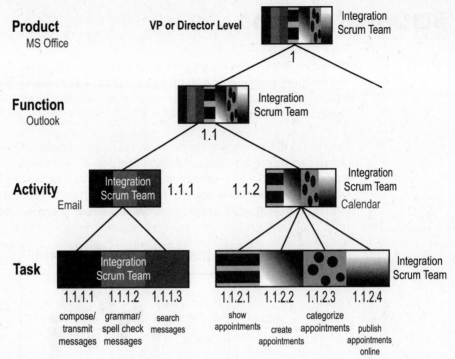

Product
MS Office

VP or Director Level

Integration
Scrum Team

1

Function
Outlook

Integration
Scrum Team

1.1

Activity
Email

Integration
Scrum Team

1.1.1

1.1.2

Integration
Scrum Team
Calendar

Task

Integration
Scrum Team

Integration
Scrum Team

1.1.1.1 1.1.1.2 1.1.1.3

compose/   grammar/   search
transmit   spell check messages
messages   messages

1.1.2.1   1.1.2.2   1.1.2.3   1.1.2.4

show   categorize
appointments   create   appointments   publish
              appointments   appointments
                                       online

FIGURE 13-2:
An enterprise
scrum team,
including an
integration team.

Take Microsoft Office as an illustration:

1. A scrum team develops the functionality for compose/transmit messages (requirement ID 1.1.1.1).

2. Another team develops the functionality for grammar/spell check messages (1.1.1.2).

3. A third scrum team develops the functionality for search messages (1.1.1.3).

4. The integration scrum team does the development work to integrate the functionality from the first three teams into a package that the Email integration team can integrate into the Email module.

5. The Outlook integration team integrates Email, Calendar, Contacts, and other modules into an Outlook package that can be integrated into the entire Microsoft Office suite.

In this example, integration teams operate as separate scrum teams, with dedicated team members for each role.

Scrum of Scrums

The scrum of scrums model facilitates effective integration, coordination, and collaboration among scrum teams by means of vertical slicing. Almost all scaling frameworks we show you in this chapter use scrum of scrums to enable daily coordination among scrum teams.

Figure 13-3 illustrates how people on one team coordinate daily with people in the same roles on other teams regarding priorities, dependencies, and impediments that affect the broader program team. The scrum of scrums for each role is facilitated by the integration-level person for each role. Thorough integration and release efforts establish a consistent, regular scrum of scrums model.

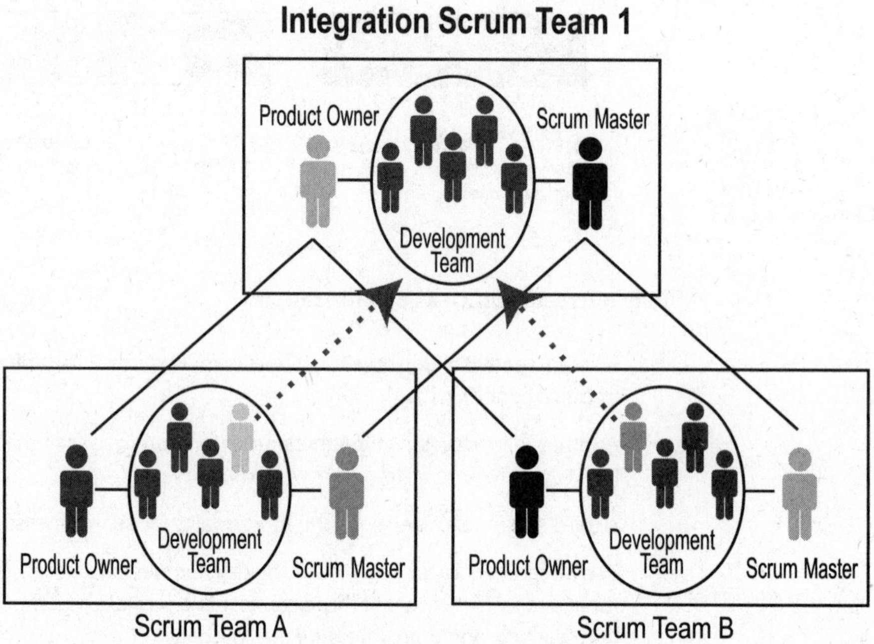

Integration Scrum Team 1

FIGURE 13-3: Scrum of scrums for coordination of scrum teams.

Each day, scrum teams hold their own daily scrums at approximately the same time, in separate locations. Following these daily scrums, scrum of scrums meetings (described in the following sections) occur.

Product owner scrum of scrums

Each day, following the scrum teams' daily scrums, the product owners from each team meet with the integration team product owner for no longer than 15 minutes. They address the requirements being completed and make any adjustments based on the realities uncovered during daily scrums. Each product owner addresses the following:

>> The business requirements that each product owner has accepted or rejected since the last product owners' meeting

>> The requirements that should be accepted by the next meeting

>> Which requirements are impeded and need help from other teams to resolve (example: "John, we won't be able to do requirement 123 until you complete requirement xyz from your current sprint backlog")

The integration team product owner makes the cross-team prioritization decisions necessary to ensure that the impediments are addressed during the daily scrum of scrums.

Development team scrum of scrums

Each day after the teams' daily scrums, one development team representative from each scrum team attends the integration team's daily scrum (which is the scrum of scrums for developers) and participates with the integration development team members in discussing the following:

>> The team's accomplishments since the last integration team scrum

>> The team's planned accomplishments between now and the next meeting

>> Technical concerns with which the team needs help

>> Technical decisions that the team has made

>> How to prevent potential issues

TIP

Consider rotating the development team members who attend the scrum of scrums (the integration team's daily scrum), daily or for each sprint, to ensure that everyone stays tuned in to the integration efforts of the portfolio.

Scrum master scrum of scrums

The scrum masters from each scrum team also meet with the integration scrum team scrum master for no longer than 15 minutes to address the impediments that each team is dealing with. Each scrum master addresses the following:

>> The individual team-level impediments resolved since the last time meeting with the integration team and how those impediments were resolved (in case other scrum masters run into the issue and can implement the solution)

WHO OWNS THE ARCHITECTURE?

Your organization should have existing architectural standards, coding standards, and style guides. This way, each team doesn't have to reinvent the wheel. But a common question is "Who is responsible for architecture in a vertically sliced program?" The answer is that it depends on which modules will be affected by the decision.

Consider an architectural decision that needs to be made and that will affect only module A. The development team of module A would make that decision. If it were going to affect multiple teams, the development team at the integration level that all affected teams roll into would make that decision. That integration level might be one level up or four levels up.

Using Figure 13-4 as an example, an architectural decision affecting two of the Email module teams (1.1.1.2 and 1.1.1.3) would be made by the Email integration team (1.1.1). A decision affecting the search messages Email module team (1.1.1.3) and the Calendar integration scrum team (1.1.2) would be made by the Outlook integration scrum team (1.1). Vertical slicing is a simple way to maintain the autonomy of each scrum team to deliver valuable functionality within a wider program context. It is also effective at helping teams have timely and relevant conversations about constraints and progress.

>> New impediments identified since the last meeting and which impediments the team needs help resolving

>> Potential impediments that everyone should be aware of

The integration team scrum master makes sure that escalated impediments are addressed after the daily scrum of scrums.

A single product backlog exists in a vertical slicing model, and team attributes are assigned to those requirements as they're broken down and move to the development scrum team. With this model, you can see the overall program and quickly filter down to your own team's piece of that program.

Scrum at Scale

This model facilitates alignment through roles with Scrum at Scale. The Scrum at Scale approach for scrum teams working together is a form of the scrum of scrums model for scrum masters and product owners, coordinating communication, impediment removal, priorities, requirement refinement, and planning. Using a scrum of scrums model for the scrum master and product owner enables daily synchronization among teams across programs.

Scaling the scrum master

Following the vertical slicing model of scrum of scrums, Scrum at Scale groups five scrum masters into a scrum master scrum of scrums. It mirrors the daily scrum for scrum teams to surface and remove impediments. With Scrum at Scale, narrowing the scope of a scrum of scrums to five scrum masters from each of five scrum teams limits the complexities for effective cross-team communication. A scrum master scrum of scrums coordinates release activities as the release team. Figure 13-4 illustrates the Scrum at Scale scrum of scrums model.

Courtesy of Jeff Sutherland & Scrum, Inc.

FIGURE 13-4: Scrum at Scale scrum of scrums model for five teams.

Figure 13-5 shows the scrum of scrums model for up to 25 teams.

When a project has more than 25 teams, an executive action team (EAT) supports a third-level scrum of scrums of scrums to remove the organizational impediments that the scrum of scrums groups can't remove themselves. The EAT is the scrum of scrums for the entire agile organization.

Figure 13-6 illustrates the Scrum at Scale third-level scrum of scrums of scrums model with an EAT.

FIGURE 13-5:
Scrum at Scale
scrum of scrums
of scrums model
for 25 teams.

Courtesy of Jeff Sutherland & Scrum, Inc.

FIGURE 13-6:
Scrum at Scale
third-level scrum
of scrums of
scrums model
with EAT.

Courtesy of Jeff Sutherland & Scrum, Inc.

Scaling the product owner

The product owners organize in a similar and aligned way through meta scrums. A first-level meta scrum brings five product owners together for meta scrum meetings to refine and plan priorities. Each meta scrum has a chief product owner (CPO) who oversees the bigger picture of the vision and product backlog and facilitates the coordination among product owners (POs) in the meta scrum. Figure 13-7 illustrates the Scrum at Scale meta scrum for product owners.

FIGURE 13-7:
Scrum at Scale meta scrum for product owners.

At the second- and third-level meta scrums, the grouping aligns with that of the scrum master scrum of scrums of scrums. An executive meta scrum (EMS) supports the meta scrums by owning and communicating the organizationwide vision, taking in technical priority feedback from the meta scrums and providing priority decisions for the program. Figure 13-8 illustrates the Scrum at Scale third-level meta scrums model with EMS.

FIGURE 13-8:
Scrum at Scale third-level scrum meta scrum model with EMS.

Figure 13-9 illustrates the aligned grouping of Scrum at Scale's third-level scrum of scrums of scrums and meta scrums model with EAT and EMS.

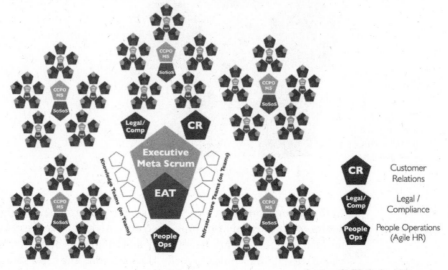

Courtesy of Jeff Sutherland & Scrum, Inc.

FIGURE 13-9: Alignment of Scrum at Scale third-level scrum of scrums of scrums and meta scrums.

A meta scrum should be a synchronization meeting that includes stakeholders. All stakeholders at the CPO level should be present to ensure alignment across the organization and support of the CPO's product backlog prioritization during every sprint.

Synchronizing in one hour a day

In an hour or less per day, an organization can align priorities for the day and accomplish effective coordination of impediment removal. At 8:00 a.m., each scrum team holds its daily scrum. At 8:45 a.m., the scrum masters hold their scrum of scrums, and the product owners hold their level-one meta scrum meetings. At 9:00 a.m., scrum masters meet in scrum of scrums of scrums, and the product owners meet in level-two meta scrums. Finally, at 9:15 a.m., the scrum master scrum of scrums of scrums meets with the EAT, and the product owner meta scrum representatives meets with the EMS.

TIP

For a complete understanding and walk-through of Scrum@Scale, visit www. scrumatscale.com/scrum-at-scale-guide/.

The beauty of scrum is that it is designed to be flexible and to scale. Scrum at Scale is the simple way to maintain the autonomy of each scrum team within a wider program context, but it's just one of many scaling models available. The following sections describe other models for managing projects of various sizes and portfolio levels.

Scaled Agile Framework (SAFe)

Scaled Agile Framework (SAFe) is a framework for scaling scrum and Agile Principles across multiple teams and their projects at the portfolio level. The SAFe Big Picture is shown in Figure 13-10.

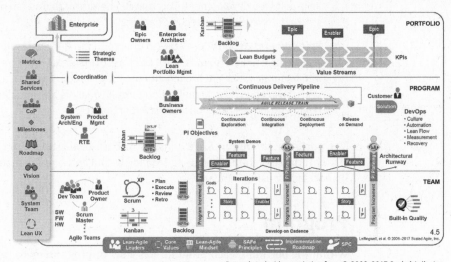

Reproduced with permission from © 2008–2017 Scaled Agile, Inc.

FIGURE 13-10: The SAFe Big Picture.

Although differences with vertical slicing exist, many similarities exist too, such as the following:

>> Development is done in scrum teams.

>> Teams are aligned in sprint lengths and cadence.

>> Scrum of scrums are used to coordinate at the program level.

SAFe has three prescribed levels of integration and coordination: portfolio, program, and team.

Portfolio

At this level, the vision and roadmap for the entire portfolio are established. Strategic themes are developed to support the vision. Budget, business objectives, and overall architecture governance are managed at the portfolio level of SAFe.

Three portfolio-level roles drive these decisions:

>> **Enterprise architect:** The enterprise architect establishes a common technical vision and drives the holistic approach to technology across programs through continuous feedback, collaboration, and adaptive engineering design and engineering practices.

>> **Lean-agile leaders:** Teachers and coaches in the organization help teams build better products through the values, principles, and practices of Lean and agile software development. This role can be similar to a scrum master or a scrum mentor, as discussed in Chapter 2.

>> **Epic owners:** We introduce epics in Chapter 3, but SAFe uses a different feature-epic relationship. In SAFe, epics are the largest requirements broken into features, which are broken into user stories. Epic owners usually drive one or two epics from identification through analysis and into decisions relating to implementation with development teams.

The portfolio backlog in SAFe consists of both business and architectural epics. The enterprise architect, Lean-agile leaders, and epic owners manage this portfolio backlog by using kanban.

Program

Within the portfolio, each program has a set of program epics from the portfolio backlog, owned and driven by an epic owner in that program. A vision and roadmap for the program are established to support the portfolio vision and backlog.

Release and product management occur at this level. The "agile release train" (ART) model is used, which is a team of agile teams delivering incremental releases of value. The train departs the station on a reliable schedule of release opportunities that each program can jump on if ready. If you miss one release, when another one comes along, you can catch it. The ART provides a fixed cadence with which the teams of the program synchronize.

At this level of integration, the work of the individual teams comes together to form release packages under the direction of shared experts such as DevOps, user experience, system architecture, and release train engineering.

The program product increment objectives artifact contains summaries of the product's business and technical goals for the upcoming release. During release planning, the team reviews the vision and goals, creates user stories for them, and plans the development necessary for the release. This plan becomes the team's product-increment objectives.

SAFe requires two working demos at the end of each iteration showing the working software or product created. The Team Demo showcases the product for the scrum team. The System Demo showcases the product for stakeholders at program level.

The release abstract showcases everything of working value in every release. Producing working product is the goal of every sprint or product increment.

Team

Programs are made up of a certain number of agile teams, each of which can be on only one program. This process works like the first layer of integration in scrum of scrums. Agile teams are essentially scrum teams, each with a development team including testers, a product owner, and a scrum master. The teams work on cadence with the other teams in the program, and their team backlogs support and align with the program backlog.

Advantages of the SAFe Model

Portfolio managers like the SAFe model because of how clear and visual it is. For larger organizations, it also provides structure for middle management's involvement with scrum teams. SAFe integrates agile techniques such as test-driven development and continuous integration.

TDD and CI

Test-driven development (TDD) is an agile software development process in which an automated unit test is written before coding begins. The developer runs the test, watches it fail, and develops enough code to pass the test without regard for efficiency. Then the developer refactors the code to remove as much coding as possible while still passing the automated unit test. This process is sometimes referred to as red, green, clean: The test fails, the test passes, the code is clean. TDD dramatically minimizes waste in code, maximizes unit test coverage, and enables seamless merging of the developer's work into the main body of work through continuous integration.

Continuous integration (CI) is a practice that code developers use where they integrate new code into a shared product. Each time code is added, it's automatically tested to ensure seamless integration.

Code quality

Another advantage of the SAFe model is that code quality is one of the core values. Any organization's ability to create quality functionality quickly requires reliable code. Creating code quality has three parts:

>> Agile architecture abstracts help organizations solve complex problems based on the nature of their large project needs. These abstracts are proven solutions for set problems that underline the importance of software architecture in any large-scale project.

>> CI at the team and system levels incorporates code from many development teams.

>> Code is tested at every increment to ensure working software at every release.

Each iteration delivers working software within a strict timebox.

As technology and customer needs change, so do the products required to fulfill those needs. In a SAFe model, refactoring is done to ensure not only current business value, but also future value.

SAFELY TRANSITIONING FROM WATERFALL

A Big Data company with offices in the United States and India made the transition from waterfall to SAFe. Market challenges existed for the company, including increased competition, changing technology, and long lead times to bring new product to market.

The company's waterfall process was so full of documentation that 25 to 40 documents had to be signed by up to ten stakeholders for anything to be approved. Multiple ongoing projects created thrashing, low visibility, and low prioritization. The firm was floundering under its own bureaucratic weight.

Within 22 months of introducing SAFe, the organization achieved the following results:

• Regrouping more than 500 employees into more than 60 agile teams

• Decreasing time to market by 27 weeks

- Decreasing time to fix errors from months to hours

- Increasing customer satisfaction and employee morale

Initially, the company was hesitant to bring in the scrum framework. It believed that scrum was only for small companies and wouldn't fit the needs of much larger companies with multinational presence. SAFe provided a scaled scrum solution that was a good fit for the company.

The company began with a few pilot teams using scrum, and after working out some organizational glitches, it achieved success. It brought in agile and scrum coaches to integrate the scrum framework into the larger organization. It began to inspect and adapt with the scrum process itself. Using pilot teams, the company started with three scrum teams, added a couple more, and eventually ran many scrum teams concurrently. Rather than leaping in with every penny and person, it incrementally scaled scrum with SAFe.

Given its success with the preceding steps, the company did a full-scale SAFe rollout. It brought in more experts, created in-house scrum training programs, and kept senior management fully in the loop.

The company dealt with its scaling issues as follows:

- Verticals were formed to leverage product owners, management, and development.

- Cubicles were redesigned into agile pods, facilitating co-location and team collaboration.

- Release trains were established, facilitating ongoing product releases coordinated across portfolios.

Large-Scale Scrum (LeSS)

Another method of incorporating the scrum framework into massive projects is Large–Scale Scrum (LeSS).

Products have been successfully developed with LeSS with as few as four to five small teams to teams that encompass 1,500 people and spanning half a dozen countries. In other words, how big would you like large to be? LeSS can scale scrum up or down to work in many environments.

At the foundation of LeSS is systems thinking, where a system is thought of as an organized entity (in this case, a product area) made up of interrelated and interdependent parts (teams). The creators of LeSS specifically see that optimizing the whole doesn't come from optimizing the parts of a whole. Optimizing parts only optimizes the parts, so LeSS optimizes collaborations between multiple teams, even across different locations.

LeSS has only a few rules and two frameworks: LeSS and LeSS Huge. The difference lies in the size of total teams involved.

LeSS framework

Figure 13-11 illustrates the basic LeSS framework. The number of development teams varies from two to eight. One product owner covers up to eight teams and each scrum master serves up to three teams.

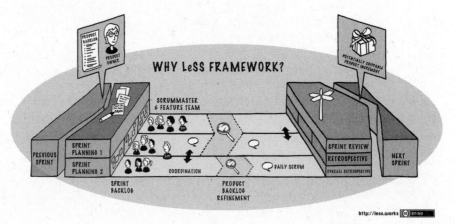

FIGURE 13-11:
LeSS framework.

Courtesy of Craig Larman and Bas Vodde

In the LeSS framework, there is one product owner and one product backlog for the complete shippable product. The product owner shouldn't work alone on product backlog refinement; she is supported by the multiple development teams that are working directly with customers/users and other stakeholders. All prioritization goes through the product owner, but clarification can happen directly between the teams and customer/users and other stakeholders.

While much of LeSS remains true to the one-team scrum framework, the differences are important:

>> Sprint Planning is split into two parts: Part 1 is common for all teams and Part 2 is for each team.

>> Sprint planning (Part 1) is limited to one hour per week of sprint length. Although not all developers are required to attend, they aren't discouraged, and at least two members per sprint team attend, along with the product owner. The representative team members then go back and share their information with their respective teams.

>> Independent sprint planning (Part 2) and daily scrums occur, and members from different teams can attend each other's meeting to facilitate information sharing.

>> Cross-team coordination is decided by the teams with a preference to decentralized and informal coordination over centralized coordination. The emphasis is on informal networks that involve cross-team talking, component mentors, travelers, scouts, and open spaces.

>> Backlog refinement is done for the overall product backlog with representatives from each development team and the product owner. Individual team backlog refinement also takes place at the individual team level but multi-team backlog refinement happens every sprint and is the key practice in LeSS.

>> Sprint reviews are done with representatives from each team and the product owner.

>> Overall sprint retrospectives are held in addition to individual team retrospectives. Scrum masters, product owner, representatives from development teams, and managers inspect and adapt the overall system of the product, such as processes, tools, and communication.

LeSS Huge framework

With LeSS Huge, the sky is the limit as far as overall project team size goes. A few thousand people could work on one project.

The scrum teams are divided into major customer requirement areas. Each area has one area product owner and four to eight scrum teams. (Having at least four teams in each requirement area prevents too much local optimization and complexity.) One overall product owner and several area product owners form the product owner team. Figure 13-12 illustrates the LeSS Huge framework.

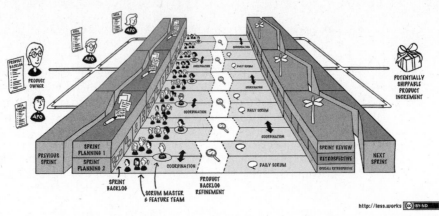

FIGURE 13-12:
LeSS Huge
framework.

Courtesy of Craig Larman and Bas Vodde

As in scrum and in smaller LeSS, you have one product, one definition of done, one (area) product owner, and one sprint. LeSS Huge is a stack of LeSS for each requirement area. Each requirement area uses LeSS, and the set of all requirement areas is in LeSS Huge. Some of the differences are

>> A product owner planning meeting happens before the sprint planning meeting.

>> Area-level meetings are added. Sprint planning, review, and retrospective meetings are done at the area level, and area-level product backlog refinement occurs.

>> Overall sprint reviews and retrospectives involving all teams are done. This review coordinates the overall work and process across the product program area.

LeSS allows for the implementation of scrum and scaling in a way that for the most part holds true to Agile Principles. Some elements of the scrum framework are upheld with empirical learning, short feedback loops, self-organization, and effective collaboration and coordination.

Leadership tools also exist in LeSS for good decisions that maximize ROI; deliver value to customers; and create happy, sustainable teams.

J.P. MORGAN AND LESS

Large in the context of J.P. Morgan means more than 3,000 employees working in multiple international locations. A group director decided to convert to LeSS. It began with small pilot projects. The results motivated the firm to get scrum rolled out on a grander scale.

The company began by choosing a single division to pilot — securities — and worked on solutions to create a customer-centric approach. Customers needed families of components rather than individual ones. Having a customer-centric approach, hugely simplified planning and coordination because groups were planned rather than individual components.

One issues was choosing the new product owners, because under the waterfall approach, business wasn't involved with development. The company solved this problem by choosing willing participants from both operations and research and development.

J.P. Morgan formed requirement areas. Each team was given a project, and a product owner was chosen. The teams were encouraged to develop cross-functionality to reduce bottlenecks and minimize the risk of losing the only person who can accomplish a task. Human resources eliminated job titles such as business analyst and tester. Even team leaders had the generic title of developer.

At the end of the initial rollout of LeSS within the securities division, increased effectiveness, customer satisfaction, and employee morale were realized. LeSS helped scale scrum up to this size of operation and continues to be used today.

Chapter **14**

Human Resources and Finance

When the winds of change blow, some people build walls, and others build windmills.

— CHINESE PROVERB

Baby Boomers are retiring at a rapid pace, new generations of employees are taking their places, and human resources (HR) has taken on high-level organizational value. Wasted funds due to failed projects indicate that a smarter way to finance projects must exist. As in so many business functions, old methods of achieving goals are becoming outdated.

Companies that can recognize their core HR and finance issues and then apply the scrum framework to the solutions are staying ahead of the pack. Many opportunities exist to increase human potential and financial effectiveness through scrum.

In this chapter, we guide you through the challenges and solutions in these critical organizational areas.

Human Resources and Scrum

In a survey conducted by the Society for Human Resource Management (SHRM), two core challenges highlight the world of HR today: retaining and rewarding the best employee and developing future leaders. These two concerns are really the same thing. Your best employees often become your future leaders.

When the surveyors asked organizations what their largest investment challenge would be, the number-one response was "obtaining human capital and optimizing human capital investments."

TIP

We always encourage the organizations we work with to refer to people as *people* or *talent* rather than *capital* and *resources.* People aren't commodities. They have individual skills, experiences, and innovations. The term *resources,* used to refer to people, is a relic. Start seeing your people as people, and see their creativity and talents as the irreplaceable value they bring to your organization.

That said, the point made by the SHRM survey is still crucial. Different types of leaders are needed. We need leaders to make the hard product owner decisions discussed in portfolio management (see Chapter 13). We need servant leaders who work collaboratively to enable and empower teams, such as scrum masters (see Chapter 2). These people empower and enable self-organizing teams to come up with the best solutions. They value iterative approaches to building products based on rapid and regular customer feedback, and they know how to pivot and respond to that feedback quickly.

Historically, technology companies have rewarded leaders who managed crisis well. In turn, these leaders promoted others who managed crisis with a sense of urgency. Although these firefighters certainly saved the day more than once, we argue that this situation caused an unbalanced shift toward crisis resolution rather than crisis avoidance.

We need leaders in development who excel by learning new skills and mentoring others as they grow. We need collaborative leaders who can work in the dynamic environment of scrum. We need people who value complementary leadership styles. Egomaniacs need not apply. Companies need cross-functional swarming scrum teams to stay competitive. In other words, we need leaders who embrace the value of change.

Reducing risky single points of failure saves money for all the reasons we've discussed so far in the book. Teams that collaborate to solve a problem get quality products to market faster than teams that use traditional methods.

Creating the Right Culture

In Chapter 4, we discuss what motivates employees most: not money, but the autonomy and trust needed to do the job, opportunities to grow, and a sense of purpose. People want what they do to mean something, and they want to work with other people who are growing and engaged in what they do.

The fruits of self-organization and self-management are the creation of an organizational culture that attracts and retains the best and the brightest. As we state in Chapter 1, these are Agile Principles 5, 8, 11, and 12.

REMEMBER

Creating the right culture has many facets. The number-one thing we look for in an effective scrum team member is versatility. Give us someone who is intellectually curious and has what we call a *contributor personality,* and we'll have success with that person. We can teach technical skills. Prima donnas who think that this thin slice of development is the only thing worthy of their time will taint the entire team. The most important job on a scrum team is the job that's necessary to ship the product. Sometimes, that job is coding; sometimes, it's quality assurance; sometimes, it's documentation. Whatever that task is, it's the highest-status, most critical job of the entire project.

Crucial to the creation of an attractive organizational culture is the attitude of executives: what qualities they embrace and how they invest in their people. Like a magnet, leaders attract people who respond to the culture they provide.

Broad organizational culture is important, but so are tactical team skills. Cross-functionality within teams, fostering the ability to swarm, is critical. The keys are aptitude and skills, not titles. A cross-functional, self-organizing team is the perfect environment for skill development. As employees grow, they can become more engaged in the organization's goal and purpose.

REMEMBER

Technology changes too fast to get stuck in the single-technology specialist mindset. The standard tech choice of today may be totally different from what's needed tomorrow. The specialty of tomorrow is the ability to learn and adapt quickly. You need team members who recognize this.

As skills are emphasized over titles, a culture is created in which you don't have to hire one person for each skill. Expertise (not specialization) is always needed. You don't need a specialist in every seat.

Situational leadership is important. If Jim has expertise in .NET, you'll probably defer to him when you're facing a .NET problem. Carol may have expertise in quality assurance. When discussing quality assurance, you may defer to Carol.

Sam may have just come back from a .NET conference, and although Jim may be strong in .NET, Sam may have learned something that Jim doesn't know.

The following sections describe two ways to examine HR and scrum.

HR and existing organization structures

In this section, we look at ways to organize and manage current employees within a scrum structure.

Incentivizing

Forced ranking and competitive incentive structures promote competition among employees. Scrum is teamcentric. The team receives praise and receives suggestions for improvement. Incentives should be on the team level too. If the team succeeds, the team gets the prize.

When a football team wins the Super Bowl, every person on the team gets a ring whether he played that day or not. If a development team has a good year, everyone on the team might get a 15 percent bonus, not just a few select people. Depending on your seniority, 15 percent could be significant.

For large teams, this practice may not work. But with scrum, development teams are between three and nine members, so it's difficult for one or two team members to fly under the radar for very long. A self-organizing, self-managing team demands the contribution of every team member so that everyone earns the prize in the end.

Compensation

If a team is cross-functional, and no titles or specialists exist, how do you create status? You create status through knowledge and being the go-to person on a subject. Someone who's a heavy lifter on the team has a lot of tasks in the Done column of the task board, and other people want to pair with those people and shadow them on tasks.

Seniority and relative compensation are established by a combination of skill depth and breadth. Each member of a development team has at least one skill. If you know how to do one skill, you're Band 1. You may be junior-level Band 1 or senior-level Band 1, but you're Band 1.

If you know how to do two skills, you're Band 2. You may be junior-level Band 2 or senior-level Band 2, but you're Band 2. If you have three skills, you're Band 3, and so on.

Each new skill gives the developer another band. As the team matures through shadowing, swarming, team pairing, and knowledge sharing, each team member should be adding skills (becoming cross-functional). As team members achieve higher levels (such as Band 2 and Band 3), their pay scales rise accordingly.

This situation is a true win–win situation because an organization can pay team members more *and* save money by having teams of cross-functional employees rather than an army of sharpshooters who know how to do only one thing.

TIP

By incentivizing developers to learn more skills and therefore increase their status, you give them the opportunity to design their own education and career path. Often, the skills they develop are those that they're most interested in or have the greatest inclination for. They may be introduced to skills that they never would have tried before but find that they have an aptitude for.

Team members have an incentive to gain more skills, and the company benefits by paying fewer people higher rates and developing scrum teams that are more effective and efficient.

Underperforming team members

If anyone on a self-organizing, self-managing team isn't pulling his weight, scrum exposes this fact quickly so that the team can correct the problem. In Chapter 4, we discuss the Hawthorne effect, which shows that a worker's performance improves when someone is watching. Visibility and performance are directly proportional. Scrum also uses information radiators such as task boards and burndown charts, which raise visibility and performance.

TIP

One client had multiple flat-screen TVs in his building's lobby. The screens were split into quadrants and showed the day's burndown of four projects at a time, refreshing with new projects every 20 seconds. Every person walking into that lobby (including suppliers and clients) could see the status of every project that the company was working on — a high-visibility situation for each scrum team and each team member.

Lack of transparency in goals and expectations can also play a role in underperformance. If a person doesn't know exactly where she's headed, it's understandable that she can get off course.

Underperformance in scrum can easily be identified in burndown charts, where daily tasks are marked as accomplished or not accomplished. New code is comprehensively and automatically tested every night through automated tests of continuous integration. With this type of visibility, in which the team is accountable as a single unit, any lapses are easily found and solved.

In a traditional model, if a developer wants to hang out on Facebook for three hours each day, he can easily do so. He can tell the project manager that he needs 4 hours to finish a 45-minute task. If the project manager says that he could do the job in less time, his response might be "Really? Show me how." Because the project manager probably doesn't have the coding skills necessary to fully understand the task at hand, his only option is to let the developer get on with whatever he wants to do. The rest of the team members figure that as long as they're doing their jobs, the problem is that developer and the project manager.

Under scrum, however, teams are held accountable as single units. If a developer spends three hours on Facebook, his teammates will hold him accountable for not doing his share.

Here are some other ways that scrum can expose performance issues:

>> In the daily scrum, before any escalation of an issue occurs, team members can suggest that a troubled developer join them in shadowing or pairing on a task. This suggestion is the team's idea and may be all it takes to solve the problem.

>> Sprint retrospectives are excellent times to identify gaps in skills and possible solutions. Causes of underperformance can be unearthed, such as team dynamics, the environment, and misunderstandings.

>> In sprint reviews, the team can encourage the struggling person to engage in the demo. In preparation for the demo, things may come to light that prompt ideas for the retrospective.

>> If all the developers know that one person isn't carrying his weight, but they're uncomfortable bringing up the issue themselves, a good scrum master will facilitate the interactions needed to address the issue.

HR and scrum in hiring

When you make organizational changes and adopt scrum practices, you'll search for and hire new employees using different criteria than you did before. Following are some things you need to consider when you're hiring for each scrum role:

>> **Developers**

- Remove titles from the job descriptions and base your searches on skills. You'll not only filter your search results based on skill keywords that candidates include in their profiles, but also filter out candidates who are more interested in touting their titles than their skills.

- Search for candidates who have curiosity and a desire to cross-train — those who have demonstrated an ability to work outside their comfort zones.

- Search for generalists who have broad skill sets and experience in moving among skills.

- Find people who seek chances to work with a team. Even the most introverted soul enjoys working with respectful teammates.

>> **Product owners**

- Look for the key characteristic of decisiveness.

- Find people who have worked collaboratively with developers and stakeholders.

- Seek the soft skills of communication and proactivity. Providing effective, timely clarification is critical to a scrum team's success.

>> **Scrum masters**

- You want soft skills such as facilitation of conflicts and demonstrated effect on previous teams' performances.

- Look for someone who can protect the team, display empathy, and mentor as a servant leader.

- Don't advertise for a project manager hoping to convert that person to a scrum master. The project manager role doesn't exist in scrum, and it may not be the right fit.

Regardless of the position you're trying to fill, search for people who have positive scrum and/or agile experience. Regularly review job descriptions and update them with appropriate scrum role terminology and Agile Principles to attract candidates who prefer working with scrum.

Performance reviews

After you have your new scrum-focused hires, performance reviews can be team-based. Reward people based on their contribution to the team, shifting the emphasis from the individual to the team.

Team-level performance reviews are a natural for scrum. Given the high visibility inherent to this framework, daily assessment is given through peers, and team output is consistent and tangible.

HOLACRACY AT ZAPPOS

Holacracy is a system of organizational governance consisting of self-organizing teams rather than traditional hierarchy. You can think of it as a hierarchy of circles, in which each circle is a self-organizing team run with democratic principles. Zappos was the largest organization (1,500 employees at the time) to embrace the ideal of holacracy with success.

John Bunch, one of the transition leaders at Zappos, said, "One of the core principles is people taking personal accountability for their work. It's not leaderless. There are certainly people who hold a bigger scope of purpose for the organization than others. What it does do is distribute leadership into each role. Everybody is expected to lead and be an entrepreneur in their own roles, and Holacracy empowers them to do so."

For a visual depiction of holacracy, check out the following figure.

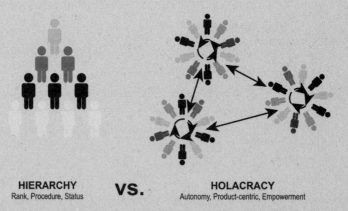

HIERARCHY
Rank, Procedure, Status

VS.

HOLACRACY
Autonomy, Product-centric, Empowerment

Ideally, Bunch says, holacracy is "politics-free, quickly evolving to define and operate the purpose of the organization, responding to market and real-world conditions in real time. It's creating a structure in which people have flexibility to pursue what they're passionate about."

Holacracy is scrum's concept of self-organizing, self-managing, cross-functional teams applied at the organizational level.

Formal annual reviews of individual employees are for the most part artifacts of traditional project management frameworks. They've proved to be ineffective for several reasons:

> ≫ People need and want regular feedback, not just a review at the end of each year. Regular coaching is the key.

>> It's difficult to assess an entire year's performance, with all its nuances and situational factors, in one review. By its nature, the review will be incomplete.

>> Poor performers should be coached and mentored early, not after a year has passed.

>> Positive, constructive feedback is much more effective than the appraisal format of an annual review.

The most logical, straightforward way to provide feedback that helps team members improve is to have each person's peers provide a 360-degree review (see Figure 14-1). On scrum teams, these peers are team members, stakeholders, and customers. Instead of being a formal performance review, a 360-degree review is a feedback tool. Each member of the team can understand the effect of her work on every other person involved. This holistic view shows how an employee is performing within the entire work environment.

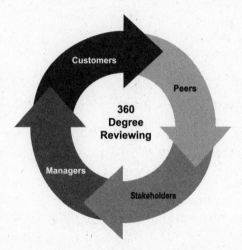

FIGURE 14-1:
The 360-degree performance review.

Use 360-degree performance reviews for determining compensation and (more important) for helping team members inspect, adapt, and improve. When you use them only to satisfy HR requirements or determine merit increases, you miss the full power of 360-degree reviews.

Some benefits of a 360-degree review are

>> Viewing an employee's performance from different angles allows for greater understanding of which skills need improving and which are outstanding.

>> Growth depends on frequent, high-quality feedback.

>> Starting points for improving skills can be identified.

>> A baseline can be set for measuring improvement.

>> Personal blind spots in an employee's behavior can be identified.

MANAGING HIRING WITH SCRUM

Scrum influences how you hire and develop talent to optimize the power of scrum. You can also use scrum for hiring and onboarding projects.

One global biopharmaceutical and medical device solution provider used scrum for a major hiring push that required 21 new hires, trained and ready to go. Developers, database administrators, business analysts, and technical writers were needed. From the start of the recruitment process to the project start date, the hiring team had only seven weeks to find, hire, and train these individuals.

Initial challenges were extensive:

- No onboarding process currently existed.

- No formal new-hire program existed.

- The current recruiting process was inefficient.

- No dedicated training department or content existed.

- New equipment was needed, such as workstations, phones, and computers.

The company incorporated the scrum framework for managing this project. To start, the product owner (the HR director) gathered all the hiring managers, the IT manager, and the HR staff for a one-day planning meeting. They identified everything they would need to do and who would do each part, such as

- Gather and create content for corporate, product, and industry overviews; agile development and software overviews; and IT and HR orientations.

- Create a weeklong, on-site training program utilizing the manual.

- Establish the new facilities.

- Purchase equipment and network and software tools.

- Recruit internal trainers (subject matter experts and managers).

- Gather and format current material that existed in various forms.

From this single day of planning, they were able to establish roadmap features and product backlog epics for

- The training program manual

- IT equipment procurement

- IT software, licenses, and credentials procurement

- Setup of the new facility

- Process for hiring new employees on time

For recruiting the new employees, they also identified the needs for

- A portal and process for reviewing resumes

- An interview schedule

- Standard tests and interview questions

The managers used one-week sprints, and each week everyone demonstrated the progress on his portion of the manual and gathered feedback from each other. IT showed their progress in the facilities and equipment needs. They created the next week's sprint goal and went back to work.

The weekly touch points with IT were important. Several times, impediments were identified on the spot, and therefore could be resolved to keep IT in line with the deadlines.

Hiring managers gave feedback to each other on the content of the training material. This way, they didn't need an exhaustive edit at the very end. By the time the training came, they knew that even if they hadn't had time to review the entire manual, their content had been inspected and adapted along the way and was already quite refined.

Sprint retrospectives were held each week, and the outcome often involved plans for improving coordination and issues with the hiring portal vendor. Issues were fixed in a timely manner because attention was given weekly. As well, someone was given the task of addressing any issue as part of the follow-up action plan.

Within this organizational framework, the hiring process was incorporated. An onboarding company provided a portal for managing candidates through the pipeline. This portal provided visibility for each stage of the hiring process they were in and helped with scheduling rooms and moving candidates from one interview stage to the next.

Results from the coordinated scrum framework included all new hires receiving the same training and their big-picture understanding of their role was complete.

After this first wave of hires, inspect and adapt was applied and improvements were made to the system. Overall, the inspect-and-adapt cycle so inherent to scrum, combined with the swarming of each feature, meant remarkable success in a potentially nightmarish hiring project.

Finance

The goal of business is to make money to provide and improve products or services. Therefore, finance lies at the heart of any successful project. Increasing competition and tightened budgets require making tough, wise funding decisions.

Billions of dollars are wasted every year on projects that failed or died somewhere along their protracted and painful development. Here are just a few examples:

» Ford Motor Co. abandoned a purchasing system after deployment, resulting in a $400 million loss.

» J Sainsbury PLC (UK) abandoned a supply chain management system after deployment, resulting in a $527 million loss.

» Hewlett-Packard experienced a $160 million loss due to problems with an enterprise resource planning (ERP) system.

» AT&T Wireless experienced problems with a customer management system upgrade, resulting in $100 million lost.

» McDonald's canceled its innovate information-purchasing system after already spending $170 million.

These are only a few examples of preventable financial waste.

A survey conducted by KPMG on global IT project management unearthed some startling findings. When respondents were asked about their experiences in delivering value in projects after receiving funding, this is what they found:

» 49 percent said they'd experienced at least one project failure in the last 12 months.

» 2 percent achieved their targeted benefits with every project in those same 12 months.

» 86 percent stated that across their entire project portfolio, they'd lost up to 25 percent of targeted benefits.

Most of this was likely preventable.

Incremental funding

Not surprisingly, companies want to fund an initial deliverable before they decide whether to keep funding a project. In scrum, product increments are produced every sprint and packaged for release every release cycle, so incremental funding is easily incorporated.

TECHNICAL
STUFF

Incremental funding is a financially driven method of funding projects. It focuses on maximizing returns by delivering sequenced, portioned customer-valued functionality to maximize a project's net present value — the present value of future incoming cash flows minus the purchase price and any future outgoing cash flows.

What used to happen in corporations is that the business team would go before a funding committee with a proposal and return on investment (ROI) numbers that team members believed were necessary to get their project funded. If they were successful, the team spent every nickel of that funding and then delivered results or asked for more funding. Few people looked at the ROI numbers from months or years earlier because the company wasn't going to get that money back anyway. Sunk costs meant that companies had to move forward at all costs.

In scrum, the product owner goes before a funding committee with his vision statement and monetized product roadmap. He might say, "I need $3 million to implement all these features." The funding committee can respond, "Okay, we'll allocate $3 million for your project. But first, we'll give you $500,000. Show us that you can deliver the ROI promised for your initial release, and we'll give you more money. But if you can't deliver on a little bit, you can't deliver on a lot."

Many companies prefer to use incremental funding for their projects with or without the accompanying scrum practices. Incremental funding is used to do the following:

>> **Mitigate risk.** Stakeholders and product owners can test the projected ROI at minimal cost to see whether they hit it.

>> **Reduce costs.** A minimal investment is used at the start.

>> **Maximize returns.** Earlier monetization leads to higher revenue.

TECHNICAL
STUFF

Another way to look at team funding is in terms of MVP (minimum viable product), which we introduce in Chapters 5 and 13. You should be able to monetize the MVP (explicit ROI). If the MVP realizes the projected ROI, fund the next MVP.

Incremental funding creates an opportunity at every release for product owners and stakeholders to examine their ROI. At each release, if problems exist, depending on the size and complexity of those problems, stakeholders can invest in fixes or terminate the project before more money is wasted.

Revenue can be started earlier. The goal is not just less waste but earlier return — and earlier return means higher return. Value is delivered to the customer earlier, and his buy-in increases. Controlling risk and cost is important; so is providing value. If you can identify ways to deliver distinct features for generating revenue in earlier time frames, you should chunk them out and deliver them first so that the customer can realize revenue before the end of the complete project. As revenue comes in, the initial costs are offset earlier, and overall revenue and profit over the life of the product are higher.

Historically, a project's ROI is projected, and funding is received based on that projection. Projects are rarely canceled because testing and customer feedback are left until the end of the development cycle. Even if problems are discovered, it's difficult to take money back after it's been allocated. Not surprisingly, ROI projections are sometimes inflated to get funding.

With incremental funding, the ROI is kept honest because it needs to be proved at each release. If the increment fails to deliver, no more money is invested.

This lower cost of failure allows developers to nurture their creativity and even form an intrapreneurial culture. Fresh ideas can be tested, and if the ROI is met, they can be continued. Company cultures change as trust is built through tangible delivery and the intrapreneurial spirit is nourished.

Failure no longer exists; it's replaced by consistent learning toward the next success when costs are low, and innovation is encouraged. Self-organizing teams have the freedom and motivation to come up with their own best designs and solutions.

The following sections discuss standard accounting practices that fall in line with this incremental approach to financing.

CULTURE OF CREATIVITY

Intrapreneurship means behaving like an entrepreneur within a large organization. This type of thinking helps companies innovate and gain competitive advantage. Organizations that encourage their employees to express new ideas and try things outside their assigned projects have resulted in some of the most useful products, including Lockheed Martin's ADP, GORE-TEX fabric, Google's Gmail, 3M's Post-its (a personal favorite), Sony's PlayStation, and Facebook's "Like" button.

Statements of position (SOP)

The American Institute of Certified Public Accountants publishes statements of position (SOPs) on accounting issues. SOP 98-1 defines the point in an internal software development at which project costs are expensed (that is, capitalized):

» Expenses in the preliminary planning stage are expensed in the period in which they occur.

» Expenses incurred during development can be capitalized or split to be included in the overall price of the software asset and then amortized as costs during the life of the product.

Scrum allows for more costs to be capitalized after planning and throughout the project, because planning and overhead are lower and value-added activities are higher. Most of a sprint is spent on value-added activities, whereas a traditional model spends as much time on planning and analysis as on the development phase.

Scrum allows the cost of doing business to occur in increments, as opposed to expensing the entire project up front. Profit can be realized much sooner when you spread initial expenses across the life of the project. The sooner you deliver value to the customer, the sooner the revenue comes in. This capitalization approach means that profit is realized sooner rather than later.

Scrum and budgets

Traditional budgeting methods, especially in private companies, entail creating a budget for the entire fiscal year. This budget is meant to capture all expenses and revenues for that year.

Management commits, tracks, and rewards based on this estimated budget projection. If a manager or product group exceeds revenue estimates or spends less than the estimated expenses, that person is group rewarded. If the manager or group falls short of revenue goals or exceeds estimated expenses, questions must be answered, but evaluating over- or underperformance is done by reflecting on what has happened in the past; it's a reactive process.

Organizations should accept a yearlong budget as what it is: an estimate. The next quarter's estimate should be the actual target and what teams measure their goals against. The team tries to meet or exceed the budget for this one quarter rather than the budget for the whole year.

Subsequent quarters are still considered to be estimates and treated as such. Teams can incorporate what they learn in the current quarter into the next quarter (inspection and adaptation in finance).

This is how Wall Street works with company estimates. Companies publish their current quarter's estimates and establish those further in the future. However, those estimates further out have less weight than the current estimate.

Chapter **15**

Business Development

It is not necessary to change. Survival is not mandatory.

— W. EDWARDS DEMING

Business development, often referred to as sales and marketing, is fundamental to the growth and health of almost every organization. After all, getting the word out about what you do and then finding prospective clients and converting them to sales keep the motor of business running.

What's the difference between marketing and sales?

Marketing is delivering information to find prospective clients to convert through the sales process. Marketing changes as new angles and methods are devised to expose your product or service to as many people as possible. Marketing is the sky over the sales funnel.

Sales is an ongoing conversation between two or more people. Sales is understanding the needs and wants of that specific person or organization and explaining how your product or service fills those needs and wants.

In this chapter, we cover how scrum works within the vital roles of marketing and sales.

Scrum and Marketing

Within the waterfall project management style, it's difficult to know whether the correct product is being built. Little to no user feedback has been sought along the way, so it's anybody's guess whether the product will be a big success.

Here's the catch: Organizations traditionally have a fixed annual marketing plan (much like the annual budgeting process we discuss in Chapter 14). Firms come out with a product with no clear idea whether it'll be a success, yet marketing is often planned a year in advance.

Additionally, markets change frequently. Given the speed of technological advances today, change is even more frequent now. Even for products that have been vetted and proved to be what the customer wants, companies might need to have their marketing angle changed along the way.

Sometimes, customers don't even know what they want until they get a product in their hands and use it. Despite the company's best intentions, a mystery remains about how and what to market.

Also, a firm may be dealing with millions of customers who have varied tastes and desires. Consider how many different styles and models of cars, clothes, and gadgets are sold in any one year. Each year, new models come out. For every buyer, marketers want to appease individual tastes.

Although the future is impossible to predict, prediction is exactly what traditional marketing asks people to do.

Marketing evolution

Like most industries and business functions marketing has evolved. As Anna Kennedy, author of *Business Development For Dummies* (John Wiley & Sons, Inc.), told us, recent changes in marketing include the following:

» Prospects can self-serve information to the extent that two-thirds of the buyer's journey happens before any formal engagement exists with the company.

» Marketing has shifted to being responsible for generating leads. Any chief marketing officer who isn't will soon be out of a job.

>> Technology allows marketers to assess where prospects are on the buyer's journey and nurture them on a one-to-one basis.

>> Social media provides a forum for conversations among brands and their influencers, prospects, and customers.

Given those trends, how can scrum help marketers embrace the changes and develop agility in responding to this shifting world?

Perhaps customers can research more on their own before engaging with a seller, which may seem to be a challenge from the seller's point of view. A marketing scrum team that makes its marketing materials trackable, however, can use analytics to inspect and adapt its marketing to fit instantaneous feedback.

In the past few years, marketing has become a primary consumer of Big Data. Being able to consolidate, analyze, and react to market data and moving trends makes scrum an ideal framework to use for marketing.

Access to feedback (potential customers' actions and interaction with marketing materials) enables a scrum team to respond and pivot more frequently and quickly than before. This feedback doesn't require a customer to attend a sprint review. A product owner has access to this feedback in real time, thanks to marketing analytics technologies.

Scrum and social media

Marketers are responsible for managing the social media images of their brands. The speed at which posts become viral is astonishing, requiring immediate tactical response. An example of this dynamic played out during the 2016 U.S. presidential election. The campaigns used social media to track and respond to trends.

A popular global charity recently faced a social media crisis and was able to respond effectively because of its investment in marketing expertise and rapid deployment strategies. A false public statement was made about the charity. Within hours, the rapidly growing false narrative endangered the charity's ability to do good in the world it served and negatively affected its donations.

Also, within hours, the charity's brand managers began producing content to correct the misconceptions. Making a social media response wasn't enough, though. The brand managers worked with all the organization's sites and developers to make sure that the charity's official position was clear and coming from the newly created content. Because the site developers were part of scrum teams, the new content became the highest priority and was deployed across the various platforms within days. If the changes had gone through a waterfall development and testing process, the story might have had an unhappy ending. Instead, the organization's message of acceptance became clearer, and a negative event was turned into a positive outcome. This story repeats on an almost-daily basis for small businesses and Fortune 500 companies.

Scrum in marketing

Before we discuss specific examples of scrum in marketing, we look at some specific ways that it can be adopted. Like the annual budgeting plan discussed in Chapter 14, the annual marketing plan is a guess that is refined throughout the year as the organization learns and adapts.

THE AGILE ADVANTAGE

In one of its annual "Agile Advantage" surveys, CMG Partners, a strategic marketing consulting firm, interviewed chief marketing officers (CMOs), marketing leaders, and agile experts and found that they overwhelmingly agreed that long-term, highly crafted marketing plans are things of the past. Today, speed and agility are key tools. Marketers need to be able to respond to changing economic landscapes and customers' shifting desires and needs.

The survey found three key benefits of using the agile framework within marketing campaigns and projects:

- **Increased business performance:** This performance increase took the form of faster speed to market and increased prioritization and productivity.

- **Increased employee satisfaction:** Self-organizing and self-managing teams, working with transparency and empowerment, lead to happier people.

- **Increased adaptability:** A hallmark of agile and scrum, adaptability came to the forefront when marketing teams adopted agile frameworks. Adaptability is sorely lacking in waterfall.

It's clear that using agile and scrum in marketing allowed greater collaboration between the end user and the marketers. The product brand could then evolve with the customer in hand, rather than hoping that at the end a fit existed.

Cost can be reduced because fewer plans fail with the new fine-tuned approach. With this increase in success rates, customer and employee satisfaction also rises.

AGILE IN MARKETING

A formal movement exists to apply Agile Principles in marketing and a set of recognized Agile marketing principles called the Agile Marketing Manifesto has been published at `http://agilemarketingmanifesto.org`. The manifesto states:

> We are discovering better ways of creating value for our customers and for our organizations through new approaches to marketing. Through this work, we have come to value:
>
> 1. Validated learning over opinions and conventions
> 2. Customer-focused collaboration over silos and hierarchy
> 3. Adaptive and iterative campaigns over Big-Bang campaigns
> 4. The process of customer discovery over static prediction
> 5. Flexible versus Rigid planning
> 6. Responding to change over following a plan
> 7. Many small experiments over a few large bets

With scrum, marketing plans can be monthly, weekly, and even daily. After each iteration, inspection and adaptation are applied based on feedback from sprint reviews and retrospectives. Marketing plans can be adjusted, change can be thought of as progress, and customers can be marketed to in a way that speaks to their changing needs.

New marketing strategies can be tested with actual users before they're released to broader audiences. In the same vein, brands can be tested within sprints, saving huge costs because branding is developed together with customers rather than presented to them at the end.

Scrum in Action for Marketing

Scrum is widely used in marketing today with astounding success. Scrum fits the wild and wooly world of shifting customer needs and technology. In the following sections, we discuss three examples of scrum and marketing.

CafePress

CafePress sells gifts and merchandise that a customer can customize, such as mugs with pictures and/or memes.

A layer of versatility was uncovered in CafePress's scrum implementation. The legal implications of customizable products meant that marketing needed a close alliance with the legal team to facilitate quick response to legal inquiries and concerns. The marketing team needed to be aware of what it could and couldn't say to avoid taking on unnecessary legal liability.

The legal department became an integral part of CafePress's marketing scrum team, making sure that marketing could get any queries answered in 20 minutes.

CafePress's strategy of bringing legal and marketing together is a great example of the benefits of aligning business with development. Sometimes, the departments' goals seem to be at odds, but with scrum, they're directly aligned with making a better product and creating more satisfied customers.

Xerox

Xerox is a household name, usually associated with office photocopying. Over the years, this firm has branched into other products and services, such as IT, document management, and software and support.

TECHNICAL STUFF

The original photocopy process of making paper copies from documents and visual images is called *xerography.* Electrostatic charges are used on a light-sensitive photoreceptor to transfer powder onto paper, thereby copying the images. Heat then seals the deal, literally. Who invented xerography? A company called Xerox.

Xerox's global interactive marketing team integrated scrum into its business framework to simplify and prioritize demand from customers and marketing teams throughout the world. The team knew that it had to respond to the changing market and customers' changing needs, and they needed to respond as fast as smaller competitors that could respond and pivot more quickly. Scrum provided the framework for Xerox to self-organize, iterate, inspect, adapt, and deliver more often.

Similar problems existed in portfolio management (see Chapter 13). Projects weren't prioritized, so developers were thrashed from project to project, and the loudest stakeholder received his product first. When new initiatives came along, the teams couldn't pivot quickly enough to take advantage of potential benefits. The teams thrashed employees across multiple projects or stopped projects to reallocate people to new ones.

With scrum, Xerox segmented the type of work to be done into three queues: new development, creative projects (such as artwork), and rapid response (service issues that take eight hours or less to resolve). Short sprint cycles and the inspect-and-adapt process enabled team members to focus each sprint on only one queue rather than all of them.

The Xerox marketing team was thrashing between sprints, but at least it was no longer thrashing within sprints. (Read Chapter 13 for information about why thrashing is undesirable.) The focus during each sprint enabled the team to deliver increments across the three queues and prioritize those that were most important. Speed to market increased because the team didn't get sidetracked before completing a project. Employee morale also increased, and customer satisfaction improved because customers got what they wanted sooner and better.

Scrum for Sales

Sales isn't an island, but part of a business development cycle that starts with defining what the market needs and the product and service that fulfills that need. Then the cycle goes through marketing, sales, delivery, and evaluation to leverage the customer for repeat sales and advocacy.

In traditional project management frameworks, sales is the classic, individualistic role. Individual quotas must be met (and ideally exceeded), and each individual's pay is based on sales-quota results. Salesperson of the Week, Month, and Year are coveted accolades. Competition is fierce, and in every organization, a few stars rise to the top. In sales, the word *team* typically refers to the staff of the department, not to the department working as a unified team for a common goal as in scrum. To apply scrum to sales, you have to figure out how to get salespeople to work together as a team rather than as individuals in a department.

Scrum takes the traditional approach to sales and turns it on its head in several ways:

>> Scrum by its nature focuses on team success. You might think of a sales team as being a group of salespeople pounding the pavement and making the same pitch. A sales team with scrum is much more. Like a cross-functional product development team consisting of designers, engineers, and testers, a sales team needs subject-matter experts and people from marketing, sales enablement, sales engineering, contracts, legal, and finance. The entire sales team has goals. If the team fails to reach its goals, the members can work together to find solutions.

- » Rewards are team-based. A traditional sales team (all salespeople) is driven by competition, with everyone working in silos. A team structure means all team members swarm around a lead to get to done (close the sale).

- » Scrum is all about results over the process to achieve those results. It's focused on reality-based inspect and adapt. You have to inspect the process and adapt for each client.

- » Results count. Burndown and burnup charts (which we discuss in Chapter 5) can be used in sales. Rather than tracking how much has been done, sales tracks how much is left to do in that sprint (burndown). Tracking cumulative sales (burnup) shows real-time progress toward the sprint sales goal.

- » Standing daily scrums work well because nobody wants long meetings. If impediments are discovered outside the team, an outside person can be invited to the daily scrum and partake in an after-party removal of the impediment (see Chapter 6).

The scrum solution

The sales process of converting leads to closed sales is also known as the sales pipeline or funnel. Figure 15-1 outlines a basic sales funnel.

A sales manager at an agile-based organization implemented a backlog item task board. Columns included the stages of the sales funnel, such as Leads, Sales Call, and Follow-Up. The sales team and management had an immediate picture of where the team was in the project. Sales estimates were inspected and adapted based on reality. Figure 15-2 shows an example of the sales funnel as a task board.

MICROCHIP

Microchip, a leading semiconductor firm, shifted its pay structure away from a traditional, variable compensation plan to one that added a small variable based on company and unit performance. Employees were paid a bonus based on their immediate team's performance, as well as on how well the overall firm did. The result was improved growth and profitability, increased employee engagement, and near-zero attrition.

In other words, the best salespeople were found to interact with others on the sales team and coordinate for the best overall results. Collective skills and even crowdsourcing were cited as methods the team used to excel. Star managers used team brainstorming with their reps, and they even borrowed ideas from other areas of the company.

FIGURE 15-1:
A classic sales
funnel depicting
the sales process
from beginning
to end.

Leads

Sales Call

Follow-Up

Conversion

Close

RELEASE GOAL: **SPRINT GOAL:**

RELEASE DATE: **SPRINT REVIEW:**

| PBI | = Product Backlog Item |
| Task | = Task |

LEADS	SALES CALL	FOLLOW-UP	CONVERSION	CLOSE
				PBI — Task Task Task / Task Task Task
		PBI — Task Task Task / Task Task Task	Task Task Task / Task Task Task	
PBI — Task Task / Task Task / Task Task / Task Task	Task Task Task / Task Task			
PBI — Task Task / Task Task / Task Task / Task Task				

FIGURE 15-2:
A sales task
board with
columns
representing
the sales
funnel stages.

A visible funnel in the form of a task board is quite valuable. The sales funnel in Figure 15-1 becomes the task board shown in Figure 15-2, as follows:

>> **Leads:** Each row (swim lane) represents one lead. Leads arrive from a variety of sources through a variety of methods, but they all land here and get discussed, vetted, and prioritized before the sales call is initiated. Taking somewhat-qualified leads and turning them into sales-qualified leads that are ready to buy is becoming a marketing function. Scrum can help bridge the traditional divide between marketing and sales through visibility and coordination of the sales team.

- **>> Sales call:** An initial sales call is made to further qualify the lead (that is, define the prospect's need and position the offering as the solution). This stage involves various tasks, which were outlined during sprint planning in the Leads column.

- **>> Follow-Up:** The lead has responded and expressed interest in the proposed solution to his need. The team coordinates, times, and executes a series of tasks.

- **>> Conversion:** Obstacles and impediments to closing the sales are identified, and the team swarms to overcome them.

- **>> Close:** The contract is won. The team clearly documents how the contract was won.

All of this is done effectively as a team. Look at the skills required to make a sale, including marketing, sales enablement, sales engineering, subject-matter expertise, contracts, legal, and finance.

Ideally, you want cross-functional team members who can do everything. But having one person who can do everything well is unusual. Having a team of people who can do everything well is even less likely. But a cross-functional team of members who can self-organize, devise plans, and swarm around a prospect, event, or contract produces better results than one person who tries to do everything alone.

Because scrum focuses on continuous communication among all parties, a scrum sales team has a clearer understanding of what prospective clients need and want. As a result, the team can present its sales ideas in a way that directly affects those prospects.

The scrum sales process

Successful salespeople are exceptional listeners and have keen observation skills. One goal is to discover prospects' problems and then show how the product or service solves those problems. To make this connection, a salesperson needs to establish a relationship based on trust. People buy things from people they know and trust.

Scrum selling is about gaining trust through teamwork. The supporting players may include presales, business development, account executives, field engineers, installers, inside sales and support, and service people. Any combination of these people can make up a scrum team and swarm to synchronize communication, supporting the effort to get the client to sign a deal. Swarming activities might revolve around the following:

>> Preparing for a trade show

>> Following up with trade-show leads

>> Developing time-bound proposals to potential solutions for a sales pitch to out-class the competition

>> Saving an at-risk sale by brainstorming and prioritizing action items

TECHNICAL STUFF

Sales cycles are more successful when a potential consumer or business is *pulled* toward a product or solution as opposed to responding to a pure outbound "cold call" approach. Pull strategies involve content marketing, webinars, trade shows, and social media marketing. Push versus pull models are discussed in Chapter 5.

The scrum sales process is high–touch and commonsense. It mirrors the roadmap to value as follows:

1. Vision

   Example: Grow gross sales in Dallas by 20 percent this fiscal year by increasing the company's social media presence and analytics. Follow up with a personal phone call or email to everyone who provides contact information.

   (The vision model we present in Chapter 2 is for product development. For sales and other nonproduct development projects, it's appropriate to tweak that model based on reality.)

2. Product roadmap (high-level) and product backlog (broken down)

   Example: High-level and low-level lists of changes are needed to make the vision a reality, such as

   - Sales strategy development

   - Acquisition of tools

   - Development of collateral

   - Sales process development and fine-tuning

   - Execution needed for specific deals in the process

   - Assigning key (detailed) social media sites to a team member

   - Finding a tool for tracking sales funnels that the team will use

   - Defining such reporting processes as analytics workflows

3. Release planning

   Example: Prioritize backlog items by month and/or quarter.

4. Sprint planning

   Example: As a team, create tasks and assignments for the backlog items.

5. Sprint

   Example: Hold daily stand-up meetings to coordinate swarming tasks for the day and identify impediments.

6. Sprint review

   Example: Demonstrate to the stakeholders (such as the vice president of sales) that the sprint is complete (the Facebook page is operational, for example, or mailing lists of past customers are compiled).

7. Sprint retrospective

   Example: Review what worked well and facilitate knowledge transfer. Service/installation people are learning how new customers are being acquired, for example, which helps them continue the company messaging that leads to the sale.

iSense PROWARENESS

iSense Prowareness is an information and computer technology consulting company (ICT) based in the Netherlands that adopted scrum throughout it sales processes. The problems that the company had been experiencing were diverse and based on a huge lack of transparency:

- The system tracked individual progress, but only the manager looked at this. The number and size of each deal were all the data that was shared, and each rep's progress was measured by these metrics alone. Every week, each individual estimated his numbers for that week, and at the end of the week, reported what he had actually achieved.

- The company had no way of knowing how individual efforts were impacting the overall team sales.

- No process indicators existed. The only measurement was the amount sold. The number of phone calls could be tracked; however, the closing rate based on these was unknown. Management had limited ways to help their sales team as they didn't know what and where the individual impediments were. The only input was to work harder, as they had no way of determining what "working smarter" meant.

- The sales reps worked hard on improving their numbers, but no structured time was spent on reflecting or on the establishment of a system to improve.

Given this quite typical sales background, iSense began implementing scrum. It hired outside consultants to help with the transition and began with

- Weekly sprints from Monday through Friday.

- Quarterly sales targets, which included 13 sprints to each "release."

- Each week, salespeople adapted what they learned from the daily scrums and sprint reviews and retrospectives.

- A scrum task board was created with a burndown chart and orders taken.

- Standing daily scrums were held in front of the task board.

After the completion of the scrum integration, revenue doubled, half of which sales managers attributed directly to scrum — an excellent return on investment for the transition to scrum.

Interestingly, important lessons learned included the ability to assess which sales tactics were working and which weren't delivering total value. Scrum's transparency made abundantly clear that there is no value to an organization being unable to fulfill a closed sale. When the sales team increased their hit rate as a result of this team-based approach, their pool of service providers had not increased to fill demand. The sales managers recognized a way that they could help recruiters fill the demand through temporary contracts, which bought them more time to permanently fill those positions.

The team just presented would cold-call to gather attendees for events highlighting the products. At the event, attendees would be turned from cold leads into warm ones, and then follow-up contact would result in some of these turning into hot leads and eventual sales. Through analyzing the process and results, the team found that they were only converting 10 percent into actual sales. This allowed the team to discuss and identify gaps in the sales process, refine the sequence, and increase sales. Before long, they doubled that conversion rate.

Through the integration of scrum, the iSense sales team made another important discovery: Making the sale was just the beginning. To truly complete the cycle, the company had to deliver on the product. Sounds simple, but through the process of sprint reviews and retrospectives, where employees from different parts of the company shared information, this gap, too, began to narrow, and the customer benefited.

The sales teams realized that instead of their primary focus being on creating new business, they had more to win with existing contacts and customers. The customers they had already done successful projects with could be used as a starting point for more business. They could become promoters of projects to other companies.

Chapter **16**

Customer Service

Get closer than ever to your customers. So close that you tell them what they need well before they realize it themselves.

— STEVE JOBS

Customer service is one of the most critical aspects of any organization and is arguably the next great horizon for scrum implementation. Positive experiences give us reason to go back to a product or refer friends and family to it. Yet customer service is the very area that many customers and clients state is the most problematic part of the experience. They like the product, but its perceived value decreases with poor service.

Customers can be internal, too. Inefficient internal support and incomplete communications lead to lost productivity as well as bad morale.

REMEMBER

Customer service equals sales. A happy customer tells friends and family members and goes back himself for more services and products.

Customer service is a huge opportunity to increase sales and, therefore, revenue. This one department can propel a firm to new heights. If customer service is neglected, it can affect a company's reputation and good will.

TIP

Knowledge of customers equals knowledge-based marketing. Finding new customers becomes more effective. Therefore, managing accounts for customers can be thought of as an extension of sales and marketing.

In this chapter, we explore opportunities to use scrum to improve both your external and internal customer service.

Customers: The Most Crucial Stakeholders

Your customers are great sources of product innovation ideas and improvements. Alienating them not only creates ill will, but also cuts off a crucial feedback loop that can lead to innovation.

Internet service providers, phone companies, and local utilities consistently rank among the highest in customer service complaints. Where service providers are limited, customer service is commonly (although not always) weaker than in other industries. Customers frequently encounter long hold times, frustrating service, and labyrinthine automated service menus. Pressures on the bottom line have caused many companies to cut the budget for customer service, yet customers are the most crucial stakeholders in any business, and they need to be provided good service. Without the customers, there's no business.

Comcast is an example of a company that has experienced bad press regarding the quality of its customer service. Instances of customers unable to get refunds for bogus charges, wait times forced until closing, and an inability to cancel subscriptions are just a few of the claims that have been made over the years.

Although the need for service is enormous, quality is often lacking, and millions of people are willing to spend the time to make others aware of their experience. Customer complaints about the handling of their service calls abound.

The service conundrum

Perhaps the number-one failure in service is that customers often report that their issues aren't even solved by the agent. Customers need and expect service representatives to be able to answer questions and solve problems regarding their companies' products. Unfortunately, all too often, training in companies fails to provide the customer service representatives with the knowledge they need to meet this need of the customers.

The service representative may not understand the problem because the customer explains it poorly, or the representative simply doesn't understand the situation the customer is describing.

TIP

Seventy-eight percent of customers state that their good customer service experience was due to the knowledge the rep had, while only 38 percent said it was due to personalization. Knowledge matters. Training development for representatives is a high priority. Preplanned answers don't carry the weight of true depth of knowledge.

The cost of losing a customer is far more than the customer's annual subscription rate. Customer service divisions are often thought of as being cost centers, but in fact they save and make their firms huge amounts of revenue. Following are some statistics that reflect how customer service can affect a business in ways that you may not have considered:

>> It's more than six times more expensive to gain a new client than to keep a current one.

>> 78 percent of customers have forgone a purchase or transaction due to poor service.

>> Loyal customers are worth up to ten times the amount of their initial purchases.

>> Twelve positive experiences are needed to make up for one negative one.

>> For every customer who takes the time to complain, 26 others tell their friends instead.

Information overload

In this day and age, too much data is quoted as a source of call center failures. Too much information can paralyze the effective functioning of a service representative. Service representatives can become overwhelmed with too much data that's hard to use, and many centers haven't managed this information so that it's useful to representatives.

Perhaps you've been on a call with one representative and been transferred to another, only to find that you had to explain the issue all over again. Often, a client's historical data doesn't get fed to the rep. It's frustrating for the customer to rehash his situation or to hear the ominous words "I have no record of your claim here."

TECHNICAL
STUFF

Getting the right information to the right people is part of the problem. Sixty percent of customer service centers say they aren't even able to get certain pieces of customer information (for example, portions of customer history) to service representatives. On top of this, more than 30 percent of representatives don't gather and record customer satisfaction data.

COMMON CUSTOMER SERVICE METRICS

When service calls are assessed, management often measures efficiency over customer needs and satisfaction. Industry standard metrics measured by percentage indicate:

- 79 percent gather average handle time.

- 75 percent measure abandonment rate.

- 71 percent measure average speed of answer.

- Less than 50 percent actually measure customer satisfaction.

Sometimes, data isn't consolidated between organizational divisions, or the data is hard to find. Firms are experts at gathering information, but timely and effective distribution of that knowledge is a problem.

Scrum and Customer Service

Most of the high-level issues listed in the preceding section can be improved by scrum. These problems seem to be daunting, but they're not insolvable. Scrum offers solutions.

Inspect and adapt through feedback

One basic tenet of scrum is the feedback loop (see Chapter 7), which facilitates inspection and adaptation. In customer service, feedback is received from customers daily, hourly, and even by the minute. This feedback is on the product as well as the customer service department itself. This feedback structure is perfect for the per-call sprint cycle.

In each sprint event, customer service teams can ask themselves whether the data they have is what they need to provide the best customer service. Teams need to know whether the tools they have best serve the customer, and whether the knowledge they have is enough to solve most problems. You can use the roadmap of value to address these issues for the customer service team:

>> **Vision:** The vision of a service call is simple: to provide customer with quality support that ends with the customer feeling better about the company.

>> **Sprint planning:** During each call, tangible steps toward solving a problem can be inspected and adapted. Each sprint might involve representatives asking

customers a certain question during a call to test their progress toward solving the broader problem. If call data shows that hold time is long, the representative might briefly ask the customer, "Do you feel that your hold time was reasonable today?" Collecting yes and no answers can validate whether progress is being made with existing processes or whether changes are required to solve the problem.

>> **Sprint review:** A team of service representatives may not find it efficient to reconvene after every call for a review. Inspecting and adapting at the end of each shift, however, gives the team and the next-shift teams real-time feedback. Here the team can assimilate the information gathered from the sprint call to prepare for future sprint calls. They reflect on what they learned from the previous shift and determine what questions they should ask in the next sprint.

>> **Sprint retrospective:** At the end of a shift, the team can ask whether a better way exists to gather information from customers. For example, do the existing questions bait the customer to provide a certain answer or are they truly objective? How well did they assess their findings? How well did they document them? What aspects of their process should they inspect for improvements?

>> **Team daily scrums:** If service teams run daily sprints, the daily scrum naturally becomes sprint review and sprint planning. If sprints are longer than a shift or a day, individual issues and impediments can be raised for the broader customer service team to solve in a daily scrum. If a rep is having a hard time transitioning into asking the research question during the call, perhaps another service representative can offer to sit with her for a few calls a day.

Many service centers have enough representatives to require multiple teams, in which case vertical slicing or other scaled scrum models would be implemented (see Chapter 13) to enable coordination and integration of activities and shared knowledge. A scrum of scrums each day would be the natural place to share lessons learned and coordinate efforts across all the teams in a quick, focused manner.

A customer service product owner would be a key stakeholder on a product development scrum team that creates the products that the product owner supports.

Customer service product backlog

Training knowledgeable customer service representatives is the most important factor in creating satisfied customers. Training isn't a one-time event. New products and services require updated training. Refreshers on how to handle complaints and miscommunication are also needed.

By making it incredibly easy for customers to provide feedback, companies can generate a product backlog containing issues that need to be resolved. These issues can be prioritized and addressed based on priority.

REMEMBER

For new-product-development teams, release planning (see Chapter 5) is the time when customer service can mobilize to prepare training for representatives about the new product as it's being developed (using the upcoming inspect-and-adapt changes to inform the training plan).

For customer service scrum teams, if a consistent customer need arises, finding a solution can be placed in the backlog and given a high priority, which shortens the triage cycle as much as possible. Customer needs can be discovered and addressed in real time. Prioritizing these needs and swarming on their solution helps customer service overcome product backlogs.

REMEMBER

Customer service is a crucial stakeholder for product development teams. Representatives' feedback should be considered to be as reliable as (if not more reliable than) market research. If customer service representatives aren't represented as integral stakeholders with product development scrum teams, product owners can't be sure that they know what customers want.

Customer service definition of done

The definition of done for customer service teams should clearly outline what it means for a customer to be satisfied with his level of service. The definition of done should include more than call length and abandonment statistics.

Going back to the roadmap to value, a customer service department should have a vision statement that specifically states what customer needs are, how the team meets those needs, and how the customer service role differentiates the organization in the marketplace and ties in to the corporate strategy. (For more on vision statements, see Chapter 2.)

The vision is the framework for defining what it means to be done when providing quality customer service one customer at a time. The customer service definition of done might look something like this:

> With each customer, I succeed in fulfilling our vision to [statement of how the need is met and differentiated] when I
>
> Fully solve the customer's problem
>
> Add the problem and solution to product documentation
>
> Thoroughly review customer history before offering a solution
>
> Update customer history
>
> Search the (ABC and XYZ) knowledge bases for answers
>
> Seek subject-matter expertise from fellow representatives and/or my supervisor

Keep my cool

Help the customer keep his cool by [stated methods used by the organization]

Follow up on promises I made to the customer

Representatives need to understand what's expected of them to provide clarity about what success looks like.

TIP

Consider what the definition of done is in providing service representatives what they need to support a product or service. Whether this material is in the form of documentation, additional training, or some other metric, clarify it and then communicate it.

Look inward

Anyone who has worked in a large company likely has felt the level of customer service frustration described in this chapter. We've grouped external and internal customers together here because many of the dynamics are the same. The following are some common complaints of both external and internal customers:

>> Companies grew too fast.

>> Budgets are cut.

>> Help desk staff has insufficient training.

>> Companies have short-term vision.

>> The feedback loops operate poorly.

Inefficient support causes lost productivity and frustration, which can lead to high turnover, missed deadlines, lost sales, and frustrated external customers. It's no longer acceptable to use excuses such as "The system is down" or "I don't have a ticket." Scrum provides an ideal framework for handling these problems by making work visible and breaking down silos of knowledge through team cooperation and communication.

We've coached help-desk teams by using scrum and one-day sprints. The transformation of the team was amazing, and the team's perception within the company went from poor to excellent in a couple of months. One group described the change in these terms:

>> Better focus every day on priorities

>> Better overall picture of the workload

>> Clearer patterns (a few issues caused most of the workload)

>> Greater transparency with customers and management

By making the work visible and applying shared knowledge, the team was able to remove some of the underlying causes of problems and received management support for future initiatives.

Information sharing is a critical component of growing proficiency. Make sure that the environment rewards knowledge sharing within the team as well as across departments. Be on the lookout for comments such as "She's the only one who can do that" and "That's not something I can do."

Inspect and adapt in practice

Historically, emails are lower-priority than calls for call centers, so it's common to hear complaints about lack of response to written inquiries. This priority makes sense in the context of Agile Principles. Customer service professionals understand the value of voice conversations compared with written conversations. Still, customers shy away from calling if they don't feel that they have time to hold to speak to a live person. Their options become email and live chat.

A customer service center that's truly inspecting and adapting looks for operational and procedural ways to make written service more successful and integral with call inquiries. After all, one rep can handle multiple chats concurrently but only one call at a time. At least one study claims that a service rep can handle up to six chats for every call.

Promptly answered voice calls that are competently handled are better than chats for providing great customer service, but chat is better than email because it provides instant response.

As we mention in Chapter 4, Albert Mehrabian, PhD, professor emeritus of psychology at UCLA, proved that 55 percent of meaning is conveyed through body language and facial expressions; 38 percent of meaning is paralinguistic, meaning conveyed by the *way* we speak; and 7 percent of meaning is conveyed in the actual words spoken.

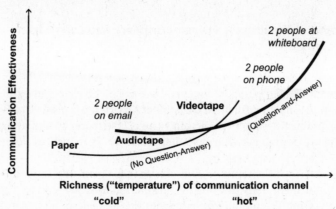

FIGURE 16-1:
Alistair Cockburn's modes of communication chart.

The importance of quality of communication simply can't be overstated. Face-to-face interaction allows for real-time questioning and clarification, cued by body language and nonverbal signals. Lack of interactivity leads to misunderstandings. Misunderstandings lead to defects, and nothing is more damaging to schedule and budget, and consequently to bottom-line profitability, than defects — whether that be product defects or customer service defects, the cost is significant.

Misunderstandings aside, the same conversation that takes days of back-and-forth responses may take as little as five minutes by standing up and walking across the floor to another office or cubicle. With customer service, constraints may only allow a service representative to put on a headset and dial a number to have a voice conversation. Voice-to-voice communication will be much more effective than chat to chat or email to email.

Given the importance of voice-to-voice communication, perhaps your definition of done for quality customer service should include communicating by voice. For instance, you might amend the definition of done that we describe earlier by adding something like the following:

>> Called an email customer after two passes back and forth to avoid further misunderstanding

>> Followed up with a customer by phone instead of email whenever possible

Scrum in Action in Customer Service

Many companies use scrum but haven't applied it to their customer service departments. These firms could greatly improve their customer service, and their bottom line, if they used scrum across the board. If an organization already uses scrum, it should have enough experience and knowledge to share with other departments.

So far in this chapter we have discussed several ways of adapting scrum through events, the definition of done, and the product backlog. Integral to this transformation is making sure that a customer service rep is present in every sprint review for product development scrum teams. Transparency and awareness stem from this integration between customer service and product development.

Service representative scrum teams can plan training and other process-improvement activities during sprints. Additionally, service representatives can learn from the product development sprint reviews and share this information with their teams.

L.A. WATER AND POWER

The Los Angeles Department of Water and Power implemented the scrum framework without calling it scrum. The goal was to enhance customer satisfaction in its net meter Solar Incentive Program. The program offers incentives to offset the cost of installing a solar rooftop system at your home or business. The department wanted to reduce delays, streamline the overall customer experience, and increase transparency.

To increase transparency, the department implemented two dashboards, called Mayor's Dashboards, to help customers stay abreast of changes and improvements. One dashboard included weekly updates on metrics, including the status of rebate checks. The second dashboard displayed the Feed-in Tariff 100-megawatt program, which the city used to purchase third-party solar power. The time and process involved in processing FiT contracts was displayed, and both dashboards displayed issues, solutions, and response times. A huge increase in transparency occurred.

These sprint backlogs were made available to all stakeholders and customers. The department also consistently inspected and adapted its process to streamline the process for reviewing applications. Results of this inspection and adaptation included increased staff to handle applications and hotline service, removed dependencies between rebate payment and turning on service, reduced review time of lease agreements through a lease compliance form, and automation of routine email communications with customers and contractors.

The main improvements streamlined existing systems and increased clarity. By enhancing the customer experience, the department greatly increased customer service. It targeted the causes of issues and set about to fix them with scrum principles.

5
Scrum for Everyday Life

Chapter **17**

Dating and Family Life

I don't want perfect. I want worth it.

— UNKNOWN

I t's easy to say the world has changed, and it has. Scrum can help any business grow and adapt along with the changing realities of the world.

In the next few chapters, we discuss some areas of your life in which you may not have considered implementing scrum. Talking about your personal life in scrum terms may seem to lack emotion, but our personal lives involve prioritizing and making critical decisions with imperfect information and an unknown future, just like in business.

As you read this chapter and Chapter 18, keep the following in mind:

» In business, the product backlog applies to a product being developed — a software or hardware product, a service, or some other deliverable. In family and personal endeavors, a product may be a vacation or wedding plan, a relationship, an education, or a retirement plan.

» When we speak of customers in business, we're talking about people who are going to use the product. In personal and family endeavors, a customer may be you, your family, your teacher, or your future self in retirement.

Don't let the terminology throw you off. It works.

In addition to benefiting you in the business world, scrum can help you develop personal relationships and make time to do the things you love. Most of us will say that our families or significant others are the most important thing in our lives, and scrum can help you prioritize those important people.

Finding Love with Scrum

People have a very real drive to seek love and relationships. Even if each person has a different kind of ideal relationship, almost everyone seeks a loving, long-term relationship. But the truth is that although dating can be fun and adventurous, finding a lasting, loving, healthy relationship can be difficult.

Relationships have evolved. In modern relationships, people are seeking honest connections. Committed relationships are no longer about being married because of societal expectations or ensuring that you don't grow old alone. People seek fulfilling, satisfying relationships based on communication and compatibility.

Although technology has played a huge role in opening dialogue in dating and providing new ways to find potential matches, it hasn't eliminated all the challenges. Despite these technological advances and conveniences, dating can be an uncomfortable subject to discuss or even to think about.

We want to show you how scrum can make dealing with dating challenges more comfortable and provide a framework for taking steps that you may have never thought possible in your pursuit of happiness. Here are a few of these dating challenges:

>> **Time:** Life is about how you spend the finite amount of time you have each day. Singles have careers, ongoing education, side jobs, personal goals, hobbies, friends, and other nondating activities. It's easy for a single person to stay late at work or take on that extra side job or project. Although many people *want* a relationship, they haven't structured their lives to have time for one. Making room for dating is about priorities.

>> **Communication:** In modern dating, communication has devolved to emailing or texting most of the time. The technological advances that facilitate making connections can also hinder relationships because they replace the face-to-face interactions that are so crucial for minimizing misunderstandings and resolving conflict. No wonder email and texting make it hard to get to know someone on a deep level or easy to get into a fight.

>> **Meeting:** Finding the right person is difficult and feels like luck half the time, but it can be broken into something simple. Most relationships that don't work out fail for one or two simple reasons: attraction and chemistry, or personality and values.

It's a problem to find someone you have genuine chemistry with and whose personality and values fit in with how you view life. These two categories oversimplify a variety of factors that affect compatibility, such as finances, selfishness, and intimacy. All these factors contribute to relationship success.

You might look at those problems and think that they have no correlation with scrum because dating is complicated! But that's exactly why scrum works for finding love. Scrum is about simplifying and working toward a vision. Here are some ways you can apply the scrum framework to romantic relationships:

>> Responding to change (such as acceptance, rejection, love, heartbreak, connection, and embarrassment)

>> Failing early and fast (wasting as little time as possible on someone who isn't compatible)

>> Inspecting and adapting (becoming the right match for someone else and refining the right match for yourself)

Almost everyone has been through heartbreak (except for the lucky few who meet the love of their life the first time around). For some people, heartbreak leads to bitterness or introversion to protect against further heartbreak. Every layer of attempted protection, however, only prevents you from getting closer to the goal of love. Love is an offensive game, not a defensive one. To be clear, inspecting and adapting based on frequent empirical evidence are your keys to finding happiness.

The following sections look at how you can overcome complications of modern dating and focus on finding love with scrum.

Setting a vision

The roadmap to value (or in this case, the roadmap to love) begins with setting a vision (see Chapter 2). As in business, you need a vision to guide you to your goal.

This area has changed dramatically in the past few years. The only purpose of any kind of romantic relationship used to be getting married and having children. Even though this vision is ideal for some people, it isn't for others. Define what you're pursuing when you pursue a relationship. Someone who defines all his interactions by the vision "I just want to have fun with someone I'm attracted to" is going to approach dating in a radically different way from someone who has the vision "I want to get married to someone I consider my best friend and soulmate."

Keep in mind that visions may change as your circumstances and stages in life change. You may desire to get married, but the thought may be so frightening that you set out to date with the vision of having fun. In that situation, you're not likely to find marriage any time soon. You may have a lot of fun, but fun won't necessarily lead to a long-term commitment or marriage until you adjust your vision.

REMEMBER

Vision statements are forward-looking internal statements. They describe how you see yourself in the future.

Having fun isn't a bad goal, but it's a bad vision if you want something else as an end state. Visions aren't met instantaneously, and simply having the goal of wanting a life partner doesn't mean that the next person you go on a date with will be that person. But knowing what you're pursuing in the long run will change your interactions during dating.

Dating in layers

Relationships evolve. You should know and clearly define what each stage of a relationship means to you. If you have a vision of finding a life partner, you'll take a series of steps toward that goal. In scrum, these steps are your roadmap, and each major milestone is a release goal. Here are some examples of release goals on a roadmap working toward a vision of finding a life partner:

>> Get ready for the dating world (update your wardrobe, start a fitness routine, change your hairstyle, or buy wineglasses, for example).

>> Create a short list of must-haves versus want-to-haves in your ideal partner.

>> Start dating compatible people.

>> Get into a relationship (as defined by you).

>> Become committed long-term (dating exclusivity, polyamorous agreement, engagement, or personal equivalent).

>> Intertwine lives (cohabitate, make joint major purchases, marry, and/or have children).

Each release goal requires you to engage in tasks and activities that move you from stage to stage. The first release goal alone can take some time.

If you can define what each stage of dating looks like, you can determine what release goal you're working toward. Use a definition of done. For example, a definition of done for readiness for dating might be accepting invitations to (and bravely showing up at) parties where you can meet new people, along with opening profiles on reputable dating networks. Each layer of a relationship should have a clear definition of done as set by you.

TIP

A definition of done for using online dating profiles that requires you to arrange and go on at least one in-person date (ideally more than one) would be a reasonable definition of done if the goal is to move forward and find someone for an in-person relationship.

A definition of done allows for clear communication and boundary setting in your dating life. The transition from dating to relationship is complicated, but you can eliminate some of the confusion by clarifying for yourself the difference between dating and a relationship. When you've dated someone to the point where the connection has evolved and has all the characteristics of your definition of done for a relationship, it's time to validate that you're in one. But the best part of using scrum to date is that you don't end up in a relationship by accident; you're an active participant moving steadily toward your goal.

WARNING

Not everyone in the dating world has the same definition of done for each stage of a relationship. Open communication and connection must be used to build trust. As you move through each release goal, you have to be open with those you date about what you're currently seeking and how you define each stage of a relationship.

Discovering companionship and scrum

With your roadmap spelled out, you have the framework for your backlog of requirements: the activities that you'll plan and take part in to accomplish your release goals and vision, starting with your initial release goal.

Part of your product backlog in preparing yourself for the dating world may be exploring activities and hobbies that you enjoy. A lot of value exists in spending this time building community and finding companionship while doing the things you enjoy. During this phase, most of the discovery is about you. What kinds of people you connect with, the community of people you build around you, and the community you find while you're doing the things that you enjoy build relationships that may connect you to people to date in the future. You also get a chance to safely connect with potential dating partners without the pressure of a dating setup.

REMEMBER

Use existing companionship and friendships to identify and refine your product backlog of what you are looking for when you move forward into dating and relationships.

Often, just putting yourself out there socially leads to dating. Dating happens naturally when you meet and spend time with people with whom you share interests. Relationships work in phases. A difference exists between friendships in communities and dating one on one, although the former can lead to the latter.

Don't forget to communicate. If you begin a relationship by spending time with someone as a friend, when the relationship evolves, you may forget to communicate about the shift in the relationship. To strengthen your ability to have good timing in potentially awkward situations, use your own definition of done to identify the difference between spending time with someone as a friend and recognizing when you've moved on to dating or even a committed relationship. Planning to have that discussion may be an example of a dating backlog item.

Be cautious about spending time with someone with all the intimacy and connection of a committed relationship — but identifying it as a casual friendship. If you struggle with this line of communication, use it as a learning opportunity to inspect and adapt and to move from the release goal of getting ready to date to dating to relationship. Poor communication is damaging to both parties and a prescription for the kind of dating drama that most people try to avoid. Use empirical evidence to refine what kind of relationship you're looking for, and use dating retrospectives such as the following to ensure that you're moving toward your goal:

>> What is going well?

>> What do we want to change?

>> How can we tangibly implement that change?

Dating with scrum

The benefits of scrum include a structured approach to a goal, empirical evidence, the inspect-and-adapt factor, and saving time. Life is full, but if you can accept that you want a partner in life, you must accept that you must make room for that person. Most people have heard (or used) the excuse that they'd love to find a relationship but have no time for it.

The good news is that your life is in your control. In the early stages of dating, you must make time for dates. In the later stages of dating, you must make room for a relationship to grow. Relationships don't happen in petri dishes. You won't find a quick way to go from having no room for a relationship to being in love and having a wonderful work-life-love balance.

Consider your life to be a product backlog. If your priority for your love-related roadmap and backlog items is always at the bottom, you'll always push it aside in favor of something else. If you decide that love is a high priority, you'll create space for it.

Continuing on the roadmap to value and using scrum in dating includes short sprint cycles, inspection and adaptation, and improvement for future sprints.

In scrum, each date is a sprint, so you're operating on a short sprint cycle meant to move you toward your release goal. Because you may not have a date every day of the week, this schedule gives you ample time between sprints to reflect (inspect) and to plan changes and improvements for the next one (adapt). The time between sprints (dates) is your opportunity for backlog refinement and process improvement.

The inspection part of inspection and adaptation focuses on how you see yourself and your date together. You can examine the following things:

>> Does this person have the qualities I'm looking for?

>> Do I have fun with this person?

>> Does this person meet my must-haves?

>> How do I act when I'm around this person?

>> What are my thoughts and feelings about this person when we're not together?

The adaptation portion is up to you. You may adapt what you're looking for (such as your vision), or you may adapt whom you're dating (such as by not going on another sprint with the same person). You may need to adapt your interaction and try another sprint with the same person based on your review. If you want to try something more fun, try a date with more lighthearted activities or something you enjoy seeing how those adaptations affect how you feel about the other person.

The best part about using scrum for dating is the inspect-and-adapt process. You and your dating partner get to form your own version of *us* — or not. As in business, the ability to cut something short based on early empirical evidence that it doesn't fit your vision saves not only time and money, but also disappointment on both sides.

Winning as a team

Unfortunately, modern dating is full of examples of game-playing, which typically pits people against one another. This mentality in dating overcomplicates interactions and closes communication. In scrum, you plan as a team, execute as a team, and are accountable based on the success or failure of the team. So, even if you feel that you're on a team of one when it comes to dating, remember that you're on a team of two. The best thing you can do for yourself is embrace scrum's concept of being a team with your date and working for the team to succeed rather than engaging in a contest against your date. With scrum, you can rise above the nonsense and avoid the games.

Honest communication is needed for any team and especially for any successful relationship. A common pitfall in contemporary dating is testing dates through loaded questions or actions. Scrum simplifies communication. Using scrum in dating means asking genuine questions and viewing the other person's answers as a chance to get to know him or her for the purpose of that sprint. In open communication, open dialogue by sharing your own views and asking your date his thoughts. As you plan your date sprints, plan questions that are genuine and encourage honest answers to help you determine whether this person is the right fit.

TIP

To work as a team, avoid putting your date in a situation in which you expect a specific behavior, but the person has no way of knowing what the goal is. Dates will often try to answer or behave the way that they believe they are expected to, many times missing the mark.

Here are some examples of behavior tests that generate skewed data:

>> You suggest a dating activity that you consider to be extreme (or uncomfortable) just to see how your date reacts, and you make a judgment based solely on that reaction.

>> A woman who believes that a gentleman should pay for a date offers to split the check, but if he accepts her offer, she's no longer interested.

>> A man who believes that physical intimacy should wait until a specific time in a relationship (a timeline defined by him but unshared) pursues being physically intimate. If the woman accepts physical intimacy, the man is no longer interested.

These examples use some gender norms, but various types of tests exist. Ask open-ended questions and share your own thoughts.

Focusing versus multitasking

Scrum is a focusing tool. One reason why scrum is so successful is that it edits out the noise of trying to do everything all at once by breaking up challenges into smaller and shorter goals. Instead of doing all projects poorly, scrum helps you focus on doing one project at a time with a higher level of quality than you'd achieve by thrashing around.

The following quote summarizes a recent study from Stanford: "Multitasking in meetings *and other social settings* indicates low self- and social-awareness, two emotional intelligence (EQ) skills that are critical to success at work." (Italics emphasis added.)

The study was examining how multitasking lowered effectiveness in a work setting — but emotional intelligence is a life skill. It will be hard to find love if you diminish your self- and social-awareness skills.

When you date two or more people at the same time, your mind and emotions are more distracted by multitasking than focused on discovering whether someone is a good match. Multitasking in dating may also mean trying to rush through multiple phases of a relationship.

Modern dating teaches everyone to date as many people as possible for as long as possible to keep all options open. The attempt to mitigate the risk that one relationship won't work out almost guarantees the risk that numerous or all relationships won't work out.

Dating multiple people can be a good thing to increase your chances of finding what you're looking for in the early stages, however. If your vision is finding the person you want to settle down with, having many relationships at the same time won't be a good fit for that vision (but it may be a good fit for a "having fun" vision).

TIP

Limit your pool of potential dates by using work-in-progress limits (see Chapters 5 and 6).

The roadmap to value takes you through the date (that is, the sprint) to the finish line (sprint review and retrospective). As you finish each date, take time to inspect the date itself (that is, your sprint review). Ask whether you liked the person and whether you liked yourself with that person. Then move to a retrospective for possible process changes, such as the way you went about planning the date, the questions you asked during the date, and the tactics or tools you used to evaluate whether your date was a good match. Your definition of done should be specific and clear enough to make it easy to inspect whether your sprints were successful and adapt your backlog for the next sprint.

When a potential relationship ends or doesn't move forward to the next release, another product backlog item (potential mate) can take its place. As in business, pivoting isn't bad as long as you pivot early to minimize investment (in terms of time and emotional drag as well as money) and as long as doing so moves you closer to your vision.

Planning your wedding with scrum

If you've already found love and are in the middle of an engagement, congratulations! Weddings are some of the biggest celebrations of life, meant to weave together families and friends and to acknowledge the beginning of a lifetime as a couple. Wedding days are full of many positive experiences, but the time leading up to the big day can put a strain on the couple that's trying to plan.

Use scrum for what it's built for: executing an important project. A wedding is the ultimate project. In wedding planning, you have a set date and (ideally) a set budget. Setting priorities and making decisions accordingly are necessary for having the kind of wedding you want. Planning a wedding successfully with scrum involves the following components:

>> Setting a vision. Talk about the ideal must-haves as part of your wedding and the experience you want to take away.

>> Setting a schedule (wedding day) and budgetary constraints.

>> Establishing and prioritizing wedding requirements (such as the venue, invitations, and cake) into a roadmap.

>> Establishing release goals (such as venue acquired, officiator scheduled, friends and family notified, decorations and place settings lined up, and photo shoots established).

>> Organizing your first sprint to address the highest-priority backlog items, breaking them into tasks, and swarming those tasks to completion).

>> Executing sprints and reprioritizing any new requirements discovered in each sprint.

>> Using sprint review to inspect and adapt (not only priorities, but also product backlog items such as remaining budget) and making new decisions moving forward.

When examining a wedding backlog, you may immediately see what needs prioritization. Some locations allow outside caterers, for example, whereas others require you to use a specific one. Also, locations frequently have strict time rules. Given that location can affect other backlog items, consider it to be a high-risk item (if not the highest-risk item) to address in an early sprint. After that item is set, it may change your existing backlog. You may make decisions toward big-budget items that you have prioritized early on to know what the remaining budget is for other items.

Toward the end of wedding planning, most couples still have long lists of small items to do. Try using a task or Kanban board to move small items forward and visualize what still needs to be addressed.

Weddings are expensive. As we discuss in terms of release planning (Chapter 5), portfolio management (Chapter 13), and financing projects (Chapter 14), using incremental funding and doing the highest-priority requirements first ensure that you finance the most critical features even if the money runs out before you complete the entire backlog. If the venue and food are already taken care of, it may not be a big deal if a few party favors have to be left off the list.

Families and Scrum

Busy is the defining word of families everywhere. With multiple levels of work and school commitments, it's difficult to find time to genuinely connect as a family. If you don't relax by connecting with your family, your stress levels remain high, lowering your effectiveness in many areas of life, including work. Connection and recreation with the family are vital parts of mental and emotional well-being.

Families can get caught up in a cycle of short-term communication via texting and long "to-do" lists. Each family member tends to work on his or her own list. Family members miss out on maximizing the amount of support they could be giving one another because of lack of communication and coordination.

The challenges facing families are as diverse as families themselves, but the following issues can apply to most families and can be addressed with scrum:

>> **Conflicting family priorities:** One member of the family wants a vacation; another wants to buy a car or go to college; yet another wants a home renovation. As in business, not all goals can be met at the same time. As in successful businesses, planning and coordinated decision-making are vital for achieving a goal.

>> **Communication:** Short text messages. Conversation cut short by a call from work. Faces buried in mobile devices sharing photos on social media during. Communication is more vital to families than even to work relationships, but exhaustion and busyness deplete real conversation.

>> **Conflicting schedules:** It's become a luxury for family members to be in the same place at the same time. Scrum can help you track who is involved in what activity and create a schedule to connect.

>> **Personal responsibility and accountability:** Every family copes with the pressures of daily life, such as chores, cleaning, errands, and paying bills. Often, one parent feels unsupported or overburdened, or one child feels too much or too little responsibility. For single parents, this problem is compounded. Scrum can help you balance responsibilities across family members.

With the challenges of modern life tugging at the bonds among family members, it's important to find innovative ways to stay connected and grounded. Stability and healthy relationships within the family affect what you do outside it, from school to career to friendships.

In the following sections, we show you concrete examples of scrum being implemented into daily life by simplifying communication, using a family vision statement, prioritizing a family backlog, making decisions as a team, and increasing responsibility through visibility and ownership.

Setting family strategy and project visions

The biggest challenge in making family decisions is conflicting priorities. In ancient times, families frequently had mottos or sayings that defined their character, and we suggest that it's time to bring this tradition back with a modern twist. Wouldn't it be nice to be able to address conflicts inside and outside the home by recognizing that the behavior doesn't fit the family strategy?

A clearly defined family strategy or mission can provide behavior, values, and structure to guide a family in all its decisions. Family strategies work especially well when all family members have ownership of the strategy statement rather than having it dictated by a parent.

As we say in Chapter 2, the vision is where the roadmap to value begins. A vision statement for a project must support the overall strategy or mission, or a disconnect occurs between project direction and overall business strategy. The situation is no different for families. As families plan projects, they start with a vision of the result of the project, and that vision ties directly into the family's strategy.

Planning and setting priorities

Most families take life a day at a time or even an hour at a time. But realizing goals takes planning and priority management. Scrum provides a framework for progressing toward goals.

As a family defines its strategy and decides on projects and activities that carry out the strategy, the projects and activities become clearer and easier to prioritize and plan. Scrum's iterative approach to planning, executing, inspecting, and adapting leads families to success.

Project planning

Families establish a strategy (if they haven't already done so) and then define the vision (see Chapter 2) for the project goal. Each family member gets to brainstorm the ideas to achieve the project vision, which becomes the roadmap for that family project. The family estimates the effort and complexity of each idea and prioritizes and orders the ideas based on their effort, complexity, value to the project, and risks involved. The roadmap is owned by the family team.

TIP

Chapter 4 describes methods for creating estimates. Family estimations may not need to use the Fibonacci sequence. Estimating is simply a way for the family to get an idea of the relative effort to complete things so that they can plan accordingly. Using affinity estimating with the more familiar concept of T-shirt sizes may be all you need.

Release planning

Families can identify minimum viable product (MVP) releases (see Chapter 5) leading up to completing a project and plan each in detail one at a time as each one is completed. When you're planning a birthday party, for example, the first release may be selecting and reserving a location. When you don't know the location, you don't know all the details of what you'll be able to do for the birthday party. When you know the location, you can send out invitations, choose a caterer, and select decorations.

Always use a definition of done when tackling each sprint and release. If a family-product backlog item is so vague that no one knows how it can be considered to be done, it shouldn't be considered to be ready to execute in a sprint. Vague or open-ended backlog items that make it into a sprint tend to sit in the Doing column for a long time. If your family backlog has items such as the following, you know that you need to break them down and quantify how they can be done:

>> Clean the house. (This item could take days, depending on the type of cleaning and the portions of the house that need cleaning.)

>> Save money for a trip to Yellowstone. (This item says nothing about how much money is needed or what means will be used to earn or save the money.)

Sprint planning

When you know the long-term goal (vision), how to get there (roadmap of how to get there), and the big steps needed to get there (releases), breaking the work into sprints is easy. Weeklong sprints are a natural cadence for families as well as businesses. For most people, work and school schedules are predictable; one day of the week usually serves as a start or end point with a logical place to reset, plan, and review. Even if you don't have a consistent break in routine, the family can establish one.

Sprint planning for a family doesn't need to take long. With a task board, a family can quickly identify the items from the backlog that can be accomplished during the week. Each family member can identify how to help with each backlog item. Members move the items from the backlog to the To Do column and talk about the tasks required for each item in the sprint backlog. Then they identify when in the week they'll be able to accomplish those tasks. (See Chapter 5 for more on sprint planning.)

Then you'll have hugs, kisses, and high-fives all around as family members agree on the plan and go to work throughout the week. Later in this chapter, we describe how to implement this type of planning into existing or natural family interactions.

REMEMBER

Visibility and transparency are every bit as important for families as for businesses. Create a family task board just as you would in a business. A tangible task board is best. Children love the satisfaction of moving a sticker, magnet, sticky note, or index card from one column to another as much as adults do. Families can use virtual task boards as well. Find what makes most sense for your family, but make sure that your board is easily accessible and visible, because family members will refer to and update it every day.

Daily scrums

Giving family members an opportunity each morning or evening to say what they did, what they'll be working on next, and what help they'll need from other family members to accomplish those tasks can happen quickly and greatly improve the chances of success for that day.

TIP

Use swarming techniques to move sprint backlog items to the Done column. A good way for older children to learn leadership and service is to allow a younger sibling to shadow them to learn a new skill. A good way to increase unity and teach cooperation and collaboration is to encourage family members to work together on backlog items.

Scrum teams are cross-functional. Embrace the concept of shadowing and pair programming in your home by having family members teach new skills when appropriate so that responsibilities can be shared. If one person is responsible for all the cooking, cook together. For the cooking project, one of the children may be able to take on the product-owner role by prioritizing and ordering the tasks for the other family members to carry out, and then practicing her decision-making skills by accepting or rejecting the work along the way. Parents can guide children throughout the process.

These projects are not only opportunities to bond, but also opportunities to pass along vital life skills that enable each member of the family to take on certain tasks.

WARNING

Thrashing occurs to families as well as businesses. Families are like large organizations in that they frequently have many projects going at the same time. (Read Chapter 14 for information about the effects of trying to do too much at once and a discussion on the hierarchy of thrashing.) Planning a family vacation, a family reunion, and a home renovation project while preparing a child to leave for college are too many projects for a family to plan at the same time. As in business, family leaders must decide which projects are highest-priority to ensure their success. You may have pressure to do all projects at the same time, but you don't have to. As a family uses scrum's planning structure to determine what projects to take on, they assess the effort and complexity of each project. Then they can determine what bandwidth they have to prioritize and order, and the big-picture view enables them to make better-informed decisions.

Thrashing on multiple projects means that completing these projects takes at least 30 percent more time. Working on one project at a time is faster than multitasking. See Chapter 13 for details.

Communicating with scrum

Scrum provides ways to increase critical communications, even when time is short. Scrum uses a variety of tools for communications, one of which is prioritizing face-to-face communication whenever possible. On a scrum team, major decisions are never enacted via text or email. This one simple change can dramatically revitalize the dynamics in a family. Parents know that when the tone and body language are present, understanding can dramatically improve!

Put down the mobile devices in your home and talk to other family members face to face. Or make it a house rule that if a conversation is taking place, no participant should be watching television, playing a video game, working on a computer, or using a mobile device. A family's mantra might be "Look up when we're talking."

Face-to-face communication works only if both people are participating in a focused conversation. Reduce miscommunication and length of conversations by quitting the habit of conversational multitasking.

To put face-to-face communication to good use, some existing family activities can provide a natural forum for sprint planning, daily scrums, sprint reviews, and retrospectives. One such activity is family mealtime.

Author and speaker Bruce Feiler presented a TED talk on "Agile programming — for your family" (www.ted.com/talks/bruce_feiler_agile_programming_for_your_family/transcript), where he discusses the dramatic change that his family achieved in minutes a day using a daily scrum model.

Think about the value that a daily scrum could add to your family in a simple 15-minute timebox! The following are some examples of benefits your family might reap from taking the time to communicate without distractions:

>> Hearing updates from every member of the family about what happened during his or her day

>> Sharing plans or goals for each person's upcoming day

>> Listening to current challenges for each member of the family

>> Providing an opportunity to problem-solve as a team or support one another through challenges

>> Celebrating accomplishments daily

Though family dinnertime is a good time slot for a family meeting, those crucial 15 minutes can happen at any time during the day. A daily scrum over breakfast, over dinner, or even before a certain television show will work as long as the time slot is consistent and limited to 15 minutes. Daily scrums aren't long enough to resolve all the issues of daily life, but they accomplish the task of opening lines of communication and establishing trust and support. That way, if greater challenges arise, the family support foundation is already in place.

Inspecting and adapting for families

Sprint reviews and retrospectives are as important for families as they are for businesses. For busy families, it may make sense to review accomplishments (sprint review) and then review processes and tools used as well as communication, relationships, and discipline techniques (sprint retrospective) during the same meeting time just before planning a new week (sprint planning).

Sprint reviews may include results from the school week; progress made toward planning the next family vacation; and successes in sports, music, and other activities. Sprint reviews are also times to review events that are scheduled for the future to identify items for the backlog to help prepare for them, like a birthday party or getting the house ready for extended-family guests who will be visiting.

For weekly family meetings, the following questions follow scrum's sprint retrospective model:

>> What worked well this week?

>> What didn't work well?

>> What can we agree to work on next week?

You may be surprised by the feedback coming from family members. During the family meeting, everyone should choose two or more improvements that they all agree to work on for the following week. This agreement is called a team agreement in the agile space.

The family may also choose what consequences should occur if rules are broken or if one member of the family doesn't meet his or her commitments. Again, rather than the traditional model in which consequences follow action, in a scrum model, the team (the family) agrees on lessons learned and how to improve them before taking on the new sprint goal. The team also agrees about the benefits or rewards of meeting new goals. The reward for achieving the family goal is a wonderful motivator.

Making chores fun and easy

It would be wonderful if chores could simply be handled without difficulty instead of escalating into arguments. Many parents are discovering how to empower their children to motivate themselves to do chores by using personal task or Kanban boards.

Human beings have an innate need to feel accomplished. Most adults make to-do lists, but we like the items that are easy to accomplish quickly so that we can cross them off the list. Children crave the same sense of accomplishment. They need to know that their contributions are important. Participating in the household is absolutely essential for helping children know that they're valued. Choosing age-appropriate ways for children to participate in running the household molds the family together as a unit. Task boards make it easy for everyone to see what it means to be successful.

TIP

If kids are struggling with larger chores, treat the larger chore as the user story and help them by breaking down important tasks. If they struggle to accomplish "Clean your bedroom," have "Clean your bedroom" be the user story, with smaller tasks such as "Organize books," "Put dirty laundry away," "Make bed," "Wash bedroom window," "Put away toys," and "Dust bookshelves." That way, children can have the user story "Clean your bedroom" in the Doing column along with other smaller tasks until all tasks are complete. They can ask for assistance with larger, more difficult tasks until they learn how to accomplish them.

As in business, family task–board requirements (user stories) should be ones that can be accomplished within a sprint, and tasks should be ones that can be completed in a day or less. For younger children, tasks should be an hour or less to set them up for success.

TASK BOARD FOR BEDTIME

Blogger Chris Scott of the Agile School (http://theagileschool.blogspot.co.uk) posted a brief video of his 5-year-old daughter using a simple task board to get herself ready for bed. Each task is represented on a piece of paper with a picture that helps her remember what the task is. Prompted by her father, she looks at the To Do column and chooses the next task, which is indicated by a photo of a puppy (representing "Wash feet"), and moves it to the Doing column. Then she then turns to her dad and tells him that it's time to wash her feet. This video is a great example of how even the youngest children can understand the basics of scrum and have fun moving themselves through their responsibilities. We know many families that struggle with putting young children to bed, but the task board helps a young child practically parent herself to bed.

Chapter **18**

Scrum for Life Goals

If you have built castles in the air, your work need not be lost; that is where they should be. Now put the foundations under them.
— HENRY DAVID THOREAU, *WALDEN*

The universal applicability of scrum is more than likely starting to become clear by now. Scrum is simple enough to be applied to any business or personal goal and adaptable enough to work for any important project you want to address.

Everyone has goals in life that end up feeling too big and too distant to approach. The best part of scrum is taking the overwhelming and breaking it into manageable pieces.

Getting to Retirement

The reality of life is that a time will come when you'll no longer be able to work full-time. But retirement can be defined as any time you reach enough financial freedom that your passive income — the income you don't actively work for — is enough to cover your expenses. If you define retirement this way, it becomes a goal to work toward at any age, and your product backlog of items and release goals supports reaching the vision of financial freedom. The farther in the future retirement is, the harder it can be to focus on the things you can do today to reach those important financial goals, as in-the-moment financial needs crop up.

A big challenge for younger generations is how to cope with rising costs of living while salaries aren't rising at the same rate. You can use scrum to address this challenge and progress toward financial security each year.

The best way to bring a long-term future goal into the present is to use the roadmap to value in developing your retirement vision, build release goals and your backlog, and use sprints to work toward each goal.

Saving for emergencies

Your first release goal toward the vision of financial independence should include saving for financial emergencies. Emergencies are bound to happen and may come at a significant financial cost. Medical bills, a job loss, repairs to your home or car, and divorce or family issues that result in unpaid time off work can cause financial strain. The only way to protect your future financial safety is to plan for emergencies now by developing a savings fund that covers emergencies, bears interest, and isn't locked into penalties if you must make a withdrawal for an emergency.

An emergency fund is one release goal in your vision of financial security. Sprints should include ways to adapt your budget, focusing on setting money aside.

The most common financial goal for emergency savings is to have the equivalent of six months of expenses in savings. To support this release, you decide sprint lengths (no more than a month) and work each sprint on backlog items that support building a savings plan.

Your income less expenses equals surplus. Surplus generating interest over time equals wealth. The equation is

$$\text{Surplus} \times \text{Interest} \times \text{Time} = \text{Wealth}$$

If you have little or no surplus at the end of each pay cycle, you need to examine your budget and reorganize your backlog of priorities to increase your income, decrease your expenses, or both. Keep in mind this motto: Live free before living well. It might be nice to have expensive things, but not if it costs you your financial freedom or future security.

When building your savings, resist the urge to use emergency funding for nonemergency reasons. It's the surest way to backpedal your progress toward your goal. Create a separate savings account for discretionary-purchase goals (such as travel, a new pair of skis, or a new car) to avoid dipping into emergency savings.

Acknowledging the need for pleasure purchases is an important step in having a sustainable plan for savings. The key is to balance short-term fun purchases against long-term security goals.

Your sprints should consistently focus on ways to open your ability to create surplus toward savings. Review the outcome of each sprint to inspect, adapt, and make changes earlier than later. Don't let yourself get stuck sprint after sprint in a passive-income endeavor that isn't achieving your goal, for example. Sprint and release goals, and your definition of done, should help you define backlog items that are specific and clear about what success is. Don't be afraid to move on with increased knowledge from your mistakes. Lean Startup (see Chapter 13) may be helpful to you if you decide to take the entrepreneurial approach to increasing your income.

Building retirement

After you have a safety net, you should shift your savings to building for retirement. This portion of your goal progression remains in progress even as you move on to other release goals. Your sprint cycle includes examining your options to get the greatest return on investment. At the end of the first sprint, if your benefits package from work includes some matching funds, for example, your product backlog should be updated with items that get you the maximum possible matching point.

When running sprints to save for retirement, focus on how to safely achieve the maximum return on investment. If you're farther from retirement, don't be shy about being more aggressive with your investments in the beginning years of your saving. You can look online for retirement resources that will help you determine how much you should be saving to have a balance between your future vision and your current budget. Keep in mind when using these tools that we define retirement as the point at which you can stop actively working because your passive income is enough to support your expenses. Although most online tools and retirement advice calculators suggest an age of 55 or 60, your retirement age is actually defined by you and your vision.

WARNING

Section 72(t) of the United States tax code allows investors to take money out of their retirement plan penalty-free before age 59½ for income, but you'll have to take substantially equal periodic payments over time. Withdrawals can be spread over your life expectancy but need to be for at least five years. This is an example of the inputs you'll use to determine the age and account balance target for your personal retirement goals.

Securing financial freedom

After you reach both release goals of emergency savings and actively saving for retirement, your next release goal is building assets. We use simple definitions for assets and liabilities. An *asset* is anything that brings money to you, and a *liability* is anything that costs you money. Building assets is a personal decision and may require several sprints to research and increase your knowledge to support your high-level vision of where you want to be. You can use a spike (agile term for research or risk assessment) as a product backlog item to research and dissect an issue to answer a question.

Examples of early sprint goals to consider include

>> Structure your budget to allow and automate a set amount of index fund purchases each month.

>> Identify ways to increase income by 5 percent by doing something you enjoy.

Your sprint goals would continue to be broken down to the requirement level, such as

>> Create a budget.

>> Set up an index-fund automatic purchase.

>> Establish a website for your online business.

Another example of a sprint goal is to determine whether purchasing a home would create an asset or a liability. Product backlog items involve steps and activities for discovering whether the purchase of a home is the best use of your money, such as the following:

>> Conduct an analysis of whether the home will bring a sufficient return on investment.

>> Determine whether another place or investment would bring a higher rate of return.

By this same measure, a large, expansive house might be nice, but it brings greater liability if it can't be easily sold at a profit. Research carefully and use early sprints to inspect and adapt toward the release goal of building assets. Building assets is about building passive income to support your vision to retire.

REMEMBER

Houses are liabilities (they cost you money) until they generate income through a rental or are sold at a profit. Your primary residence is likely not an asset; you need to live somewhere.

In using scrum for building financial freedom, you use empirical evidence and the inspect-and-adapt process in the same way that a software project would. You can see if you're tangibly moving toward the goal and determine how you can achieve the goal faster. You can see what roadblocks are in your way and come up with a plan for removing them.

A perfect example of asset building and addressing roadblocks is considering academic education. If your educational status prevents you from moving forward financially, examine the potential asset outcome against the liability. Some questions to consider are

>> How much will the education I'm considering cost (actual cost plus opportunity cost)?

>> How much income will it generate when I'm finished?

>> Does the income it will generate greatly outweigh the cost of getting the education?

As with purchasing a home, you should have a clear financial asset outcome for getting additional education before you embark on it.

DIGGING A WHOLE

A recent Federal Reserve study (www.federalreserve.gov/releases/g19/current/default.htm) shows that members of the class of 2016 graduated from college with an average of $37,172 in student loans. Members of that class who are now 20 to 30 years old have an average monthly payment of more than $350.

Total U.S. student loan debt is $45 trillion with more than 44 million borrowers. According to Gallup (http://news.gallup.com/businessjournal/188984/americans-big-debt-burden-growing-not-evenly-distributed.aspx), "the situation is indeed dire for the one-third of millennials (35%) who carry student loan debt." Additionally, 64 percent of millennials carry consumer debt, and when student loans are put into that mix, the average debt balance for millennials is $40,000.

Retiring debt

Another part of financial independence for you may be some form of being debt-free. Scrum can be an effective strategy to pay off debts by breaking the achievements into small, measurable increments such as the following:

» Treat paying off a loan or credit card like a release goal.

» Pay more than minimum balances so that overall principal goes down.

» Retrospectively look at progress and have a party when you achieve your goal.

Achieving Fitness and Weight Goals

If fitness is a goal, using scrum to achieve your vision is one of the best ways to succeed. The struggle many people have with weight loss and fitness is the so-called yo-yo effect. Many people can start a fitness-and-diet regimen, but often after achieving the result they slowly but surely slide back to where they began.

One reason why this happens is focus. The drawback is that in weight loss, this focus is often on an extreme, regimented situation. After you fall off the wagon, so to speak, you immediately begin unraveling your hard-earned work. Scrum allows for focus, but that focus is in small, measurable, and achievable segments. In other words, scrum is about taking steps toward your goal and achieving it sustainably, not just jumping on an extreme roller coaster and then burning out.

Work through the roadmap to value, just as you would with any other major project. Following are some examples of applying the roadmap to value to weight loss and fitness, which you can tailor to your own vision and goals:

» **Set a vision.** You want to be back to your physical shape in college, which was 185 pounds, 32-inch waist, running a mile in 7 minutes, and bench-pressing 200 pounds.

» **Create a product roadmap.** Initial roadmap items may include things such as losing 10 pounds (you may have this item several times, because incremental improvement is the goal), running 3 miles without stopping, or lowering your blood pressure.

» **Create a product backlog.** This backlog might include making new recipes to cook, joining a gym, and having diet and exercise plans.

» **Set your first release goal.** In two months, you may want to have lost 3 pounds and be able to run 1 mile.

>> **Determine sprint lengths.** A sprint may last a week, for example.

>> **Choose what to bring into the first sprint.** You may decide to cut soda volume by 50 percent, eat dessert only three times a week, walk a mile three times a week, and do aerobic activity at least once a week.

At the end of each sprint, review your progress toward the goals, update your product backlog with what you have learned throughout the sprint, and adapt the next steps to be in line with your release goal.

Even after one sprint, you should use the sprint retrospective to inspect and adapt. Ask yourself the three sprint retrospective questions:

>> **What went well?** You might say, "The cooking website I used has good recipes. I should keep using it. The mobile calorie tracking app is easy to use. My family is being really supportive."

>> **What do I want to change?** You might say, "I don't like to do cardio on days I eat sweets. Nighttime workouts are hard to stick to. My lunch group gives me a hard time about my new health goals, which is discouraging."

>> **How can I achieve that change?** You might say, "I'll establish set days of the week for sweets, which won't be cardio days." You might try morning workouts the next sprint to see whether it's easier to be consistent at that time of day, cut lunch groups to once per week or not at all, or find a new lunch group.

Run your next sprint incorporating both what you want to improve and the new items from your backlog. At the two-month mark, review the whole release to examine whether you've achieved your goal and to determine your next release goal.

The key in using scrum to move forward on your weight-loss goal is recognizing that each step is a small but truly incremental step. At any time, not meeting your goal isn't a failure, but an opportunity to find a new way to move forward. Even if you fall back on bad habits, getting back on track isn't a massive commitment because the sprint cycles are so short.

Consider a high-visibility task board for items that have the specific status of Done. To continue the preceding example, you could have three workout tasks, each of which gets moved over each time you complete your exercise. Giving yourself a visual depiction of completing also helps you identify opportunities (exercises that you enjoy) and bottlenecks (exercises that you avoid), and it helps you create ideas for your next sprint.

An example of a visible and achievable plan which has brought success to many is a novice plan to participate in a half-marathon (www.halhigdon.com/ training/51131/Half-Marathon-Novice-1-Training-Program). Every week the Sunday goal is clear and incremental.

TIP

Keeping Life Balance

One big challenge in life is managing emotional and mental well-being. Life can be a roller coaster, and it's your responsibility to find a way to minimize volatility and maximize enjoyment and fulfillment.

Mental and emotional health is a wide category, covering everything from a temporary increase in life stress to diagnosable mental health issues. Scrum is a framework for addressing goals and prioritizing issues, not a substitution for mental or emotional health services. You'll probably want to team up with someone whom you trust to provide ongoing support and accountability as you build your vision, roadmap, and backlog and work through the scrum events. Don't go it alone.

If life becomes overwhelming, the source can be from a variety of places (some of which are addressed in Chapter 17, as well as those in the previous examples in this chapter). The building blocks of our lives get moved and shifted over time. With stress, everyone has a breaking point. For one person, a bad breakup might be the building block that makes the other stressors in life seem like too much. For another person, financial hardship or the loss of a job is the building block that, along with other life factors, ends up feeling like too much.

When stressors are becoming burdensome, use scrum to find solutions. Here are some questions to ask yourself as you start defining your vision, roadmap, and backlog:

> » What are my stressors?
>
> » Why are they causing such high stress right now?
>
> » What stressor makes me feel overwhelmed?

Asking yourself these questions allows you to identify the source of the issues and the factor that currently creates the most stress. From this identification, you begin to move through the roadmap to value.

Using the current highest stressor as the priority, you build a vision of what you'd like to see in your life. From this point, you break down your first release and then identify sprint goals and tasks that you can take toward achieving that release.

As in sprints in any other life goal endeavor, you consistently return to inspection and adaptation. You may ask, "Is this still the highest stressor and the one that I need to focus on solving to feel more balanced?" If so, keep working until you achieve the release goal. If not (AC + OC > V; see Chapter 5), finish that release, and set a new release goal.

REDUCING LIFE STRESS

John is in his early 30s; he's struggling with feeling overwhelmed and doesn't know how to address the many frustrations in his life. First, he examines his stressors and discovers the following:

- Work is very stressful and a negative environment; additionally, it doesn't pay well, causing financial stress.

- His current apartment is a stressful, unsafe place to live, but he feels that he can't move because he doesn't earn enough from work.

- He frequently feels alone, and although he wants a relationship, he hasn't found the right person to be with and doesn't feel that he's ready to be in a relationship. His friends and family members feel distant because of how stressed he is at work and home.

John decides that his bad work situation is the worst of these factors (priority decision). He writes a vision statement that reflects what he wants: "I want a job that pays at least $80,000 a year, with full benefits and a steady work schedule, not the long and unpredictable hours that I currently work." (This vision is clear and specific.)

His first release goal may be to begin searching for new jobs. His first sprint may include dedicating one hour per night to updating his résumé and applying to five new jobs during the sprint. He may also include tasks such as reconnecting with acquaintances, looking for job leads, or searching for positions starting at $80,000 with specific working hours.

After several sprints of focusing on applying to new jobs, John moves to the interviewing phase. After each sprint (that is, each interview), he holds a review and uses inspection and adaptation to adjust his job search or reexamine what stressor needs focus.

At any point during any given sprint review, John could decide that he's reduced his stress enough to release that goal and focus on a new stressor. The point of using scrum to keep mental and emotional balance is that it combines the concept of taking measurable steps to address a need with the sprint review to inspect and adapt those steps or, if necessary, address another issue from the product backlog of stressors.

As you move through sprints, addressing one issue at a time, you may find to your surprise that you feel less stress, but another item has taken priority, and it's time to focus on that item to feel more mentally and emotionally stable.

REMEMBER

Thrashing among projects not only increases time by at least 30 percent, but it's also overwhelming. With your mental and emotional well-being, focusing on one thing at a time is your best bet.

As you progress through the roadmap to value, use the following questions to define your vision, release goals, and sprint goals:

>> **Vision:** What do I ultimately want my situation to look like?

>> **Release goal:** What smaller milestone would progress me toward that vision?

>> **Sprint goals:** What items can I bring in from the product backlog to work on first that would mean I am taking steps toward achieving that release goal *right now?*

Planning Travel

Vacations are amazing opportunities for relaxation, exploration, and connection as a team. Even travel for business can accomplish similar objectives. All too often, however, teams, families, and friends struggle with frustrations about financing and finding time for travel, as well as differing opinions on what to do and how to relax. Also, circumstances can change at any time with travel, both before and during the trip. Scrum is a major planning tool that is perfect for this kind of project. Think about it: You have an exact date and often a fixed budget; everything else is prioritization of the scope of the trip. Instead of one person calling all the shots and hoping that everyone likes the decisions made, working together as a team brings about engagement and satisfaction from everyone. For example, everyone would work together to come to a consensus on the following things:

>> Create a vision plan of the trip or vacation.

>> Set calendar dates.

>> Know your budget.

>> Create a vacation backlog of items from the stakeholders (such as family members and travel companions).

>> Prioritize the backlog to achieve the best result possible.

With family travel, every member of the family can and should participate in what an ideal vacation looks like to them. Keep in mind that if taking a trip becomes a family habit, this year's vacation vision may not have the same ideal qualities as last year or next year, and that is the point. Reviewing the plan as a family provides insight on how to focus the budget.

As in any scrum project, the vacation budget is the factor that you want to fix first. If family members are focused on activities that cost a higher value, the family can examine more budget-friendly places to do them. If a specific location is the highest priority as a family, the vacation can be planned around more budget-friendly options in an ideal location.

Don't be afraid to include children in discussing priorities according to budgeting. Although they may or may not have the responsibility of saving the money in the bank or setting the total budget, they should be involved in a trade-off decision as a team. You might say, "We can snorkel in Hawaii or go ziplining, but not both. Which would you like to do? It's important to teach kids that setting financial priorities and sticking to a budget are major family life skills. Scrum thrives when everyone involved has ownership of decisions.

TIP

Rather than a simple vote structure, in which each member only says yes or no, try fist of five (see Chapter 4), followed by dot voting. In fist of five, you show your support for an idea. Putting up one finger means total resistance to the idea, whereas displaying five fingers means it's a great idea. For a decision to pass, everyone in the family should at least have three fingers up, meaning that even though they may not love it, they don't hate it and are willing to support the decision. Using fist of five voting first allows narrowing a pool of options that no one in the family hates. You follow with dot voting for a final decision. In dot voting, all family members have five votes each. They put dots on the choice they want vote for, and they can put all dots on the same option or one on different options, indicating a preference for certain decisions.

Items from the product backlog need to be executed by each family member. Reservations need to be set, but changes based on the reality of availability or price, or perhaps changes in expected weather, need to be addressed on an ongoing basis. This approach allows the major items with higher risk to be done early, with risk declining as the date gets closer.

As dates for vacation grow closer, fewer large decisions will be in progress, and vacation planning will evolve into tasks that need to be accomplished before departure. Keep an eye on the calendar and establish short sprints to accomplish any remaining items. Break the product backlog items down so that items are easily moved to the Done column. Shopping for the appropriate clothing and also packing for the trip can't be done in the same week without causing stress and chaos, for example. Place shopping in a sprint that's long enough before the trip so that when it's time to pack, items are available. In fact, in an earlier sprint, do a mock packing activity to help you identify things that you'll need to shop for so that no surprises occur during the real packing the night before you leave.

VACATION PLANNING WITH SCRUM

Travel — both business and pleasure — can be unpredictable. One of our coaches planned an anniversary vacation to Hawaii a few years ago with scrum. He scored some last-minute (less than two weeks in advance) travel deals and didn't have much time to plan the trip in detail. He and his wife had never been to Hawaii, so he asked friends and family for ideas about what to do and where to eat. With luggage, plane tickets, hotel and car reservation, and a list of potential things to do (roadmap) in hand with a general budget amount in mind, they boarded the plane. The vision was simple: Relax with no pressure to see or do everything.

On the plane ride, finally catching their breath, they took out their trip backlog of activities and places to eat. They planned the first day and estimated about how much of the budget it would take. Then they enjoyed the rest of the flight.

At the start of the next day, they crossed off the things they did on the list and identified a few other things that sounded interesting. One of those things involved making a tour reservation, so they scheduled it for three days out.

Each day, they did the same thing, adding to the list, crossing off completed items, and adjusting the priority based on their interests. Some items never reached the top of the list or got thrown out as their interest in the item decreased. The process hardly felt like planning.

They were fortunate to have had open-ended return date (not a prerequisite for using scrum). They found that after eight days instead of their projected ten days, they had had enough, accomplished their vision for the trip, did the things they wanted to do, and ate where they wanted to eat. They returned home fully satisfied (AC + OC > V).

Studying

Learning is a necessary part of life from birth until death. Theoretical physicist Albert Einstein is quoted as saying, "Once you stop learning, you start dying." Human curiosity propels us toward the life we want to lead. Primary school is a structured format of learning from the age of 5 (or less for some learners) until the 12th grade, but formal learning often goes beyond primary school through trade certifications, undergraduate or graduate studies, and professional education.

In the United States, the school system is meant to unify basic competency skills for children and help them identify potential areas of interest for further exploration. As we examine in Chapter 10, scrum can help schools at administrative levels and teachers at classroom levels. Although schools and teachers work to improve things at those levels, students themselves can use scrum to enhance their experiences with their own education.

Students can use the roadmap to value to work toward their goals. They develop a vision, generate a backlog of items from an overall roadmap, identify a first release, run short sprints against that release, and use a sprint review to inspect and adapt their product (such as homework) for the next sprint. They run a sprint retrospective to inspect and adapt their processes and tools to help them optimize progress with their education. This process allows students at every step to refine their product backlog or adapt their study sessions as needed.

Learning early

If you're a parent or a teacher, you see kids struggle with learning in some form or another. Depending on their ages, it can be hard for kids to feel like they need to learn something difficult because they don't always have the sense of how it applies to their future. If they don't see a connection between their learning and what they want, it's hard for them to want to fight through the difficulty. Even young children can use scrum. Scrum is simply three roles, three artifacts, and five events. It empowers children and makes it fun to get through their own backlog of items. In this section, we address early learners as students in grades kindergarten through grade 8.

Helping young learners identify a vision and correlating that vision to their own lives are keys to getting them to engage. Help them correlate things they're interested in and like to do with what they're studying. We have a friend whose 6-year-old wakes up in the morning and pulls out all the supplies to bake a cake. But the same daughter gets frustrated when learning numbers and counting. Her mother saw an opportunity to help her see that baking a cake involves numbers.

After that small lesson, her daughter was much more willing to put in the work required to learn numbers.

Early learners can benefit from using task boards to work through their homework on many levels, because task boards are easily adaptable as the homework changes and the student grows.

We talk about thrashing in just about every chapter, especially in Chapters 6, 13, and 15. Multitasking reduces quality and effectiveness, and scrum reduces that error margin by focusing on one project at a time. Students of all ages are thrashed across many subjects at the same time. The key to using scrum for students is running short sprints against certain topics or projects. Perhaps sprints last several days or even a single day to enable students to focus on one item at a time.

Regardless of sprint length, students can use the Pomodoro technique (see Chapter 2) to shift tasks more easily. The Pomodoro technique creates a natural resting point and provides an easy opportunity for task switching. When using the Pomodoro method, a student can easily see whether the task needs to be continued after a break or whether it's time for a new task to begin.

Teaching children early how to inspect and adapt is crucial. One of our coaches has a daughter in third grade. She came home and showed her dad her spelling test grade for the week. She was normally a perfect speller, so when he noticed that she missed four words, he was surprised. He first acknowledged that she still got a relatively good score but asked why she missed more than usual. After attempting to blame other students for distracting her, she admitted that she'd been rushing through her tests and hadn't been practicing as much as she could have each day between the pretest and the final test.

Instead of treating her as having done something wrong, he asked her how she thought she could do better on next week's test and avoid rushing through it. She remembered that at the beginning of the year, she was doing short practice tests every day of the week, not just at the beginning and the night before the test. They agreed it would be good to try that again, and she implemented her new plan the following week. She was able to learn from her own experiences and own the solution for improvement.

Graduating from high school

High school students have a specific set of needs geared toward their vision of life after high school. Until graduation, most students focus on grade-by-grade or school-level movement, but at high school level, they're taking electives and beginning to steer themselves toward their own vision. High school is an opportunity for students to take hold of the reins and guide themselves. A student in high school may have many kinds of vision statements, from wanting to go to a four-year university to wanting to work right away and everything in between. The best way to achieve that vision is to use each year as a stepping stone.

In this section, we focus on the popular goal of getting into college. If a student's vision is to attend college, a specific backlog geared toward college requirements needs to be set. Items on this list should include all the nonscholarly work that needs to be done. Researching schools takes longer than a student might expect, for example, and should be done as early as possible so that future sprints can include activities tailored toward meeting admission requirements. Task boards are effective tools for progressing on important product backlog items.

Prioritization for high schoolers is key. Few students can take every academic subject, play every sport, score perfectly on exams, and participate in every activity — and they definitely can't do these things at the same time. By using prioritization, a student can edit out items that don't directly support his vision and focus on release goals that are important both personally and for getting into the right college. Using these release goals in working toward his vision helps him create milestones. Having release goals allows him to organize decomposed requirements into sprints.

Here's how this breakdown might look for a high school student:

>> **Vision:** Get into a four-year university.

>> **Release goal supporting vision:** Score more than 2,200 on the Scholastic Aptitude Test (SAT).

>> **Sprint goal supporting release goal:** Score more than 720 on five practice SAT math tests.

>> **Requirement level supporting sprint:** Find an SAT tutor, spend three hours studying the SAT book this week, focus on SAT math concepts, and ask the tutor about SAT-level geometry.

Expectations are high, and students are expected to become knowledgeable in a broad base of subjects. Also, competition to make it into college and receive scholarships is extremely high. Students have various mixtures of teachers and classes, so workloads vary from student to student and from term to term.

The sprint cycle of inspecting and adapting provides the framework that students need to adjust to varying loads and situations from term to term as they work through their roadmap.

In 2014, a guest blog post written by Alexis Wiggins went viral detailing the challenges she noticed as she shadowed first a tenth-grade student and then a twelfth-grade student for one day. Of primary concern to her were the constant strain of sitting all day and the passivity expected from learning. By incorporating scrum into at-home study, a student can take charge of learning in another way. While students can't control in-class lectures, they can find alternative ways aside from sitting and memorizing when at home. This is also where a student's product backlog can heavily influence progression. If extracurricular activities are an important factor in your vision, try choosing one that allows for physicality such as sports or a tactile club, such as art, to allow different methods of learning into goal progression. If, for some reason, physical extracurricular activities aren't appropriate or available, try incorporating physically active breaks when using the Pomodoro technique for studying.

PERSONAL EDUCATION VISION

A student's vision may change throughout the course of her educational career. Consider the following vision set by a student as a freshman and notice how it evolves as she inspects and adapts along the way. At the start of ninth grade, she knows that she wants to graduate from high school with a minimum 3.8 grade-point average (GPA) to qualify to attend an Ivy League school.

She may not have done much research on what's required of Ivy League schools. She may not know that more than just a certain GPA is required to get into college. She may not even know what career she wants after graduation. This vision is still a fine start, however.

By the end of her ninth-grade year, she knows that a 3.8 GPA probably won't be enough. She learns what test scores she needs for entrance, as well as what extracurricular leadership, service, and activities are required. She enjoyed a couple of social-sciences classes that gave her some insights into what she wanted her career to be. To start tenth grade, she has an updated vision: to qualify to attend Yale, Stanford, or Harvard after high school.

Her roadmap and backlog includes things such as "earn a minimum 4.2 GPA, score at least 30 on my ACT and a 2,200 on my SAT, and save enough money to pay for half of a trip to South America (Mom and Dad will pay for the other half) for humanitarian work before the end of my junior year."

At the end of each year, this student's vision and roadmap will probably evolve because she knows more than she did when she started. Regularly inspecting and adapting at logical intervals allows her to seek guidance from trusted parents and advisers to make informed decisions.

Achieving in college

College is the perfect opportunity for a student to use scrum. For any college student whose vision includes employability after graduation, implementing scrum practices helps with preparation for the business world.

The curriculum for each class may be decided by a teacher, but the overall educational content is up to the student. Deciding what to major in is a huge task for a student, regardless of the decisions being made before or during college. Inspection and adaptation still influence students on the sprint level to improve their learning, but with college, these tasks need to be brought to release or even vision level. A student may find at the end of a semester (release level), for example, that biology isn't a study that he wants to continue to pursue and that another subject has become a high-priority interest. As his interests evolve, he adjusts his vision and roadmap so that they provide the boundaries and direction for each release (term) and sprint (week).

College is also a time to pursue team building within a scrum framework. College group projects are an opportunity to use scrum for planning, reviewing, coordinating, establishing team agreements, and responding to changes. Holding scrum events and using a task board give immediate visibility of who is working on each portion of the project and how the project is progressing. Students should keep group meetings as short as possible by using daily scrums. If the group needs to address an impediment or swarm on a sprint backlog item that has lagged, that visibility allows the project to progress quickly.

In addition, students can tailor successful completion of projects to their own learning styles. College-level projects are frequently defined by a definition of done (the rubric provided by the professor), but getting to done is left up to the learner.

TIP

Team-building and pair-programming techniques apply in collegiate study. Students don't have to have a group project to review one another's work before completion. They can use sprint reviews to elevate their work before final submission (the release to the customer, who is the teacher).

Subsets of release and sprint goals are similar to what was done at the high school level, but in the collegiate atmosphere, goals may include building relationships with professors who can refer you for scholarships or jobs or seeking specific internships to gain job skills. Students can build a strong working relationship with professors by including their feedback and using it to improve their own work.

TIP

Credit hours, like velocity (see Chapter 4), may tell only part of the story. Just because a student took 12 credits last term doesn't mean that 12 credits is the right number next term. A three-credit class last term may not require the same amount of effort outside class as a totally different three-credit class next term. Doing an internship next term may require taking fewer credits than last term. Perhaps a student can take more online credits next term than last term.

SPRINT CYCLE FOR A COLLEGE STUDENT

Scrum for students breaks sprints into one week each. Students review the roadmap and focus on the current release, selecting backlog items for the sprint, which are broken into activities that can be done in a day or less. If 30 pages need to be read for class B, the total might be broken down to 10 pages per day for three of the seven days of the sprint. At the end of the first day of reading, the student knows whether 10 pages is the right amount for the remaining days. Another requirement for the sprint might be to research a specific topic for an upcoming writing assignment.

Some of these activities may need to be timeboxed. The research may need to be done in two hours or less, for examples. Because of work and class schedules, a student may have only enough time for 60 minutes of reading. Based on time available and work left to be done, each day the student has to decide how he can best use that time.

At the roadmap, release, sprint, and daily levels, students prioritize and order their work to be done and adjust as needed.

At the end of each sprint, a student reviews her work completed against what the goal and adjusts the remaining product backlog accordingly. She also reviews her process and identifies impediments that keep her from attaining goals. Perhaps reading is taking too long, and she explores options for improving speed, such as a speed-reading course. Note-taking workshops are probably offered through the school, or perhaps a tutor is needed for one subject. This review of goals and processes for attaining those goals happens every week, and tweaks and adjustments can be made against a limited amount of work — quickly, rather than the typical cramming required to make up for procrastination.

6

The Part of Tens

Chapter 19

Ten Steps to Transition to Scrum

Throughout this book, we highlight the fact that scrum is very different from traditional project management. Moving an organization from water-fall to scrum is a significant change. Through our experience guiding all types of companies through this kind of change, we've identified the following important steps to take to become a more agile organization and successfully implement scrum.

Conduct an Audit

Before you plan where you want to go, you need to know where you currently stand. A third-party audit of your current processes, methods, practices, and structures not only tells you some things you don't know about how you currently operate, but also validate some things that you already know, with added insights you may not have considered.

An *implementation strategy* is the output of an audit and a plan that outlines how your organization will transition to scrum from where it is today. A thorough implementation of scrum includes analysis and recommendations for

- >> **Current processes:** Examples include how your organization runs projects today, what it does well, and what its challenges are.

- >> **Future processes:** Examples include how your company can benefit from scrum, what additional agile practices can enhance scrum in your organization, what key changes your organization will need to make, the organizational and personnel implications of those challenges, and what your transformed company will look like from a team and process perspective.

- >> **Step-by-step plan:** Examples include how you'll move from existing processes to scrum, what will change immediately and in six months or a year or longer. This plan should be a roadmap of steps getting the company to a sustainable state of scrum maturity.

- >> **Benefits:** Examples include the advantages that scrum will provide for the people and groups in your organization and for the organization as a whole. Knowing the benefits will be a valuable resource as you promote the transition to senior management and the organization.

- >> **Potential challenges:** Examples include the most difficult changes, the departments or people that will have the biggest trouble with scrum, whose fiefdom is being disrupted, potential roadblocks, and how you'll overcome these challenges.

- >> **Success factors:** Examples include organizational that factors will help you while switching to scrum, how the company will commit to a new approach, and which people or departments will be champions of scrum.

Your implementation strategy serves as your roadmap to a successful transformation.

Identify and Recruit Talent

Scrum roles, although unique, are becoming more common, but not all recruiters know how to find people who can fill them. Getting people who know what they're doing requires working with recruiters to understand the scrum knowledge necessary to separate the fabulous from the fakers.

Cross-functional developers continue to learn new skills and recognize the need to expand their skill sets rather than restrict their knowledge to a single area. The talent is available. For your transition to scrum to be effective, you need to get the right people in the right seats.

You should look for people who already have certifications and training such as Certified Scrum Master (CSM), Certified Scrum Product Owner (CSPO), and

Certified Scrum Developer (CSD). When looking for a scrum coach, look for a Certified Scrum Professional (CSP-SM, CSP-PO) or a Certified Scrum Coach (CEC or CSC). The certifications are from the Scrum Alliance (www.scrumalliance.org) but certifications are available from other sources as well. For more detail on certifications, see Chapter 23.

Ensure Proper Training

Training is a critical step in adopting scrum. The combination of communicating in person with a scrum expert and working through exercises with scrum is the best way to help people to absorb and retain the skills needed to run a successful scrum project.

Training works best when the members of the project team can train and learn together. Training provides a common vocabulary to use during the transition. As scrum trainers and mentors, we've overheard conversations between project team members that start with, "Remember when Mark showed us how to . . .? That worked when we did it in class. Let's try that and see what happens." If the development team, product owner, scrum master, and project stakeholders can attend the same class, they can apply lessons to their work as a team.

Even stakeholders benefit from training. See Chapter 13 to understand how crucial senior management priority decisions are to making scrum successful. Some of our clients have seen so much value in this training with their scrum masters, product owners, and developers that they send their entire executive team and creative, sales, marketing, finance, and HR personnel to the same training so that the entire company could be on the same page and speak the same language.

Mobilize a Transition Team

Identify a transition team of decision-makers within your company who can be responsible for the scrum transformation at the organization level. This team is made up of company executives who have the ability and clout to improve processes systematically and can report requirements and performance measurements across the organization.

The transition team creates change by using scrum to run transition efforts, just as the development team creates product features within sprints. The implementation strategy from the audit is the transition team's roadmap, outlining what needs to be done for a successful transformation. The transformation team focuses on the highest-priority changes in each sprint and demonstrates its implementation (when possible) during a sprint review.

When you begin, the transition is a good time to engage an experienced scrum coach or mentor to help you through these first awkward steps. A good coach can work with the pilot teams as well as the transition team as a follow-up to group training.

Figure 19-1 illustrates how a transition team's sprints align with the pilot scrum team's sprints (see the next section), and how the impediments identified in the sprint retrospective of the pilot team become backlog items for the transition team to resolve as process improvements for the pilot team.

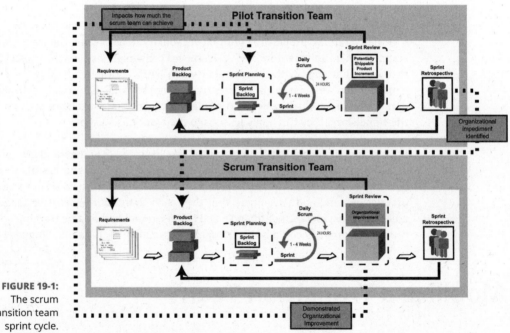

FIGURE 19-1:
The scrum transition team sprint cycle.

Identify Pilot Project

Starting your transition to scrum with one pilot project is a great idea. Having one initial project allows you to figure out how to work with scrum with little disruption to your organization's overall business. Concentrating on one project to start also lets you work out some of the kinks that inevitably follow change.

When selecting your first scrum project, look for an endeavor that has these qualities:

>> **Appropriately important:** Make sure that the project you choose is important enough to merit interest within your company. Avoid choosing the most important project coming up; you want to have room to make and learn from mistakes. See the note on the blame game in Chapter 20.

>> **Sufficiently visible:** Your pilot project should be visible to your organization's key influencers, but don't make it the most high-profile item on their agenda. You need the freedom to adjust to new processes; critical projects may not allow that freedom.

>> **Clear and containable:** Look for a product with clear requirements and a business group that can commit to defining and prioritizing those requirements. Try to pick a project that has a distinct end point rather than one that can expand indefinitely.

>> **Not too large:** Select a project that you can complete with no more than two scrum teams working simultaneously.

>> **Tangibly measurable:** Pick a project that you know can show measurable value within sprints.

TECHNICAL STUFF

People need time to adjust to organizational changes of any type, not just scrum transitions. Studies have found that with large changes, companies and teams see dips in performance before they see improvements. Satir's Curve, shown in Figure 19-2, illustrates the process of teams' excitement, chaos, and finally adjustment to new processes.

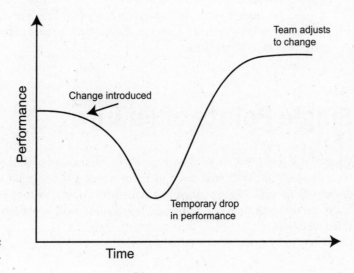

FIGURE 19-2: Satir's Curve.

After you've run one scrum project successfully, you'll have a foundation for future successes, expanding to more projects and teams.

Maximize Environment Efficiency

Having identified a pilot project, make sure that the work environment is one that sets it up for success. Your implementation strategy from your audit will likely outline the things to address, which may include

>> **Co-location:** If you're putting together a new team, put one together that's co-located, including the product owner and scrum master. Even if your organization typically has dislocated teams, this project is an opportunity to step back and evaluate whether dislocated teams are optimal.

>> **Work spaces:** Make sure that the pilot team has a work space that promotes collaboration and face-to-face communication. Team members need an area that not only allows them to focus uninterrupted on tasks, but also makes collaboration and swarming convenient and effective. Cubicle walls may not be ideal. Tables with shared monitors and other shared work spaces may be better. Whiteboards and plenty of tools such as sticky notes, 3x5 cards, pens, and markers effectively facilitate collaboration.

>> **Technology:** For improved collaboration with any stakeholder or other project team member not co-located with the scrum team, technology minimizes productivity loss. Videoconferencing, recording, screen sharing, and virtual whiteboard equipment are key factors in supporting a pilot scrum team to develop a quality product with the efficiency needed to demonstrate success. Consider investments in the technology that suits your team's needs, which may include monitors, cameras, virtual meeting-room software, microphones, and headsets.

Reduce Single Points of Failure

Your pilot scrum team needs to be as cross-functional as possible to be successful. Identify skill gaps with each team member where a single point of failure exists on any given skill. Make immediate plans for training so that everyone on the team can do more than one thing and no required skill is possessed by only one team member.

Training may include formal training or pairing with or shadowing another developer for a certain period. Training can be done during the first sprint(s) and doesn't need to delay the pilot team kickoff (see the section "Kick Off Pilot Project").

REMEMBER

You won't have a completely cross-functional team on day one. But the goal should be to get started on day one and to inspect and adapt along the way. Make cross-training and pair programming a priority and resist the pressures to meet arbitrary deadlines at the expense of a cross-functional team.

Establish Definition of Done

No doubt you'll be excited to get the project team started right away. But before diving in headfirst, make sure that the team's definition of done is . . . well, defined. The definition won't be perfect at first. The team will revise it often at first until it finds what makes sense. Making the definition a topic of conversation at each sprint retrospective is important.

Make sure that the team is clear about what done means for each requirement at the sprint and release levels. Make sure that the definition of done is always visible and referred to by all team members for every requirement to prevent many problems down the road. See Chapter 4 for details on creating a definition of done.

Kick Off Pilot Project

When you've chosen your pilot project, don't fall into the trap of using a plan from an old methodology. Instead, use scrum and other common practices from the roadmap to value that we introduce in Chapter 1. These practices include

>> Project planning

>> Agreeing on the vision

>> Creating a roadmap with estimations

REMEMBER

Although you'll have a long-range view of the product through the product roadmap, you don't need to define the product or project scope up front to get started. Don't worry about gathering exhaustive requirements at the beginning of your project; just add the features that the project team currently knows. You can always add requirements later.

- » Release planning

- » Identifying major minimum viable product (MVP) releases

- » Planning the first release

- » Sprint planning: Planning the first sprint and going to work

WARNING

In Chapter 7, we outline why you can't plan away uncertainty. Don't fall victim to analysis paralysis; set a direction and go!

Throughout the first sprint, be sure to consciously stick with scrum events. The following things should occur during your first sprint:

- » Have your daily scrum every day, even if you feel that you didn't make any progress. Identify roadblocks and communicate them promptly to the transition team.

- » The development team needs to remember to manage itself as a team of peers and not look to the product owner, the scrum master, or anywhere except the sprint backlog for task assignments.

- » The scrum master needs to protect the development team from outside work and distractions, especially while other members of the organization get used to having a dedicated scrum team.

- » The product owner needs to become accustomed to working directly with the development team, being available for questions, and reviewing and accepting completed requirements immediately.

In the first sprint, expect the road to be a little bumpy. That's okay; empiricism is about learning and adapting.

See Chapter 5 for details on planning releases and sprints.

Inspect, Adapt, Mature, and Scale

This step is about moving forward, taking what you've learned to new heights. If you follow the steps in the preceding sections, you'll start out with a solid foundation. As outlined in Chapter 7, empiricism will drive your continued adoption of scrum and transformation to scrum.

Inspect and adapt sprint 1

At the end of your first sprint, you'll gather feedback and improve with two important meetings: the sprint review and the sprint retrospective (see Chapter 6).

TIP

The sprint review and sprint retrospective are critical events. The product owner should spend time making sure that members of the development team are clear about what it means to demonstrate working software for the stakeholders, and he or she should prepare questions to ask the stakeholders to draw out feedback and show them the value of attending this review. Ensuring stakeholder attendance may take several invitations and reminders.

TIP

The scrum master should study resources such *Agile Retrospectives*, by Esther Derby and Diana Larsen (Pragmatic Bookshelf), to make sure that he establishes the right atmosphere and facilitates a retrospective that prevents venting and rehashing but promotes celebrating successes and identifying plans of action for improvement.

Maturity

Inspection and adaptation enable scrum teams to grow as a team and to mature with each sprint.

Agile practitioners sometimes compare the process of maturing with the martial-arts technique Shu Ha Ri, a Japanese term that means "maintain, detach, transcend." The term describes three stages in which people learn new skills:

>> **Shu:** In the Shu stage, students follow a new skill as they were taught, without deviation, to commit that skill to memory and make it automatic.

New scrum teams can benefit from closely following scrum until those processes become familiar. During the Shu stage, scrum teams may work closely with a scrum coach or mentor to follow processes correctly.

>> **Ha:** In the Ha stage, students start to improvise as they understand more about how their new skill works. Sometimes, the improvisations work, and sometimes, they don't. Students learn more about the skill from these successes and failures.

As scrum teams understand more about how scrum works, they may try variations on processes for their own project.

During the Ha stage, the sprint retrospective is a valuable tool for scrum teams to talk about how their improvisations worked or didn't work. In this stage, scrum team members may still learn from a scrum mentor, but they may also learn from one another, from other agile professionals, and from teaching agile skills to others.

>> **Ri:** In the Ri stage, the skill comes naturally to the former student, who knows what works and what doesn't, and can innovate with confidence.

With practice, scrum teams get to the point where scrum is easy and comfortable, like riding a bicycle or driving a car. In the Ri stage, scrum teams can customize processes, knowing what works in the spirit of the Agile Manifesto and Principles.

Scale virally

Completing a successful project is an important step in moving an organization to scrum. With metrics that prove the success of your project and the value of scrum, you can garner commitment from your company to support new scrum projects.

To scale scrum across an organization, start with the following:

>> **Seed new teams.** A scrum team that has reached maturity — the people who worked on the first scrum project — should have the expertise and enthusiasm to become scrum ambassadors within the organization. These people can join new scrum project teams and help those teams learn and grow.

>> **Redefine metrics.** Review, identify, and unify measurements for success (see Chapter 22) across the organization with the creation of each new scrum team and with each new project.

>> **Scale methodically.** Producing great results can be exciting, but company-wide improvements can require process changes. Don't move faster than the organization can handle.

>> **Identify new challenges.** Your first scrum project may have uncovered roadblocks that you didn't consider in your original implementation strategy. Update your strategy (that is, your transition team roadmap) as needed.

>> **Continue learning.** As you roll out new processes, make sure that new scrum team members and stakeholders have the proper training, mentorship, and resources to participate effectively in scrum projects.

To support your long-term effort to improve and mature with scrum, engage with an experienced scrum coach to jump-start mentoring leadership and teams in making the recommended changes from your audit. Also, begin searching for CSP+ talent — Certified Scrum Professional (CSP also CSP-SM and CSP-PO), Certified Scrum Coach (CTC and CEC), or Certified Scrum Trainer (CST) — to sustain long-term transformation. Establish this internal role as a source for clarification, ongoing training, and development, and embed this talent to work one on one with teams.

Chapter **20**

Ten Pitfalls to Avoid

Scrum teams can make common but serious mistakes when implementing scrum. This chapter provides an overview of some typical problems and ways for scrum teams to turn them around.

REMEMBER

As you may notice, many of these pitfalls are related to lack of organizational support, lack of training, and falling back on old project management practices. If your company invests in transition support and supports positive changes, if the project team is trained, and if scrum teams make an active commitment to upholding the scrum framework and agile values, you'll have a successful transition.

Faux Scrum

Sometimes, organizations say that they're "doing scrum." They may go through some of the scrum events, but they haven't embraced the principles of agile and are ultimately creating waterfall deliverables and products under false scrum titles. What these organizations are doing is sometimes called *faux scrum* and is a sure way to miss the benefits of scrum.

Trying to use scrum in addition to waterfall processes, documents, and meetings is another faux scrum approach.

Double-work agile results in quick project-team burnout. If you're doing twice the work, you aren't doing scrum or adhering to Agile Principles.

Solution: Insist on following scrum. Garner support from management to avoid using non-Agile Principles and practices.

Lack of Training

Investment in a hands-on training class provides a quicker, better learning environment than even the best book, blog, or white paper. Lack of training often indicates overall lack of organizational commitment to scrum.

REMEMBER

Training can help scrum teams avoid many of the mistakes in this chapter.

Solution: Build training into your implementation strategy. Giving teams the right foundation of skills is critical to success and is necessary at the start of your scrum transition.

Ineffective Product Owner

No scrum role is more different from traditional roles than that of the product owner. Scrum teams need a product owner who's an expert on business needs and priorities and can work well with the rest of the scrum team. An absent or indecisive product owner quickly sinks a scrum project.

Solution: Start the project with a person who has the time, expertise, and temperament to be a good product owner. Ensure that the product owner has proper training. The scrum master can help coach the product owner and may try to clear roadblocks preventing the product owner from being effective. If removing impediments doesn't work, the scrum team should insist on replacing the ineffective product owner with one who can make product decisions and help the scrum team be successful.

Lack of Automated Testing

Without automated testing, it may be impossible to fully complete and test work within a sprint. Most manual testing is a waste of time that fast-moving scrum teams don't have. Automating your regression testing validates that your past work isn't broken by your new work and is critical to preventing a backup of technical debt.

Solution: You can find many low-cost, open-source testing tools on the market today. Look into the right tools and make a commitment as a development team to using those tools.

Lack of Transition Support

Without the support of professionals and executives who can help guide scrum teams through new approaches, new scrum teams may find themselves falling back into old habits.

Solution: Enlist the help of an agile mentor — from your organization or from a consulting firm — who can support your transition. Implementing process is easy, but changing people is hard. It pays to invest in professional transition support with an experienced partner who understands behavioral science and organizational change.

Inappropriate Environment

When scrum teams aren't co-located, they lose the advantage of face-to-face communication. Being in the same building isn't enough; scrum teams need to sit in the same area.

Solution: Take action to co-locate the team. Examples include the following:

>> If the members of a scrum team are in the same building but not in the same area, move them together.

>> Consider creating a room or annex for the scrum team.

>> Try to keep the scrum team area away from distractors, such as the guy who can talk forever or the manager who needs just one small favor.

>> Before starting a project with a dislocated scrum team, do what you can to enlist local talent.

See Chapter 4 for more information on co-locating.

Poor Team Selection

Scrum team members who don't support scrum, don't work well with others, or don't have the capacity for self-management may sabotage a new scrum project from within.

Solution: When creating a scrum team, consider how well potential team members will enact Agile Principles. The key is versatility and willingness to learn.

Lax Discipline

Scrum projects need requirements, design, development, testing, and releases. Doing that work in sprints requires discipline.

Solution: Build in the habits of creating working functionality with the definition of done from the project start. You need more, not less discipline to deliver working products in a short iteration. Progress needs to be consistent and constant. To help develop good habits:

>> Use the daily scrum to help ensure that progress is occurring throughout the sprint.

>> Use the sprint retrospective as an opportunity to reset approaches to discipline.

>> Review and refine the team's definition of done regularly.

Lack of Support for Learning

Scrum teams succeed as teams and fail as teams; calling out one person's mistakes (known as the *blame game*) destroys the learning environment and destroys innovation.

Solution: Scrum teams can make a commitment at the project start to leave room for learning and to accept success and failures as a group.

Watered-Down Process

Watering down scrum roles, artifacts, and events with old waterfall habits erodes the benefits of agile processes until those benefits no longer exist.

Solution: When making process changes, stop to consider whether those changes support the scrum framework, Agile Manifesto, and Agile Principles. Resist changes that don't work with the manifesto and principles. Remember to reduce waste by maximizing the amount of work not done.

Chapter **21**

Ten Key Benefits of Scrum

REMEMBER

This chapter lists ten important benefits that scrum provides to organizations, teams, products, and individuals.

To take advantage of scrum benefits, you need to trust in empiricism, find out more about the scrum framework by using it, and continually inspect and adapt your implementation of scrum.

Better Quality

Projects exist to accomplish a vision or goal. Scrum provides the framework for continual feedback and exposure to make sure that quality is as high as possible. When we talk about quality, we aren't talking only about passing a defined set of tests. Building the right product and building it well involves interactions with customers and subject-matter experts. Scrum helps ensure quality through the following practices:

» Defining and elaborating on requirements just in time so that knowledge of product features is as relevant as possible.

>> Incorporating daily testing and product owner feedback into the development process, allowing the development team to address issues while they're fresh.

>> Regular and continuous improvement of scrum team output (product or service) through sprint reviews with stakeholders.

>> Conducting sprint retrospectives, allowing the scrum team to continuously improve such team-specific factors as processes, tools, relationships, and work environments.

>> Completing work by using the definition of done that addresses development, testing, integration, and documentation for each backlog item.

>> Reducing context switching through focusing on small iterations creates less errors and allows testing within a few days of the change.

Decreased Time to Market

Scrum has been proved to deliver value to customers 30 percent to 40 percent faster than traditional methods. This decrease in time is due to the following factors:

>> Earlier initiation of development due to the fact that the up-front documentation phases of waterfall projects (which typically take months) are forgone by having a dedicated product owner embedded within the scrum team to progressively elaborate requirements just in time and provide real-time clarification.

>> Highest-priority requirements are separated from lower-priority items. Incrementally delivering value to the customer means that the highest-value and highest-risk requirements (see Chapters 5 and 6) can be delivered before lower-value and lower-risk requirements. You don't need to wait until the entire project is complete before releasing anything into the market. Build only the features that will be used and deliver the most business value.

>> Functionality is swarmed to completion each sprint. At the end of every sprint, scrum teams produce working product and service increments that are shippable.

Increased Return on Investment

The decrease in time to market is one key reason why scrum projects realize higher return on investment (ROI). Because revenue and other targeted benefits start coming in sooner, earlier accumulation means higher total return over time, which is a basic tenet of net present value calculations (see Chapter 14). In addition to providing time-to-market benefits, scrum increases ROI through the following:

>> Regular feedback through sprint reviews directly from stakeholders (including customers) enables course corrections early, which is less costly and time-consuming than later in the process.

>> Fewer costly defects due to automation and up-front testing mean less wasted work and faster deployments.

>> Costs of failure are reduced. If a scrum project is going to fail, it fails earlier and faster than a waterfall project would.

Higher Customer Satisfaction

Scrum teams are committed to producing products and services that satisfy customers. Scrum enables happier project sponsors by

>> Collaborating with customers as partners and keeping customers involved and engaged throughout projects.

>> Having a product owner who is an expert on product requirements and customer needs. (Chapters 2 through 6 discuss the product-owner role.)

>> Keeping the product backlog updated and prioritized to respond quickly to change. (You can find out about the product backlog in Chapter 3.)

>> Demonstrating working functionality to internal stakeholders and customers in every sprint review. (Chapter 6 shows you how to conduct a sprint review.)

>> Delivering product to customers faster and more often with every release, rather than at the end.

>> Incrementally funding projects instead of requiring large up-front commitments. (Chapter 14 tells you about incremental funding of projects.)

Higher Team Morale

Working with happy people who enjoy their jobs can be satisfying and rewarding. Self-management puts decisions that would normally be made by a manager or the organization into the hands of scrum team members. Scrum improves the morale of team members in these ways:

>> Being part of a self-managing and self-organizing team allows people to be creative, innovative, and acknowledged for their expertise.

>> Development teams may organize their team structure around people with specific work styles and personalities. Organization around work styles provides these benefits:

- Allows team members to work the way they want to work

- Encourages team members to expand their skills to fit into teams that they like

- Increases team performance because people who do good work like to work together and naturally gravitate toward one another

>> Scrum teams can make decisions tailored to provide balance between team members' professional and personal lives.

>> Having a peer relationship with a business representative (product owner) on the same team aligns technical and business priorities and breaks down organizational barriers.

>> Having a scrum master who serves the scrum team removes impediments and shields the development team from external interferences.

>> Focusing on sustainable work practices and cadence ensures that people don't burn out from stress or overwork.

>> Working cross-functionally allows development team members to learn new skills and to grow by teaching others.

>> Encouraging a servant-leader approach assists scrum teams in self-management and actively avoiding command-and-control methods.

>> Providing an environment of support and trust increases people's overall motivation and morale.

>> Having face-to-face conversations helps reduce the frustration of miscommunication.

>> Ultimately, scrum teams can agree on rules about how they work to get the job done.

REMEMBER

The idea of team customization allows scrum workplaces to have more diversity. Organizations with traditional management styles tend to have monolithic teams on which everyone follows the same rules. Scrum work environments are much like a salad bowl. As salads can have ingredients with wildly different tastes that make a delicious dish, scrum projects can have people on teams with diverse strengths that make great products.

Increased Collaboration and Ownership

When scrum teams take responsibility for projects and products, they can produce great results. Scrum teams collaborate and take ownership of quality and project performance through the following practices:

» Having the development team, the product owner, and the scrum master work closely together on a daily basis

» Conducting sprint planning meetings, allowing the development team to organize its work around informed business priorities

» Having daily scrum meetings in which development team members organize around work completed, future work, and roadblocks

» Conducting sprint reviews, in which the product owner outlines his prioritization decisions and the development team can demonstrate and discuss the product directly with stakeholders

» Conducting sprint retrospectives, allowing scrum team members to review past work and recommend better practices with every sprint

» Working in a co-located environment, allowing for instant communication and collaboration among development team members, the product owner, and the scrum master

» Making decisions by consensus, using techniques such as estimation poker and the fist of five

You can find out how development teams estimate effort for requirements, decompose requirements, and gain team consensus in Chapter 4. You can discover more about sprint planning and daily scrum meetings in Chapter 5. For more information about sprint reviews and retrospectives, check out Chapter 6.

More Relevant Metrics

The metrics that scrum teams use to estimate time and cost, measure project performance, and make project decisions are often more relevant, more visible, and more accurate than metrics of traditional projects. On scrum projects, metrics are more relevant because

» Those who will be doing the work, and no one else, provide effort estimates for project requirements.

>> Timelines and budgets are based on each development team's actual performance and capabilities.

>> Using relative estimates, rather than hours or days, tailors estimated effort to an individual development team's knowledge and capabilities.

>> In less than one minute a day, developers can update the burndown chart, providing daily visibility of how the development team is progressing toward a sprint goal.

>> At the end of every sprint, a product owner can compare the project's actual cost (AC) plus the opportunity cost of future projects (OC) against the value that the current project is returning (V) to know when to terminate a project and begin a new one. You don't need to wait until the end of a project to know what its value is. (See Chapter 5 for more on AC + OC > V as a termination trigger.)

You may notice that velocity is missing from this list. *Velocity* (a measure of development speed, as detailed in Chapter 4) is a postsprint fact, not a goal. It's a metric, but only for the individual scrum team. Scrum teams can use this input to determine the amount of work that they can accomplish in future sprints, but it works only when it's tailored to an individual team. The velocity of Team A has no bearing on the velocity of Team B. Also, velocity is great for measurement and trending, but it doesn't work as a control mechanism. Trying to make a development team meet a certain velocity number only disrupts team performance and thwarts self-management.

If you're interested in finding out more about relative estimating, check out Chapter 4. Chapter 22 shows you ten key metrics for scrum projects.

Improved Progress Visibility and Exposure

On scrum projects, every member of the project team (which includes the scrum team and stakeholders) has the opportunity to know how the project is going at any given time. Transparency and visibility make scrum an exposure model to help the project team accurately identify issues and more accurately predict how things will go as the project progresses. Scrum projects can provide a high level of progress visibility through the following:

>> Placing a high value on open, honest communication among the scrum team, stakeholders, customers, and anyone else within an organization who wants to know about a project.

- >> Daily scrums that provide daily insight into the development team's immediate progress and roadblocks.

- >> Daily scrums around task boards that enable developers to self-organize and identify the highest-priority tasks for the day.

- >> Using the information from daily scrum meetings, sprint burndown charts, and task boards to track progress for individual sprints.

- >> Using sprint retrospectives to identify what's working well and what's not to make action plans for improvement.

- >> Demonstrating accomplishments in sprint reviews. Anyone within an organization may attend a sprint review, even members of other scrum teams.

Improved project visibility can lead to greater project control and predictability, as described in the following sections.

Increased Project Control

Scrum teams have numerous opportunities to control project performance and make corrections as needed because of the following practices:

- >> Adjusting priorities throughout the project at each sprint interval rather than at major milestones allows the organization to have fixed-time and fixed-price projects while accommodating change.

- >> Embracing change allows the project team to react to outside factors such as market demand.

- >> Daily scrum coordination allows the scrum team to quickly address issues as they arise and swarm together to get requirements to done.

- >> Daily updates to sprint backlogs mean that sprint burndown charts accurately reflect sprint progress, giving the scrum team the opportunity to make changes the moment it sees problems.

- >> Face-to-face conversations remove roadblocks to communication and issue resolution.

- >> Sprint reviews let project stakeholders see working products and provide product owners the feedback they need to ensure that the project stays on track.

- >> Sprint retrospectives enable the scrum team to make informed course adjustments at the end of every sprint to enhance product quality, increase development team performance, and refine project processes.

The many opportunities to inspect and adapt throughout scrum projects allow all members of the project team — development team, product owner, scrum master, and stakeholders — to exercise control and ultimately create better products.

Reduced Risk

Scrum helps mitigate the risk of absolute project failure — spending large amounts of time and money with no return on investment — by delivering tangible product early and forcing scrum teams to fail early if they're going to fail at all through the following practices:

>> Having the highest-risk items done first provides the longest runway to work through issues or fail early and inexpensively.

>> Developing in sprints, ensuring a short time between initial project investment and either failing fast or validating that a product or an approach will work.

>> Having a working product increment starting with the very first sprint, so that even if a project gets terminated, the highest-value and highest-risk requirements have been developed and could be delivered to the customer if desired.

>> Developing requirements to the definition of done in each sprint so that project sponsors have completed, usable features, regardless of what may happen with the project in the future.

>> Providing constant feedback on products and processes through

- Daily scrum meetings and constant development team communication through co-location

- Regular clarification about requirements and review and acceptance of features by the product owner

- Sprint reviews, with stakeholder and customer input, about completed product features

- Sprint retrospectives, in which the development team discusses process improvement

- Releases, in which the end user can see and react to new features on a regular basis

Chapter **22**

Ten Key Metrics for Scrum

With scrum, metrics can be powerful tools for planning, inspecting, adapting, and understanding progress over time. Rates of success or failure can let a scrum team know whether it needs to make positive changes or keep up its good work. Time and cost numbers can highlight the benefits of agile projects and provide support for an organization's financial activities. Metrics that quantify people's satisfaction can help a scrum team identify areas for improvement with customers and with the team itself.

WARNING

Double-work agile is the practice of management expecting to see traditional status reports and meetings in addition to scrum artifacts, events, and appropriate metrics. This practice is one of the top pitfalls of scrum projects. Management is looking for one thing while teams are trying to do another. As a result, decisions are made based on the wrong information, teams burn out from doing double the work, and the benefits of scrum become minimized.

This chapter describes ten key metrics to help guide scrum project teams.

Sprint Goal Success Rates

One way to measure scrum project performance is with the rate of sprint success. The sprint may not need all the requirements and tasks in the sprint backlog to be complete to minimally realize the sprint goal. However, a successful sprint should have a working product increment that fulfills the sprint goal and meets the scrum team's definition of done: developed, tested, integrated, and documented.

Throughout the project, the scrum team can track how frequently it succeeds in reaching the sprint goal and use success rates to see whether the team is maturing or needs to correct its course. Teams should always be stretching themselves, so 100 percent of the sprint backlog isn't necessarily the goal. Making sure that individual requirements started get 100 percent done is important, but teams should always be stretching themselves, so success rates less than 100 percent sprint backlog completion should be considered to be opportunities to learn and improve. Scrum masters should always be looking for ways to reduce drag on the team so that the team can set and accomplish higher goals as it continues to accomplish more and more in each sprint. Sprint success rates are a useful launching point for inspection and adaptation.

TIP

Velocity isn't a goal; it's a postsprint fact. An increasing velocity and an increasing sprint goal completion rate are key indicators that a scrum team is continually improving efficiency.

You can find out more about setting sprint goals in Chapter 5 and reviewing them in Chapter 6.

Defects

To be truly agile, scrum teams need to implement agile practices such as test-driven development and continuous integration (see Chapter 13). Without quality practices such as these, scrum teams are ineffective at delivering quality as fast as the market demands due to the overhead of manual testing before each release and the number of defects introduced that automation could easily catch.

It's unlikely that any scrum team will be able to accomplish perfection in these areas, so any project is likely to have some defects. Agile techniques combined with the scrum framework help development teams proactively minimize defects.

Tracking defect metrics can let the development team know how well it's preventing issues and when to refine its processes. To track defects, it helps to look at the following numbers:

» **Defects during development:** If the development team uses practices such as automated testing and continuous integration, it can track the number of defects at the build level in each sprint.

By understanding the number of build defects, the development team can know whether to adjust development processes and environmental factors.

» **User-acceptance testing defects:** The development team can track the number of defects that the product owner finds when accepting requirements in each sprint. By tracking defects, the development team and the product owner can identify the need to refine processes for understanding requirements. The development team can also determine whether adjustments to automated testing tools are necessary.

» **Defect rates:** In addition to seeing how many issues are discovered, it's useful to look at the frequency per user story (stories delivered/defects found). Two defects out of 20 stories paints a different picture from 2 defects out of 2 stories. As a team increases its work effort, see whether the rate of defects goes up as well.

» **Release defects:** The development team can track the number of defects that make it past the release to the marketplace.

By tracking release defects, the development team and the product owner can know whether changes in the user-acceptance testing process, automated testing, or the development process are necessary. Large numbers of defects at the release level can indicate bigger problems within the scrum team.

The number of defects and whether defects are increasing, decreasing, or staying the same are good metrics to spark discussions about project processes and development techniques at sprint retrospectives.

Time to Market

Time to market is the amount of time that a project takes to provide value by releasing working products and features to users. Organizations may perceive value in a couple of ways:

» When a product directly generates income, its value is the money it can make.

» When a product is for an organization's internal use, its value is the employees' ability to use the product and contains subjective factors based on what the product can do.

When measuring time to market, consider the following values:

>> Measure the time from the project start until you first show value to the customer.

>> Some scrum teams deploy new product features for use at the end of each sprint. For scrum teams with a release with every sprint, the time to market is simply the sprint length, measured in days.

>> Other scrum teams plan releases after multiple sprints and deploy product features in groups. For scrum teams that use longer release times, the time to market is the number of days between the start of development of a feature and the next release.

Time to market helps organizations recognize and quantify the ongoing value of scrum projects. Time to market is especially important for companies with revenue-generating products because it aids in budgeting throughout the year.

Return on Investment

Return on investment (ROI) is income generated by the product, less project costs — money in versus money out. On scrum projects, ROI is fundamentally different from ROI on traditional projects. Scrum projects have the potential to generate income with the first release (which can be as soon as the end of the first sprint) and can increase revenue with each new release.

To fully appreciate the difference between ROI on traditional and scrum projects, consider two scenarios with the same project costs that take the same amount of time to complete. We're ignoring the additional documentation, meetings, and other expenses of a waterfall project and assuming that they could be kept at the scrum level to simplify the comparison. Both scenarios begin on January 1 and have the potential to generate $100,000 in income every month when all the requirements are finished.

Scenario A is waterfall and releases when all requirements are finished on June 30 of the same year. It enjoys monthly revenue of $100,000 per month for each month thereafter through the end of the year (six months, $600,000 revenue).

Scenario B begins releasing the highest-value and highest-risk features incrementally on January 31 after four one-week sprints, five months earlier than Project A. Monthly revenue is less as it builds up each month from the first release (that is, $50,000 in February, $60,000 in March, $70,000 in April, $80,000 in May, and $90,000 in June) until the entire project is complete.

This extra revenue in each of the five months from February through June gives the project $950,000 in revenue for the year, $350,000 more than scenario A.

REMEMBER

Like time to market, ROI metrics are a great way for an organization to appreciate the ongoing value of a scrum project. ROI metrics help justify projects from the start because companies may fund projects based on ROI potential. Organizations may track ROI for individual projects as well as for the organization as a whole.

Total project duration and cost

To calculate ROI, first calculate duration and cost, which can themselves be effective inputs and metrics for scrum projects. Scrum projects should get done faster and be less costly than traditional projects.

A higher ROI as a result of decreasing project durations and costs should be a good indicator that scrum teams are increasing swarming, reducing thrashing, and improving overall efficiency.

New requests within ROI budgets

The ability to quickly generate higher ROI gives organizations that use scrum a unique way to fund additional product development. New product features may translate to higher product income.

Suppose that in the preceding example, the project team identified a new feature at the beginning of June that would take four one-week sprints to complete and would boost the product income from $100,000 a month to $120,000 a month, which results in increased revenue of $120,000 for the year in both scenarios. In scenario B, if the new feature had been identified earlier, ROI would have increased even more.

If a project is already generating income, it can make sense for an organization to roll that income back into new development and see higher revenue. Tracking ROI provides the intelligence required to make that decision.

Capital Redeployment

When the cost of future development is higher than the value of that future development, it's time for the project to end.

The product owner prioritizes requirements in part by their ability to generate revenue. If only low-revenue requirements remain in the backlog, a project may need to end before the scrum team has used its entire budget. The organization may use the remaining budget from the old project to start a new, more valuable project. The practice of moving a budget from one project to another is called *capital redeployment*.

To determine a project's end, you need the following metrics:

>> The value (V) of the remaining requirements in the product backlog

>> The actual cost (AC) for the work to complete the requirements in the product backlog

>> The opportunity cost (OC), or the value of having the scrum team work on a new project

When $V < AC + OC$ (or $AC + OC > V$, as described in Chapter 5), the project can stop. The cost you sink into the project is more than the value you receive from continuing the project or starting the next project.

Capital redeployment allows an organization to spend efficiently on valuable product development and maximize the organization's overall ROI.

Satisfaction Surveys

A scrum team's highest priority is to satisfy the customer, both early and often, by delivering value. At the same time, the scrum team strives to motivate individual team members and promote sustainable development practices.

A scrum team can benefit from digging deeper into customer and team member experiences. One way to get measurable information about how well a scrum team is fulfilling its purpose is through satisfaction surveys.

Customer satisfaction surveys measure the customer's experience with the project, the process, and the scrum team. The scrum team may want to use customer surveys multiple times during a project, including at the beginning to establish a benchmark for future comparisons. The scrum team can use customer survey results to examine processes, continue positive practices, and adjust behavior as necessary.

Team satisfaction surveys measure the scrum team members' experience with the organization, the work environment, processes, other project team members, and their work. Everyone on the scrum team can take team surveys. As with the customer survey, the scrum team may choose to give team surveys throughout a project. Scrum team members can use team survey results to regularly fine-tune and adjust personal and team behaviors. The scrum team can also use results to address organizational issues. Customer survey results over time can provide a quantitative look at how the scrum team is maturing as a team.

You can put together informal paper surveys or use one of the many online survey tools. Some companies even have survey software available through their human resources department.

Team Member Turnover

Scrum projects tend to have higher team member morale. One way to quantify morale is to measure turnover. You can look at the following metrics:

>> **Scrum team turnover:** Low scrum team turnover can be one sign of a healthy team environment. High scrum team turnover (resulting from things such as burnout, ineffective product owners who force development team commitments, personality incompatibilities, or a scrum master who fails to remove impediments, making the development team look bad in sprint reviews) can indicate problems with the project, the organization, the work, individual scrum team members, or overall team dynamics.

Team members may be quitting, or managers may be stealing team members away to other projects. Either way, the result is increased thrashing that exposes organizational issues that should be addressed.

>> **Company turnover:** High company turnover, even if it doesn't include the scrum team, can affect morale and effectiveness. High company turnover can be a sign of problems within the organization. As a company adopts scrum, it should see turnover decrease.

When the scrum team knows turnover metrics and understands the reasons behind those metrics, it may be able to take actions to maintain morale and improve the work environment.

Project Attrition

Organizations with project portfolios should look at the rate of projects being cut short. Capital redeployment shouldn't be confused with thrashing teams between projects at the whim of senior managers. Tracking project durations against capital redeployment analyses may expose trends of ending projects prematurely or letting them run longer than needed.

From these trends, portfolio managers can look into reasons why projects are getting cut short. High attrition may indicate such issues as thrashing, planning, prioritization, impediments, and cross-functionality.

For more on how scrum improves portfolio management, see Chapter 13.

Skill Versatility

Strong scrum teams are typically more cross-functional than weaker scrum teams. By eliminating single points of failure on a scrum team, you increase its ability to move faster and produce higher quality. Tracking skill versatility allows scrum teams and functional managers to gauge *growth* of cross-functionality. Chapter 14 talks about incentivizing and encouraging skill development for scrum teams.

When starting, capture the existing skills and levels contained at each of the following organizational structures:

>> Per-person skills and levels

>> Per-team skills and levels

>> Per-organization skills and levels

Over time, as each person increases the quantity and level of skills, each team and the organization will increase its skill levels. The most important factor isn't how many managers or directors you have by title in the organization that can deliver quality products and services to your customers. Your focus should be having team members who can contribute to the sprint goal each day without the risk of single points of failure.

Manager:Creator Ratio

Typically, the larger the organization is, the more likely it is to have a heavy middle layer of managers. Many organizations haven't figured out how to function well without managers to handle personnel, training, and development issues. However, you need to strike the right balance of managers and individuals who produce product.

REMEMBER

Every dollar spent on someone who manages organizational processes is a dollar not spent on a product creator.

Track your manager:creator ratio to help you identify bloat and ways to minimize the investment that you're making in people who don't create product.

Chapter **23**

Ten Key Resources for Scrum

Many organizations, websites, blogs, and companies exist to provide information about and support for scrum. To help you get started, we've compiled a list of key resources that you can use to support your journey with scrum.

Scrum Alliance

http://scrumalliance.org

The Scrum Alliance is a not-for-profit professional membership organization that promotes understanding and use of scrum. The alliance achieves this goal by promoting scrum training and certification classes, hosting international and regional scrum gatherings, and supporting scrum user groups. The Scrum Alliance site is rich in blog entries, white papers, case studies, and other tools for learning and working with scrum. Scrum Alliance certifications include

» Certified ScrumMaster (CSM)

» Advanced Certified ScrumMaster (A-CSM)

- » Certified Scrum Product Owner (CSPO)

- » Advanced Certified Scrum Product Owner (A-CSPO)

- » Certified Scrum Developer (CSD)

- » Advanced Certified Scrum Developer (A-CSD)

- » Certified Scrum Professional (CSP)

  - CSP for ScrumMasters (CSP-SM)

  - CSP for Product Owners (CSP-PO)

  - CSP for Developers (CSP-D)

- » Certified Team Coach (CTC)

- » Certified Enterprise Coach (CEC)

- » Certified Agile Leadership (CAL)

The Agile Alliance

`http://agilealliance.org`

The Agile Alliance is the original global agile community, with a mission to help advance the 12 Agile Principles and common agile practices, regardless of approach. The Agile Alliance site has an extensive resources section that includes articles, videos, presentations, and an index of independent agile community groups across the world.

Scrumguides.org

`http://scrumguides.org`

Jeff Sutherland and Ken Schwaber, co-creators of scrum, offer *The Scrum Guide: The Definitive Guide to Scrum: The Rules of the Game* in more than 30 languages at `http://scrumguides.org`. *The Scrum Guide* is available in both online and PDF formats and is free to use. In fewer than 20 pages, the guide outlines scrum theory and defines each scrum role, artifact, and event.

Scrum.org

http://scrum.org

Scrum.org provides tools and resources for scrum practitioners to deliver value through assessments and certifications, including

>> Professional Scrum Master (PSM I, II, III)

>> Professional Scrum Product Owner (PSPO I, II)

>> Professional Scrum Developer (PSD)

Scruminc.com (Scrum at Scale)

http://www.scruminc.com

Jeff Southerland and his team offer scrum training, resources, and certifications, including Scrum at Scale.

ScrumPLoP

http://scrumplop.org

Pattern Languages of Programs (PLoP) are methods of describing design practices within fields of expertise and often have conferences organized around them for shared learning. ScrumPLoP publishes patterns written by scrum professionals, many of which were written by Jeff Sutherland, co-creator of scrum. These practical patterns have been used successfully by organizations to get started with scrum.

Scaled Agile Framework (SAFe)

http://scaledagileframework.com

The Scaled Agile Framework (SAFe) is a knowledge base for implementing agile practices and one framework for implementing scrum at scale. Use the interactive

"Big Picture" graphic on the landing page to click through to see highlights of the roles, teams, activities, and artifacts.

SAFe is a registered trademark of Scaled Agile Inc.

LeSS

`http://less.works`

Large-Scale Scrum (LeSS) is a scrum-scaling method that provides two frameworks, known as LeSS and LeSS Huge. Like SAFe, LeSS provides a graphic interface that highlights the frameworks.

InfoQ

`www.infoq.com/scrum`

InfoQ is an independent online community with a prominent scrum section offering news, articles, video interviews, video presentations, and minibooks, all written by scrum domain experts. The resources at InfoQ tend to be high-quality, and the content is unique and relevant to the issues facing scrum teams.

Platinum Edge

`http://platinumedge.com`

Visit our blog to get the latest insights on practices, tools, and innovative solutions emerging from our work with Global 1,000 companies and the dynamic agile community.

We also provide the following services:

>> **Agile audits:** Auditing of your current organizational structure and processes to create an agile implementation strategy that delivers bottom-line results.

>> **Recruiting:** We help you find the best fit for your needs to bootstrap your scrum projects, including scrum masters, scrum product owners, and scrum developers.

>> **Training:** We offer public and private customized corporate agile and scrum training and certification, regardless of your level of knowledge:

- Certified ScrumMaster classes (CSM)
- Certified Scrum Product Owner classes (CSPO)
- Certified Scrum Developer classes (CSD)
- SAFe Scaled Agile training and implementations

>> **Transformation:** Follow up on agile coaching and training with agile mentoring to ensure that the right practices occur in the real world.

TIP

You can use the online Cheat Sheet as a companion to this book as you start implementing the scrum framework outlined in the preceding chapters. You'll find helpful resources there for staying on track with scrum. Visit www.dummies.com and search for this book's title.

Index

applications
  publishing, 191–192
  software, 147–153
applying scrum in publishing industry, 192–193
approval, as a step for building requirements, 52
architecture
  emergent, 146–147
  owner of, 232
art, in video-game development, 151
ART (agile release train) model, 239
artifacts, 13
Atos Origin, 20
AT&T Wireless, 258
audits, conducting, 327–328
automated testing, 338–339
automobiles, 164
autonomy, in Saab Jet Fighter, 169
average handle time, as a metric, 280
average speed of answer, as a metric, 280

B

behavior tests, 296
"being in the zone," 41
benefits
  in implementation strategy, 328
  of scrum, 343–350
bids, in construction, 157–158
Big Data, 202–208
Bigollo, Leonardo Pisano (Fibonacci)
    (mathematician), 74
Blanchard, Kenneth (author)
  The New One Minute Manager, 38
Blueprint High School, 186
body language, 285
Boesch, Jordan (app developer), 147
bots, 209
bring in outside applications (BYOA), 208
bring your own device (BYOD), 208
budgets, 261–262, 317
Build, Measure, and Learn pattern, 227
building retirement, 309

Bunch, John (transition leader), 254
burndown chart, 100–101
burnup chart, 94
business alignment, with technology, 143–145
business development
  about, 263
  marketing, 264–269
  sales, 269–275
Business Development For Dummies (Kennedy), 264
business performance, increased, as a benefit of
    using agile framework, 266
BYOA (bring in outside applications), 208
BYOD (bring your own device), 208

C

CafePress, 268
CAL (Certified Agile Leadership), 362
Canon, 155
capacity, backlog, 101–102
capital redeployment, 355–356
Carpentier, Andrée (app developer), 147
CEC (Certified Enterprise Coach), 362
CEC (Certified Scrum Coach), 329, 336
certainty, need for, 125–126
Certified Agile Leadership (CAL), 362
Certified Enterprise Coach (CEC), 362
Certified Scrum Coach (CEC/CTC), 329, 336
Certified Scrum Developer (CSD), 328–329,
    362, 365
Certified Scrum Master (CSM), 328–329, 361, 365
Certified Scrum Product Owner (CSPO), 328–329,
    362, 365
Certified Scrum Professional (CSP), 362
Certified Scrum Professional (CSP-SM, CSP-PO),
    329, 336
Certified Scrum Trainer (CST), 336
Certified Team Coach (CTC), 362
CFDs (cumulative flow diagrams), 94
challenges
  for development team, 143
  in education, 180–182
  family life, 299

I

life goals *(continued)*
    retirement, 307–312
    studying, 319–324
    travel, 316–318
    weight, 312–314
Lockheed Martin, 260
Los Angeles Department of Water and Power, 286

M

maintenance, in IT management, 213–214
maintenance type, of backlog item, 59
malware, 209
manager:creator ratio, 359
"Managing the Development of Large Software Systems" (Royce), 139–140
manufacturing
    about, 164–165
    fastest to market, 165
    shareholder value, 165
    strategic capacity management, 166
marketing
    about, 264
    adopting scrum in, 266–267
    Agile Advantage surveys, 266–267
    defined, 263
    evolution of, 264–265
    scrum and, 264–269
    scrum in action, 267–269
    social media, 265–266
    speed to, 165
    in video-game development, 150
The Marshmallow Challenge (TED talk), 19
maturity, importance of, 334, 335–336
maximizing environment efficiency, 332
McDonald's, 258
measurability, of pilot projects, 331
medical devices, manufacturing and safety of, 178–179
meeting, as a dating challenge, 291
Mehrabian, Albert (professor), 69, 284
mentoring program, 210

metrics
    customer service, 280
    redefining, 336
    relevancy of with scrum, 347–348
    for scrum, 351–359
Microchip, 270
Microsoft Office, 229
migration, large-scale, 202–208
military, scrum and, 186–188
minimum viable product (MVP), 85, 207, 259, 301
Mission Command, 186–187
mistakes, reduced, in healthcare, 175
misunderstandings, 285
MMBD (Multi-Mission Bus Demonstrator) project, 168
mobilizing transition teams, 329–330
modular architecture, in Saab Jet Fighter, 169
monetization, faster, as a general benefit of scrum, 173
Moore, Geoffrey (author)
    Crossing the Chasm, 36
Mortensen, Brady (news professional), 194
motivating creativity, 133
Multi-Mission Bus Demonstrator (MMBD) project, 168
multitasking
    about, 116
    focusing *vs.,* 296–297
music industry, 190
MVP (minimum viable product), 85, 207, 259, 301

N

National Public Radio (NPR), 194, 195
Negotiable, as a user story quality, 62
Nelson, Admiral, 187–188
"New New Product Development Game," 155
news media
    about, 194–195
    defining "done," 195–196
    sprint flexibility, 197
    team for, 196–197
"The New New Product Development Game," 15

W

X

Y

Z

About the Authors

Mark C. Layton, known globally as Mr. Agile®, is an executive and board of directors advisor with over 25 years in the project/program management field. He is the Los Angeles chair for the Agile Leadership Network and is the founder of Platinum Edge, LLC — an organizational improvement company that supports businesses making the waterfall-to-agile transition.

Prior to founding Platinum Edge in 2001, Mark developed his expertise as a consulting firm executive, program management coach, and in-the-trenches project leader. He also spent 11 years as a cryptographic specialist for the U.S. Air Force, where he earned both Commendation and Achievement medals for his accomplishments.

Mark holds MBAs from the University of California, Los Angeles, and the National University of Singapore; a B.Sc. (*summa cum laude*) in behavioral science from University of La Verne; and an A.S. in Electronic Systems from the Air Force's Air College. He is also a distinguished graduate of the Air Force's Leadership School, a Certified Scrum Trainer (CST), a certified scaled agile program consultant (SAFe SPC), a certified Project Management Professional (PMP), and a recipient of Stanford University's advanced project management certification (SCPM).

When he isn't overseeing client engagements, Mark is a frequent speaker on Scrum, eXtreme Programming (XP), Lean, and other agile solutions. He lives in Las Vegas, Nevada.

Additional information can be found at www.platinumedge.com.

David Morrow is an Executive Agile Coach, helping leadership and scrum teams work through their roles in ensuring agile transformation success. David is a Certified Scrum Professional (CSP) and Certified Agile Coach (ICP-ACC), and he has more than two decades of experience building and coaching teams to be more powerful and successful. He is a software development veteran who has an economist mindset, which gives him a unique perspective on team dynamics.

David served as the CEO of Devnext for 15 years before moving into coaching full-time for Platinum Edge. Now he can be found speaking about scrum to anyone who will listen, and he frequents local agile user groups and pubs.

Dedication

To the knockout of my life. Thanks.

— Mark C. Layton

To my beloved wife and family. You love me so well.

— David Morrow

Authors' Acknowledgments

We'd like to again thank the numerous people who contributed to the first edition of this book and helped make it a reality.

Thank you to everyone who added even more value to this second edition. Steve Ostermiller, your experience and guidance was crucial to our success. Dean Kynaston for your experience and technical refinements; the industry advisors whose input showed scrum's broader uses: Amber Allen (LAUSD) and Renee Jumper on education; Anna Kennedy (author of *Business Development For Dummies* [published by John Wiley & Sons, Inc.]) on business development and sales; Brian Dreyer on video-game and business development; Adi Ekowibowo, Farid Kazimi, Charles Park, and Scot Kramarich on video-game development; Kelly Anderson on talent management (HR); Melani Chacon on customer service; Hiren Vashi, Lisa White, Doc Dochtermann, and Sunil Bhandari on health care; Lowell Feil, Rob Carstons, and Steffanie Ducher for enterprise resource planning (ERP); Brady Mortensen on publishing; Mogenns Gilmour, Joe Justice, and J.J. Sutherland on hardware development; Elana Glazer on manufacturing; and Dean Leffingll, Alex Yakyma, Patrick Roach, Bas Vodde, and Craig Larman on enterprise scaling models.

A special thanks to Jeff Sutherland and Ken Schwaber, the co-creators of scrum. We all work better because of you.

We'd also like to say thank you to the amazing team at Wiley & Sons: Charlotte Kughen, whose patience and wisdom made this happen, and the many, many others who contributed their time and expertise to making this book the guide we hoped it would be.

Publisher's Acknowledgments

Acquisitions Editor: Amy Fandrei

Project Editor: Charlotte Kughen

Copy Editor: Kathy Simpson

Technical Editor: Dean Kynaston

Production Editor: Siddique Shaik

Cover Image: ©MissTuni/Getty Images

Take dummies with you everywhere you go!

Whether you are excited about e-books, want more from the web, must have your mobile apps, or are swept up in social media, dummies makes everything easier.

Find us online!

Dummies is the global leader in the reference category and one of the most trusted and highly regarded brands in the world. No longer just focused on books, customers now have access to the dummies content they need in the format they want. Together we'll craft a solution that engages your customers, stands out from the competition, and helps you meet your goals.

Advertising & Sponsorships

Connect with an engaged audience on a powerful multimedia site, and position your message alongside expert how-to content. Dummies.com is a one-stop shop for free, online information and know-how curated by a team of experts.

- Targeted ads
- Video
- Email Marketing
- Microsites
- Sweepstakes sponsorship

20 MILLION
PAGE VIEWS
EVERY SINGLE MONTH

15 MILLION
UNIQUE
VISITORS PER MONTH

43%
OF ALL VISITORS
ACCESS THE SITE
VIA THEIR MOBILE DEVICES

700,000 NEWSLETTER
SUBSCRIPTIONS
TO THE INBOXES OF
300,000 UNIQUE INDIVIDUALS
EVERY WEEK

# of dummies

Custom Publishing

Reach a global audience in any language by creating a solution that will differentiate you from competitors, amplify your message, and encourage customers to make a buying decision.

- Apps
- Books
- eBooks
- Video
- Audio
- Webinars

Brand Licensing & Content

Leverage the strength of the world's most popular reference brand to reach new audiences and channels of distribution.

For more information, visit dummies.com/biz

PERSONAL ENRICHMENT

9781119187790	9781119179030	9781119293354	9781119293347	9781119310068	9781119235606
USA $26.00	USA $21.99	USA $24.99	USA $22.99	USA $22.99	USA $24.99
CAN $31.99	CAN $25.99	CAN $29.99	CAN $27.99	CAN $27.99	CAN $29.99
UK £19.99	UK £16.99	UK £17.99	UK £16.99	UK £16.99	UK £17.99

9781119251163	9781119235491	9781119279952	9781119283133	9781119287117	9781119130246
USA $24.99	USA $26.99	USA $24.99	USA $24.99	USA $24.99	USA $22.99
CAN $29.99	CAN $31.99	CAN $29.99	CAN $29.99	CAN $29.99	CAN $27.99
UK £17.99	UK £19.99	UK £17.99	UK £17.99	UK £16.99	UK £16.99

PROFESSIONAL DEVELOPMENT

9781119311041	9781119255796	9781119293439	9781119281467	9781119280651	9781119251132	9781119310563
USA $24.99	USA $39.99	USA $26.99	USA $26.99	USA $29.99	USA $24.99	USA $34.00
CAN $29.99	CAN $47.99	CAN $31.99	CAN $31.99	CAN $35.99	CAN $29.99	CAN $41.99
UK £17.99	UK £27.99	UK £19.99	UK £19.99	UK £21.99	UK £17.99	UK £24.99

9781119181705	9781119263593	9781119257769	9781119293477	9781119265313	9781119239314	9781119293323
USA $29.99	USA $26.99	USA $29.99	USA $26.99	USA $24.99	USA $29.99	USA $29.99
CAN $35.99	CAN $31.99	CAN $35.99	CAN $31.99	CAN $29.99	CAN $35.99	CAN $35.99
UK £21.99	UK £19.99	UK £21.99	UK £19.99	UK £17.99	UK £21.99	UK £21.99

dummies.com

dummies
A Wiley Brand